WHILE THE U.S.
SLEEPS

WHILE THE U.S. SLEEPS

Squandered Opportunities and Looming Threats to Societies.

Winston Langley

To order additional copies of this book, contact:
Xlibris
844-714-8691
www.Xlibris.com
Orders@Xlibris.com
823052

To Eunny whose life has been dedicated to protecting children from this sleep.

CONTENTS

Acknowledgements...ix
Introduction xi

1. Arms Limitation, Third-Party Dispute Settlement, and Security.................1
2. Economic Models Chosen and Pursued 16
3. Race and Class: Their Bearing on Social Rights 43
4. Education: Political and Popular Culture 61
5. The Environment: Our Home and Ourselves 81
6. The Will to National Power or Global Leadership? 98
7. A Final Chance: Common Security..120

Epilogue 141
Bibliography 143
Endnotes 157
Index 187

Acknowledgements

*Without belittling the courage with which
men have died, we should not forget those acts
of courage with which men have lived.*
— J. F. Kennedy, *Profiles in Courage*

This book came from a deep concern about my adopted country, the United States of America, especially its seeming blindness to its own weaknesses, including claims about and beliefs in itself that have served as opiates to society in the face of evidence contradicting those claims and beliefs and the development of social ills that now threaten its very existence. Because, especially after World War II, the United States became and, to an extent, remains the leading nation-state in international affairs, threats to its existence also bear with them fundamental threats to the world.

There are values that the United States espouses that are important to the world and the future of humankind. Given those values, along with many that other countries likewise (separately or collectively) offer to the world, should they become the defining grounds for interpersonal, inter-societal, international, and global societies, the promise that tomorrow could hold for everyone would be quite bright. There is no such brightness, however, and storm clouds are being formed domestically and globally. Those storm clouds are the offspring of many years, sometimes centuries, of accumulated bypassing, as if we were in a sleep. The clouds can be removed if we wake up and heed the call to a number of required individual and social acts of courage.

The author offers thanks to the Boston Athenaeum, where some of the research for the book was conducted. Thanks go also to the Boston University Law School Library, the Lamont Library at Harvard University, the Healey Library at the University of Massachusetts Boston, and the Moorland-Spingarn Research Center at Howard University. Special thanks go to Marc Miller, whose editorial assistance was invaluable.

Introduction

As the 2018 congressional midterm elections neared in the United States, the news media posed a question: "What kind of candidate can defeat President Trump?"[1] It is a question that elites, the country at large, and observers worldwide continue to ask as the 2020 election approaches. In part, those asking it seek to identify candidates to whom they might offer help in removing a president whose fitness for office they doubt—mobilizing voters, shaping policy positions, overcoming mistaken assumptions about the 2016 electorate, inveighing against (or championing) the wing of the Democratic Party from which a candidate may emerge, or pointing to the person whom President Trump might least wish to face as he campaigns for reelection. Some or all of these factors as well as others may be involved.

However, the question is grounded on a superficial understanding of leadership, the issues confronting the United States, and the extent to which any individual head of the nation can address those issues effectively. My own research and reflection suggest that replacing President Trump will do little to tackle the major problems that the United States faces; nor will solutions be found in any leader or political party.

For well over a century, both political parties and a long succession of U.S. leaders have failed to embrace countless opportunities across a variety of areas to make a major contribution to either national society or the world at large. Those failures haunt U.S. society and the world today. *While the U.S. Sleeps* looks at six of these areas. In each, the failure to grasp opportunities constitutes a form of sleep, even a lack of basic understanding of the profound implications of rejecting or circumventing those opportunities.

Consider, for example, the area of arms limitation and disarmament. Occasions to pursue these goals came with the Hague Conferences of 1899 and 1907 and continued with the Kellogg–Briand Pact of 1928, certain terms of the League of Nations Charter, U.S. responses to the 1986 Reagan–Gorbachev disarmament initiative in Reykjavik, Iceland, and the 2017 Treaty on the Prohibition of Nuclear Weapons.

The United States also failed to seize opportunities for domestic and international progress with regard to economic development. This becomes clear when viewing all three general models of development pursued by the United States through a lens of fairness in the distribution of economic returns. For over 140 years, the United States pursued a mercantilist model of development, using it, especially after World War I, to ensure the nation's international ascendency, even while surviving the Great Depression and other challenges to development. The next model was liberalism as it came to dominance after World War II. Late in the war, forty-four nations created the Bretton Woods System, a new way to control the value of national currencies and hence the international economy. The United States' Marshall Plan bypassed that system, and later, it collapsed in the 1970s. Perhaps most importantly, the United States rejected the Global South's proposal for a new international economic order (NIEO) and pursued in its stead liberalism's offspring, neoliberalism, which is the third model of economic development.

A further broad area of lost opportunities comes with the deliberate manipulation of economic, social, and cultural emphases, along with the U.S. denial, domestically and abroad, of social rights, and instead, it pursued actions that preserved racial cleavage. Lost were opportunities to challenge racism during and after World War I (including during the New Deal), after World War II (especially surprising in light of the war's racial atrocities), at the beginning of the modern human rights movement, during the 1960s civil rights movement, or in conjunction with the 1976 adoption of the United Nations (UN)–sponsored International Covenant on Economic, Social, and Cultural Rights (ICESCR), the 1976 International Covenant on Civil and Political Rights (ICCPR), and the Carter administration's 1979 decision to make human rights a cornerstone of U.S. foreign policy. Across these instances, far from dealing with our society's deep racial issues, the United States sought to preserve immoral claims of racial superiority. It fought off efforts to adopt statements on racial equality and supported principles that spoke in terms of nondiscrimination rather than racial equality.

When the United States finally accepted the ICCPR in 1992, the adoption came with a fundamental limitation: the covenant could not add to rights already present under the U.S. Constitution. At the same time, the United States continued its long-standing de-emphasis of social class, substituting racial identities in its stead, with incentives for white ethnics to focus on their whiteness. U.S. political leaders have never even brought up the ICESCR for discussion. That covenant could have promoted a sense of community and helped confront the nation's ugly history of racial discrimination.

In the fourth area of lost opportunities, the history of racism couples with the use of education, more properly termed political culture and political socialization. Education in the United States has eroded early Puritan values that promoted the self-making, truth-seeking person, one committed to the social good; it has replaced that person with the consumer, a more or less passive individual, with ego-driven concerns for material things but little interest in the social good. The realms of information and communication as well as the advent of "captains of consciousness," the rise of the advertising industry, have joined in this socialization and, along with social media, now seek to produce and manage human experiences with the aid of artificial intelligence.

The fifth area centers on the national and international history of the environmental movement, the 1983 National Academy of Sciences report entitled *Changing Climate*, and Washington's responses to those developments. Particularly important are the 1992 United Nations Conference on the Environment and Development (UNCED or the Rio Summit) and other international conferences. In case after case, the United States sought to limit efforts to build an international legal and policy infrastructure on environmental matters. Before Rio, an emerging consensus had developed for the United States to lead worldwide efforts toward that goal. The United States' failure to accept leadership in 1992 and its subsequent behavior stand in contrast to the struggle of domestic subnational leaders, including state-level and nongovernmental individuals and organizations, to redress, at least in part, the poor record of the national government. Washington continued its pattern of missed opportunities with its responses to the 2015 Paris Agreement, reports from the UN's Intergovernmental Panel on Climate Change (particularly its 2018 report as well as a parallel report from the U.S. government itself), and the link of the UN's Millennium Development Goals with those of the environment.

The final area of lost opportunities centers the U.S. march to global leadership and the extent to which that leadership reflects national interests over global ones. Looking at the United States in terms of a "will to power" suggests that its claim to represent a larger humanity, dating from the time of George Washington, in fact, shields a tight focus on augmenting national power. A comparison with the United Kingdom and the latter's own idea of empire is informative in the context of today's many challenges to the collective future of humanity: ongoing demographic changes and transborder movements of peoples; the nature of the social compact that societies must embrace if they are to survive; the capacity of economic systems to accommodate that compact while generating promise for the complex political future that humanity appears to seek; the acceptance of humanity's place in the earth's ecology; the relationships among education, technology, and society; and our common security, including security conferred by the rule of law. Chapter 7, using a redefined concept of security, suggests a possible last chance for the United States.

My approach throughout is primarily historical, with a focus on the linkage between domestic and international affairs. To explore those linkages, I have relied primarily on the positions and policies of decision makers, looking at presentations by presidents to Congress, for example, as well as court decisions, international treaties, political memoirs, and political theoreticians and thinkers (Alexander Hamilton and Reinhold Niebuhr, for example). The failure to recognize national–international linkages has often been a cause for a mistaken separation of U.S. behavior from its consequences. On issue after issue, the results of the United States' rejection of proposals for change and its failure to seize opportunities to improve national and international society have returned to haunt the nation and the world. There appears to be little understanding of this fact and, thus, little or no preparation to deal with any of the fundamental issues it raises, hence the title: *While the U.S. Sleeps.*

1

Arms Limitation, Third-Party Dispute Settlement, and Security

The United States is both the world's dominant economy and its dominant military power, spending more on national security than all the major and second-tier military powers combined. However, dual supremacy has not resulted in security in either sphere. On the contrary, it has made the United States less secure in many ways, nationally and internationally, and within U.S. borders, militarism threatens the very democracy that armed might was to ensure.

This state of affairs was not inevitable; indeed, the United States has subverted a number of opportunities in the past century and earlier to bequeath to the present and future a different nation and, quite likely, a different international system and different paths for the world.

The Hague Conferences of 1899 and 1907

Named after the Dutch city where they took place, the Hague Conferences of 1899 and 1907 aimed at "limiting the progressive development of existing armaments" and serving as a means of "assuring to all the peoples [of the world] the blessings of real and lasting peace," in the words of Tsar Nicholas II, who called for the first gathering.[1] The Russian's actions caught political leaders off guard and even elicited anger from some. Many tried to ascertain his motives.

For the United States, the first of the two initiatives, May 7–July 29, 1899, could not have come at a worse time: just after the 1898 war with Spain. However, U.S. political leaders had no alternative but to attend the conference. Tsar Nicholas's call captured popular opinion against war, and his action reinforced a strong, vocal peace movement that had emerged in Russia, Europe, and the United States. At the first conference, the leaders spent much of their time publicly lauding the tsar and suggesting a strong attachment to peace.

The United States, through Pres. William McKinley's nuanced voice, tried to indicate that the conference proposal to limit arms (which he termed an "exalted proposal") was really directed at the nations of Europe, although "it behooves us as a nation to lend countenance and aid to the beneficent project."[2] The president voiced the prevailing reasoning among U.S. foreign policy elites that "the active military force of the United States, as measured by our population, territorial area, and taxable wealth," was so "conspicuously less than that of European powers" during times of peace that the tsar's project could not conceivably have any practicable application.

The U.S. delegation, especially through the leading voice of Capt. Alfred T. Mahan, joined with that of the United Kingdom, which, as the dominant power, wanted little by way of arms limitation. Together, they shaped a consensus merely to study arms limitation further. According to Sir Julian Pauncefort, the British delegate to the conference, Mahan had already indicated to the British that the United States would, "on no account, even discuss the question of any limitation on naval armaments."[3] Mahan considered U.S. vital interests to follow primarily an East–West trajectory in international relations rather than a North–South frame. Further, he thought the United States would be "compelled, by fact if not explicit policy, to take a leading part in the struggle for Chinese markets," a course of action that would entail "considerable increase in her [U.S.] naval forces in the Pacific."[4]

On behalf of the United States, Mahan voted no on whether governments should prohibit the use of projectiles, the principal purpose of which was, Tate wrote, the "diffusion of asphyxiating gasses."[5] With that vote, Mahan weakened the conference's core objective: limiting arms. Because projectiles could have a decisive effect during war, Mahan believed that denying a country the right to use them was the equivalent of denying the advantage of such weapons, a line of reasoning that continued with the advent of U.S. military preeminence.

On the matter of devising a means of ensuring peace for all, the conference focused on arbitration as a peaceful, third-party way to settle disputes. A third-party mode of settlement would help end the morally and legally corrosive practice of having states serve as judges of their own causes and actions, and it would build a greater sense of fairness into international relations. The conference did agree on creating an arbitration court, now called the Permanent Court of Arbitration, but only after overriding strong German and British opposition. Both claimed that war entailed fixed schedules, so arbitration might only buy time for powerful rivals to overcome any advantages that those schedules might confer.

The disappointment of peace activists and others over the limited achievements in disarmament was, in part, balanced by gains in the sphere of arbitration.

Governmental and nongovernmental peace groups deepened their engagement in the debates as well as in peace congresses (1904, 1905, 1906) and peace societies in France, the United Kingdom, Italy, Germany, Scotland, and the United States, among other countries.

The activists began to demand that governments publicly commit to arbitration and sometimes compulsory arbitration, a principle that gained ground between the first and second Hague Conferences. Denmark, for example, entered into arbitration treaties with Holland (1904) and Italy (1906); Norway entered into a treaty with its then rival Sweden (1905), and those two countries also demilitarized their frontiers. These developments prompted UK prime minister Sir Henry Campbell-Bannerman to declare in 1905 not only that he had cause to "rejoice that the principle of arbitration had made great strides" but also that his nation had conquered a most important psychological barrier: "It is no longer counted a weakness for any of the Great Powers to submit to a higher tribunal."[6]

Amid these speeches and decisions, however, other international developments provided cause for concern and even dismay. For example, the United Kingdom refused to submit its differences with South Africa to arbitration, and the nations went to war (Boer War, 1899–1902). Also, the wanton destruction of people, institutions, and property, with foreign powers playing a major role, followed the Boxer Uprising in China (1899–1901). Panama, with U.S. help, forcefully separated from Columbia in 1903 to facilitate the building of the Panama Canal. Even more dangerous in terms of international peace and security were the Russian–Japanese War (1904–1905) and the Moroccan Crises in 1905 and 1906, which threatened to ignite an all-European war. Augmenting the fear and tensions associated with these events was an escalating arms race as Italy, France, and Germany steeply increased their military spending and the United Kingdom doubled the spending of all three nations put together.[7]

Rising arms spending, increasingly lethal weapons, and the outbreak or threat of wars made the cause of worldwide, third-party dispute settlement all the more compelling and urgent. It is one thing to have bilateral agreements for resolving differences between two states; it is quite another to have a universal commitment to settling disputes.

In the United States, the Lake Mohonk Conference on International Arbitration was among the peace groups and societies pushing to strengthen international arbitration by making it compulsory, unlike the voluntary kind agreed to in 1899. Consisting of a number of wealthy people, mostly philanthropists, who had privileged access to presidents, Congress, and other leading organs and members of government, the Mohonk Conference brought considerable pressure to bear on Pres. Theodore Roosevelt, and he indicated that he was favorably disposed to arbitration on a number of occasions during this period.[8] The president also made promises in 1904 to both the Universal Peace Congress and the Inter-Parliamentary

Union (which counted members of Congress among its members) that he would call for another international gathering to deal with arms reduction and arbitration.

With some degree of public concern about the U.S. Navy's expansion following the war with Spain, President Roosevelt, on December 6, 1904, informed Congress that he had asked other countries to join in a second Hague conference. "It is hoped that the work already begun at the Hague may be carried some steps further toward completion," he declared.[9] Those steps would entail both arms limitation and the compulsory third-party settlement of disputes.

In the same speech, President Roosevelt noted that the "maxim of law that for every wrong, there was a remedy" was not yet applicable to international law and would not be without a "judicial way of enforcing a right in international law."[10] He went further: until some method was devised of "international control over offending nations," it would be "a wicked thing for most civilized powers to disarm." Doing so would mean the immediate "recrudescence of barbarism of one form or the other."[11] Compulsory arbitration would not satisfy all the requirements, but it would be a major step on the way.

The idea that Roosevelt would call a second Hague conference became even more promising in 1905 after he mediated the end of the Russo-Japanese War. That achievement brought him and the United States considerable world recognition and prestige, including the 1906 Nobel Peace Prize for the president. He played a similar role in the 1905 Moroccan Crisis involving France, Germany, and the United Kingdom, raising his international standing even further. Indeed, Carl Schurz, a reformer and Republican Party leader, congratulated the president on his successful mediation between Japan and Russia and asked him to use his influence, in the service of humankind, to promote the "gradual diminution of the oppressive burdens imposed upon nations by the armed peace."[12]

On September 13, 2005, Roosevelt received a memorandum from Russia indicating that the time was favorable, given the conclusion of the Russo-Japanese War, to extend the work of the 1899 Hague Conference. However, the president, then singularly able to exercise a persuasive influence on other countries at such a conference and who had promised to call one, yielded the initiative to Tsar Nicholas. That decision proved to be most unfortunate. First, it discouraged and weakened the influence of peace groups, especially the Inter-Parliamentary Union, which had obtained the president's promise to lead a second Hague conference. Second, it allowed an internationally diminished Nicholas II, reeling from defeat by Japan and then politically and morally enfeebled by domestic uprisings seeking to overthrow the monarchy, to lead where and when he was least able to. For example, the tsar, who had become politically dependent on the Russian military after a 1905 uprising at home, could not seriously push for arms limitation, the major failure from the 1899 Hague Conference. The military, after the Russo-Japanese War had exposed its weakness, could hardly be expected to press the case for arms reduction. Just as important, the Russian economy depended deeply on European finance, especially from France but increasingly the United Kingdom as well. London, the main opponent to any change in the distribution of power, staunchly supported the status quo. France, observing Germany's growth in armaments, especially in defeating France in the Franco-Prussian War of 1870, resisted any limitation of its arms as long as Germany continued increasing its military power. Berlin, for its part, was not about to freeze a status quo favorable to the United Kingdom. The latter, which had remained neutral during the Russo-Japanese War, had begun courting Russia (at France's prompting) in pursuit of an alliance against Germany, leading to the Triple Entente in August 1907.

In this broad context, before the second Hague Conference convened on June 18, 1907, the major powers struck understandings to say little about arms limitation. Instead, they would focus on improving the Permanent Court of Arbitration. Efforts to secure compulsory arbitration of differences between and among states failed.[13] The nations did agree to some limitation on floating mines, the bombardment of undefended towns, and the dropping of explosives from the air. Also, they secured a prohibition against using poison gases, but the conference left nations to continue the arms race.

The failure of the 1907 Hague Conference was vexing, both morally and spiritually, for a number of reasons. The first conference had set in motion profound expectations. Never before had nations gathered to discuss peace for all human beings.[14] The gathering represented a qualitative change in the very nature of international relations, and when both President Roosevelt and Tsar Nicholas spoke of furthering its work, it was in the spirit of this change. Although the 1899 conference did not limit arms or military budgets, it stirred a movement and set the stage for deeper and wider deliberations by peoples and governments.

To limit the disappointments after the 1907 conference, the delegates envisioned a third conference for 1914. President Roosevelt, the self-acknowledged believer in and advocate for the "most civilized powers," claimed that they would accept limits to their armaments and military budgets if there were greater "international cohesion and sense of international duties." In fact, Roosevelt had the opportunity to take the lead in effecting that greater cohesion. Not only did he have strong domestic support for such a venture, but also, he could point to the U.S.–Canada demarcation as the world's longest demilitarized international border as an example. Moreover, he retained considerable trust among governments, especially after his mediatory interventions in the Moroccan Crisis and the Russo-Japanese War.

Roosevelt's failure to accept the opportunity coincided with the expiration of the time for another conference as World War I began. Merze Tate writes, "[T]he most highly civilized nations of the world possessed of the most powerful and deadly means of destruction devised to that time . . . engaged in one of the most ghastly annihilations in history."[15]

Why did President Roosevelt refuse to lead the second conference? His offered reason to Secretary of State Elihu Root was that he did "not want to appear as a professional peace advocate."[16] While this partly captures his position, it masks a larger complex of factors that induced him to sacrifice an opportunity for peace in preference for his search for great power status for the United States: the idea of "frontier"; the matter of U.S. identity; the emulation of great powers, especially the United Kingdom; and the notion of U.S. exceptionalism.

For Roosevelt, the expansion from the Atlantic Ocean across the American West had changed and shaped the U.S. character and culture into one of courage, adventure, conquest, and faith in progress. With the apparent closing of this frontier, what would happen to the most distinctive qualities of the "American spirit"? Complementing this territorial outlook was an inherited geopolitical frontier defined by President Washington (and buttressed by President Monroe), urging a focus on the Americas while avoiding entangling political intercourse with European powers. Roosevelt as well as many of his influential supporters sought new frontiers to ensure the continuing development of the American character and "manhood."[17]

In the matter of identity, racial and other, concern was rising about the perceived waning of the nation's Anglo-Saxon heritage, defined by intelligence, courage, valor, self-sacrifice, high-mindedness, and broad heroic achievements, including conquest in warfare. Sentiments of the kind, about a "softening" of the republic, are found in Roosevelt's fourth annual message to Congress: "Many times, peoples who are slothful or timid or shortsighted, who have been enervated by ease and luxury . . . have shrunk in unmanly fashion from doing duty that was stern and needed self-sacrifice"; these persons have instead "sought to hide from their own minds their shortcomings, their ignoble motives, by their love of peace."[18] In short, Roosevelt did not want to reinforce sentiments for peace, especially when pushing for a new frontier, including the frontier that came with the Anglo-Saxon virtues displayed by Admiral Dewey in defeating Spain in the Philippines.[19]

Emulation and exceptionalism offer complementary reasons for Roosevelt's reluctance to lead the second Hague Conference. The president admired and sought to emulate the United Kingdom, a fellow Anglo-Saxon country, especially in the area of naval supremacy and its expansive links to the rest of the world. He also admired the Dutch and their place in what is today Indonesia, the French in Algeria, the Russians in Turkistan, and the Japanese in Taiwan. In his view, these nations were doing the "world's work," and the United States should share in that endeavor beyond the Caribbean and the Atlantic into the Pacific. Above all, he sought, especially by enlarging the U.S. Navy, to expand U.S. influence throughout the world or, phrased differently, assume "her rightful place" among the great powers.[20]

In pursuing this aim, Roosevelt expressed not only his own views but also those of a broadening political and psychological terrain among political elites, including the following: members of the Senate, where Henry Cabot Lodge's views on the U.S. role in the world were at least as expansive as Roosevelt's; the House of Representatives, where Speaker Thomas Read had lost broad support because he opposed increased military spending, especially for the navy; and secretaries of state and military thinkers who imbibed the scholarly work of Captain Mahan, including his influential book *The Influence of Sea Power upon History, 1660–1783*.[21] In fact, a few months after the second Hague Conference ended, the United States sent the Great White Fleet—fourteen thousand sailors, eighteen battleships, and their supporting cast—around the world to emphasize U.S. industrial and military power. How would a public leader of a conference for peace appear when so avidly pursuing military expansion?

Between 1898 and 1904, those expansive ideas extended to U.S. sponsorship of the building of the Panama Canal, taking control of Cuba, Puerto Rico, Guam, and the Philippines and annexing Hawaii—but no official use of the term *imperialism* or even *expansionism* ever characterized U.S. foreign policy. Those terms were reserved for Europe. Henry Cabot Lodge simply referred to "the large policy" to distinguish Europeans' actions from those of the United States. Roosevelt and others saw the United States as better and more decent than other nations. Never part of the unending dynastic struggle of Europe, the United States instead opened its borders to and developed from refugees, people fleeing persecution and corruption.[22] This nation was exceptional; it had a special mission.

The Interwar Years: Arms Limitation and Criminalization of War

During the Hague Conferences' clamors for limiting arms, the United States contended that it could not follow the actions recommended by some countries, nongovernmental groups, and popular sentiments unless an organization or internationally recognized institution could enforce decisions resulting from international deliberations and agreements. Such a third-party enforcer emerged in the period between World War I and World War II, but the United States, bent on global supremacy as the United Kingdom's dominance waned, found other reasons for resisting, until it was too late, the type of arms control needed and sought.

The first significant development in the domain of international organization was the League of Nations. Articles 10 and 16 of the league's covenant, which went into effect in 1920, provided for collective action—in the form of financial,

7

economic, and military sanctions—to repel attacks by any nation that might impair the political independence and territorial integrity of member states. However, the United States did not join the league, which President Coolidge called a "foreign agency" that would limit Washington's freedom and independence.[23] This reaction to the league, despite its creation to help ensure international peace in part by enforcing international law and policy, came even after other nations had made unprecedented concessions to the United States. The wording of Article 21 provided for international recognition of U.S. domination of the Americas and the Caribbean: "Nothing in the Covenant shall be deemed to affect the validity of international engagements . . . or regional understandings like the Monroe Doctrine, for securing the maintenance of peace."

For years, the United States had used the Monroe Doctrine to justify high levels of military spending, but this did not affect a line of reasoning that Senator Borah of Idaho advanced against joining the League of Nations. He argued that one "cannot yoke a government whose fundamental maxim is that of liberty to a government whose first law is that of force and hope to preserve the former," and he inveighed against committing the United States "to a scheme of world control based on force."[24] In other words, the United States could not accept arms limitations without institutions for international enforcement of law and policy, yet given such an institution, even a relatively weak one that could not succeed without U.S. participation, it was described as a form of "world control," contrary to liberty.

The United States did join the league's Permanent Court of International Justice—sort of. The court, which came into being under the league's covenant in 1920, had an optional clause. It bound a state accepting that clause to compulsory arbitration of international disputes. The United States became a signatory to the optional clause, but it never became a member of the court despite the immense prestige its membership would have conferred on the court, multiple assertions since 1899 about Washington's commitment to a law-governed world, and many promises to join.

The United States had come out of World War I as a creditor nation for the first time in its history, and its industrial capacity and balance of payments surpassed those of the entire British empire. This newly won status made the United States the world's banker, and every country would have to seek its favor.[25] Washington was not prepared to subordinate this position to any international organization regardless of what even the most limited subordination could mean for the world.

Two other developments in the interwar years are of concern here: continuing efforts at arms control or limitation and a revolutionary step that made war a crime. At the end of World War I, people throughout the world and many national leaders resolved that changes should be effected in the suicidal armament policies defining the decades preceding 1914. As a result, the postwar settlements incorporated policies to avert or limit future arms races. To give a concrete expression to these policies, the settlements provided disarming the defeated powers, especially Germany and its allies, and simultaneously taking the unprecedented step of obligating the victors to voluntarily reduce their own armaments.[26]

Germany, which joined the League of Nations in 1926, was honoring the terms of the Treaty of Versailles, which required it to reduce its arms to a level consistent with self-defense. Reminiscent of today's nonproliferation treaties, Germany understood (and repeatedly asserted) that it and its former allies should not be expected to observe the "self-defense only" condition indefinitely in the absence of good faith actions on the part of other major powers, especially the United States and the other victors. Indeed, Germany began to insist, with justification widely recognized by other nations, that all league members should make their promised contributions to international security.[27]

Pres. Franklin Delano Roosevelt seemed to agree at first, apparently bypassing a series of excuses the United States had given in the 1920s for not giving greater support to disarmament. On May 10, 1933, he informed Congress that he thought offensive weapons, which had the capacity to overwhelm defenses—aside from causing unacceptable, recurring budget challenges—were a source of people's and nations' fear. Therefore, he would share with other nations a plan to reduce weapons, with the understanding of the "simple fact that invasion of any nation or the destruction of national sovereignty can be prevented only by the complete elimination of the [offensive] weapons that make such a course possible."[28] He further contended, without acknowledging the need for an organization to help provide security for all, that "[t]he way to disarm is to disarm. The way to prevent invasion is to make it impossible" by getting rid of offensive weapons.[29]

Roosevelt's proposal was prompted by the rise of Hitler in Germany. Unfortunately, he put forth no specific plan for enforcing any disarmament agreement. France, for example, which would be among the most vulnerable countries were Germany to rearm, objected on the grounds that the approach to disarmament required a different sequence. Before disarmament must come a mechanism to ensure the enforcement of agreements. However, before and during FDR's administration, the U.S. position opposed granting the league any powers of supervision or control in matters of disarmament. With the world's most powerful country unsupportive of enforcement[30] and other leading nations uncertain and even fearful about their capacity to resist aggression, the league was crippled—as was seen when Japan invaded Manchuria in 1931 and then withdrew from the league the next year. Hitler apparently learned much from Japan's model. In October 1933, he withdrew from the league, blaming the other major states for refusing to act in good faith to disarm.

While disarmament failed for many reasons, the unfortunate lack of substantive U.S. support was the principal cause. That lack was particularly painful because the 1928 Pact of Paris took the first steps to inaugurate a new order in matters of war and peace.[31] In contrast with the Hague Conferences, the League of Nations, and disarmament or arms limitation talks, the pact was not concerned with finding ways to make wars less brutal or more morally acceptable. Rather, it was concerned with nothing less than criminalizing and abolishing war. Article 1 specifically stipulates that states "condemn recourse to war for the solution of international controversies and renounce it as an instrument of policy in their relations with one another." Article 2 states that "the settlement of all disputes and conflicts of whatever nature or whatever origin they may be, which may arise among them, shall be sought by pacific means."[32]

It would have been far more effective for the United States to have insisted on complete disarmament with league enforcement based on the Pact of Paris rather than tinkering with the "old order" of arms limitation and arms reduction. After all, the United States was a joint author of this important international instrument, which appealed to the highest normative instincts in international relations and which had the shared support of the world at large, including Germany and Japan. Continuing the old-order approach confused rather than helped clarify the emerging new order that Washington had helped give birth to. Under the Pact of Paris, in fact, neutrality was illegal under the new order in contrast to the old regime that accepted war as legal.[33]

The United States, which had historically benefited commercially from neutral stances, refused to take the position that wars were criminal pursuits that made neutrality impossible. Instead, when Japan had invaded Manchuria, the United States, seeking to protect the interests of U.S. citizens in China, merely issued a statement of non-recognition of Japanese activities.[34]

What if the United States had labeled Japan's acts in Manchuria (and later Italy's in Ethiopia) as criminal in nature? What if, as a result of criminal courses of conduct, Washington called on other states to cut off trade with Japan? Aside from the major powers, members of the league's general assembly were, as a group, outraged by the failure of the league's council to punish Japan and would have supported a U.S.-led initiative within or outside the league. This would have given pause to other countries contemplating aggression. One may even contend that the principle of a crime against peace, grounded on the Pact of Paris (and that later served as the basis for trials and convictions of German and Japanese military leaders after World War II), would have been better known to the world and have far greater influence today. The principle was partly weakened after World War II because it wore the appearance of something used by victors against the defeated instead of a widely, publicly, and popularly recognized legal and moral norm of international life.

Along with other international understandings, a recognition of crimes against peace might have contributed to the creation of a new, mutually beneficial order among nations. Instead, that failure helps preserve a vague demarcation between the old and new orders, one in which the United States can use its military and economic ascendency to a perceived, indefinite advantage.

The 1986 Gorbachev–Reagan Initiative and the 2017 Nuclear Ban Treaty

Between World War II and 1986, competition to develop nuclear weapons proceeded incessantly, with little regard for voices of caution, dissent, and warning.[35] Weapons piled on weapons, delivery systems upon delivery systems, levels of destructiveness upon levels of destructiveness, and theory after theory of nuclear deterrence.[36] It was as if moral sensibilities had become nonexistent, as the nuclear utilization thinkers (NUTs), who believed that a nuclear war could be fought and won, inveighed against the mutual assured destruction thinkers (MADs), who felt that weapons would deter foes who understood how a nuclear war would end.

In 1985, the Soviet Union gained a new leader, Mikhail Gorbachev. Intellectually able and imaginative and, at the age of fifty-four, relatively young for a general secretary of the Communist Party, he was born in rather modest circumstances but rose to the highest levels of leadership—what Americans would call living the American dream. He had seen and experienced the excesses of Soviet authoritarianism, come to understand how poorly his country's economic system was performing, and seen that many billions of rubles went to supporting the military while his country's social and cultural ills increased. Perhaps most profound of all, he came to recognize the decline of the moral and psychological passion and historical truth the Soviet Union was to have embodied. He had become an unbeliever.

The West, led by the United States, believed that the Soviet Union continued to pose strong military and political threats even if it was becoming economically weak.[37] Washington sought to limit Soviet actions in the political and military domains and to allow social and economic deterioration to continue.[38] Mikhail Gorbachev would have none of what the United States envisioned. In 1985, he introduced two major programs. Glasnost (openness) had to do with making Soviet society's goings-on transparent through radio, television, publishing, schools, churches, public discussions, debate, and the transborder movement of peoples, among other things. Perestroika (restructuring) sought to dismantle the Stalinist state machinery and remove the Communist Party's stranglehold, replacing them with institutional structures, especially in the economy, that would transform an authoritarian state into a social democratic system, not unlike certain Western European societies.[39] Few people in either country had believed such changes were possible in the Soviet Union.

Gorbachev also sought to put in place a vision (albeit with few details) of reorganized relations among nations. Partly, this was to deal with what he saw as the Soviet Union's low levels of investment, lack of innovation, inefficiencies in production, and wasteful military spending. In this context, he made a dramatic proposal after largely prevailing against those in his own country who believed that Moscow should always be prepared to win a nuclear war because deterrence might not work. To effect his international vision, Gorbachev needed a partner and thought he saw one in the U.S. president.

Five years before Gorbachev took office, Ronald Reagan had won the election chiefly on a promise to restore America's military strength, and he then oversaw considerable increases in military spending that augmented U.S. self-confidence about its military prowess.[40] In 1983, President Reagan had presented the Strategic Defense Initiative (SDI, popularly known as Star Wars), seeking to create a space-based defense system to protect the United States from a strategic nuclear attack. By the time Gorbachev had become general secretary, SDI research was well underway, with billions of dollars being invested in it. While this might make him an odd partner to Gorbachev, Reagan's 1983 language about the SDI suggested otherwise. He was persuaded that "the human spirit must be capable of rising above dealing with other nations and human beings by threatening their existence."[41]

In fact, the threat of a nuclear exchange had generated severe anxiety in both countries, with the Soviet buildup of its strategic offensive weapons capabilities during the 1970s and early 1980s, the similar U.S. buildup during that period and into the Reagan administration, and tensions generated by wars in Afghanistan, the Middle East, Central America, and Southern Africa, among other areas—wars that either directly or indirectly implicated both Moscow and Washington. Further, for Gorbachev, the April 1986 nuclear reactor explosion at Chernobyl, releasing more than a hundred times the radiation of the atomic bombs dropped on Hiroshima and Nagasaki, reinforced his conviction of the need for bold steps to deal with nuclear weapons as part of his overall focus on transforming the Soviet Union.

At a summit meeting in Reykjavik, Iceland, on October 11–12, 1986, the Soviet general secretary proposed to the U.S. president that their nations eliminate *all* offensive strategic nuclear weapons within a decade.[42] Within the first five years, the two nations would eliminate 50 percent of the weapons, with the remainder eliminated over the next five years. Complementing this effort would be a collaboration between the two superpowers in the area of common security.

Gorbachev's initiative had one condition. Under the terms of the 1972 Anti-Ballistic Missile Treaty, the United States would forego "testing in space of all space components of the missile defense" and confine itself to "research and testing in laboratories."[43] Gorbachev's proposal astonished the U.S. delegation.

Defense Department officials rejected it, as did many on the National Security Council, although in a more nuanced way. However, the State Department, led by George Shultz, urged consideration. The president accepted Shultz's counsel, having decided to test the Soviet leader in responding to a pre-Reykjavik letter from Gorbachev.[44]

Gorbachev was willing to make almost every concession the United States asked for, including retreating on matters calculated to reassure his own allies, many of whom would be as anxious as U.S. leaders about the proposal. However, Gorbachev refused to drop his opposition to the SDI. For him, ending the SDI would be a test of U.S. good faith. If the two nations were eliminating offensive weapons, why would the United States require a space defense system, and how consistent would the SDI be with the very language used to justify research into its feasibility? Did not President Reagan give as a reason for SDI research "the ultimate goal of eliminating the threat posed by strategic nuclear missiles"? Eliminating these missiles—all of them—would eliminate their threat.

The path-breaking significance of Gorbachev's proposal was clear. Reagan, on finding Gorbachev immovable on the SDI, asked his team to reexamine matters. He especially sought to move the more conservative members of the U.S. delegation who, like Reagan himself, deeply mistrusted the Soviet Union.[45] They stood firm on the SDI, however, and Reagan said no to Gorbachev.

That refusal has had deep repercussions. The vicious arms buildup cycle has continued (despite some here-and-there rounds of arms reduction), with technology, including artificial intelligence, assuming ever greater roles in military and civilian thinking and escalating the lethality of weapons systems. For example, on July 7, 2017, 122 countries voted to approve the Treaty on the Prohibition of Nuclear Weapons, forbidding states to "use or threaten to use nuclear weapons or other nuclear explosive [devices]" and prohibiting states from developing, testing, or stockpiling nuclear weapons.[46] However, the United States, abdicating moral leadership, has been the treaty's leading opponent. Washington refuses to ratify or become a party to the treaty because it disregards the "reality" of the international security environment, which it says proves the necessity of nuclear weapons.[47]

Further, in March 2018, the Trump administration proposed creating a "U.S. Space Force" that would be separate from the U.S. Air Force.[48] This would violate the 1967 Outer Space Treaty, which forbids the use of space for military purposes. The open move into space underscores the failure of the United States to accept complicity in the Cold War and the military rivalry it had entailed. In the U.S. view, this nation had simply reacted to threats from others. In fact, as forcefully stated by the "father of containment," George Kennan, "[i]t was we who first produced and tested the device [atomic bomb]; we who were the first to raise its destructiveness to a new level with the hydrogen bomb; we who introduced the multiple warheads; we who declared the principle of 'first use'; and we alone, so help us God, who have used the weapons in anger against others and against ten thousands of helpless non-combatants at that."[49] Will the United States now add to these steps backward, among others, and become the first to initiate an outer space force? This step began many years ago, although Washington now uses China and Russia as the rationale as they emulate and try to catch up with the United States.[50]

The United States rejected the idea of common security, proposed by Gorbachev, along with its associated abolition scheme. The general secretary continued, after Reagan, to work with George H. W. Bush to urge the abolition of the North Atlantic Treaty Organization (NATO) and the Warsaw Pact, but the United States felt that doing so would undermine U.S. worldwide preeminence. As Rozanne Ridgway, then U.S. ambassador to East Germany, argued, substituting a common security for strategic missiles "would change the way we walked down the street."[51] It would indeed transform the way Americans see themselves and other see them; it would change the U.S. identity.

The rejection of Gorbachev's grand proposal revealed the U.S. government's lack of interest in his democracy project for the Soviet Union despite laudatory comments from Washington and other Western leaders.[52] Gorbachev got almost no material help from the United States despite his risk-taking to effect radical civil and political changes within the Soviet Union, along with his external focus on arms reduction and elimination. Even the image he sought to build of a leader who had won Western approval was defeated, at least in part, when the United States refused to allow him to speak to the American people—even as he had given some U.S. leaders access to his nation.[53]

A number of observers, including former secretary of state George Shultz, have downplayed the impact of wasting the Reykjavik opportunity, suggesting that Gorbachev's proposal was not genuine. Shultz argued that Gorbachev had made so many concessions because he feared the SDI and went to Reykjavik to kill it,[54] yet Shultz not only misrepresents actual events but also gives a considerable impetus toward more SDI spending. While the SDI itself, by 2017, had "barely made it past the concept stage,"[55] interest escalated in military activities in outer space, although just as much for offense as for defense.[56]

In another rewriting of the events surrounding and following Reykjavik, political scientist Francis Fukuyama ascribed the dissolution of the Soviet Union to liberalism's victory over communism.[57] On the contrary, the fall is directly attributable to some of Gorbachev's reforms, such as deliberately weakening the Communist Party's control of the state and society.

The rejection of Gorbachev's proposal may have even contributed to growing militarization within the United States. With the dissolution of the Soviet Union, Washington celebrated not so much a victory for liberalism as an ideology or set of values but the triumph of U.S. military power—power used to reshape the world in a manner consistent with perceived U.S. interests.[58] Contrary to Reagan's announced intent for the SDI, the United States has not come to feel that it can rise above threatening the existence of other human beings, countries, or nature. In 2002, the United States unilaterally abandoned the 1972 Anti-Ballistic Missile Treaty with Russia, and the Trump administration has withdrawn from the 1987 Intermediate-Range Nuclear Forces Treaty, negotiated by Reagan and Gorbachev, requiring the banning of short- and intermediate-range missiles from land. The security sought by the 2014 NSA Report, on which many security concerns since then has relied, is nowhere in sight.[59]

The U.S. objective has been to reduce Soviet power and reinforce its own ascendency; aggravating the Soviet Union's social and political problems would further that end. Only a few years after the Soviet Union had broken up, the United States aided Boris Yeltsin, inviting the first president of the Russian Federation to speak to a joint session of Congress in 1992. Under the guise of creating a market economy, Yeltsin had opened Russia to cruel exploitation, led by oligarchs. In U.S. eyes, this new order, which passed for a market economy, was more important than democracy.

Gorbachev, on the other hand, while committed to democracy, had wanted social democracy that was roughly comparable to that practiced in Western Europe. Like his countryman Boris Pasternak wrote in *Doctor Zhivago*, Gorbachev saw communism as the "god that had failed" and felt that a new form of society would have to be created not only to vindicate the suffering of all who had sacrificed for the romantic ideal of the classless society but also to find a way to ensure human dignity and societal self-fulfillment. The Russia that the United States had sought and Yeltsin had offered promised none of this. How different would the world, Russia, and U.S. relations with Russia have been had Gorbachev's vision come to pass?

2

Economic Models Chosen
and Pursued

In its development and its success in achieving domestic affluence and international economic dominance, the United States has embraced three models of political economy: mercantilism, liberalism, and neoliberalism. None of the three has been "pure," but each, within the broader system called capitalism, has had its clear outline, impact, and influence on what the nation has been, is, and may become. These models, especially the last two, have deeply affected the world through emulation, imposition, and bilateral or multilateral institutional arrangements.

Mercantilism, largely followed in the pre-modern era but especially elaborated in the global West, is an outlook or doctrine and body of practices urging or expressing the broad regulation of economic activities in the interest of national societies and the state's wealth, usually in the form of accumulated capital (e.g., gold, silver, currency, general infrastructure). The state pursues the augmentation of its own power and the ascendency of polity over economy: economic regulation is broad, grounded on the view that a principal role of the state is translating individual interests on behalf of the general or common good.

Liberalism, a competitor of and successor to mercantilism, emerged as the feudal order, and its landed aristocracy declined in the West, gradually replaced by the ascending, soon-to-be-dominant commercial class. Often referred to as the bourgeoisie, this class, consistent with its commercial interests, emphasizes the freedoms of travel, inquiry, and exchange as well as freedoms from old customs, hierarchical arrangements, and special favors that monarchs and like leaders granted, often based on blood or some preferred status. In the latter sense, liberalism has become associated with equality. At its center is the idea of liberty, often defined as "negative freedom" and broadly understood as the freedom from state-imposed restrictions. Complementing this negative freedom, a defining attribute of American conservatism, is an affirmative one, long associated with American liberals: freedom as the capacity, which governments can foster, to realize human potential.

Adam Smith, in *The Wealth of Nations*, captured the heart of liberalism's economic outlook. He argued that wealth is best accumulated not through government regulations of commerce or investment but through the unlimited liberty of individuals to engage in exchanges consistent with self-interest, including the exchange of labor and the operation of specialization. Further, the drive and passion resulting from individual self-interest bring about competition; this, in turn, supervises the quantity and quality of goods and other features of commercial activities. Thus, Smith contended, the wealth of nations and the common good are best served by competition and the freedom that allows for that competition, not by government regulations.

Neoliberalism "updates" Smith to make liberalism's operation all the more pervasive and effective. It argues that human and societal well-being can best be assured and advanced by releasing (liberating) the skills, entrepreneurial bent, and imaginative faculties of individuals and private organizations to pursue self-chosen goals. Because these faculties are often unknowable in advance, they cannot be properly regulated within well-defined institutional arrangements, including the law. "Well-defined" in this context suggests that liberty is fostered when the actors know in advance what is normatively expected.

Neoliberal institutional arrangements, bearing close resemblance to those under nineteenth-century laissez-faire capitalism, include widely shared values of private property rights, free trade (the self-regulating market), and the sanctity of contracts. These comprise the core of the commitment to the rule of law. At both the domestic and international levels, this outlook has been translated to mean, among other things, open markets (everything, ideally, including labor, should be subject to the market), free trade, deregulation and the privatization of public-owned entities, and an expanded private-sector role in civil society (public schools, for example). Neoliberalism sees the self-regulating market as not only providing greater human freedom but also a check on the polity—some would say to ensure that economy dominates polity, the reverse of mercantilism.

Despite their differences, the three models reflect continuity in the development of the United States around achieving one goal: economic preeminence. The quest for and operation of that status has not only caused much suffering within and beyond U.S. borders but also alienated allies and threatened the models' ostensible ends, and now it bodes ill for domestic social stability and the stability of the international economic system.

17

The Mercantilist Period: 1789–1930

The Founding Fathers knew they were creating a unique polity: a republic, as opposed to the then all-pervading presence of monarchies. They also consciously intended to put in place the basis for a great nation. The "greatness" to which they directed their attention—borrowing from many political cultures, including ancient Rome, Athens, and Sparta—was the emerging grandeur of the United Kingdom, minus its monarchical system and its perceived corruption.

Pres. George Washington, in his 1796 farewell address, expressed that sentiment and the ambition, provided that the young republic could deal with what he saw as geographic sectionalism and political factionalism and carefully manage foreign affairs. What would await such success, "at no distant period," would be "a great nation, to give to mankind the magnanimous and too novel example of a people always guided by an exalted justice and benevolence."[1]

Besides Washington, the person who had helped lay the foundation for this sought greatness was Alexander Hamilton. His theoretical and pragmatic policy focus set the stage for a mercantilist model of economic development, and it commanded the direction of U.S. policy and society from 1789 to 1930. Bearing in mind that a strong national government was necessary for what he had envisioned, Hamilton devised and pursued a three-pronged plan with a view to defeating those who—like Thomas Jefferson, James Madison, and others—preferred a relatively weak central government, a focus on agriculture, and less emphasis on manufacture.

Hamilton carried out his plan as secretary of the treasury, the largest and most important department of the government at the time. First, he had the federal government assume debt incurred not only during the Confederation Period before the ratification of the U.S. Constitution—and there was debt at every level of government—but during the revolutionary period as well. The latter included debts to Holland and France; the success of the American Revolution had depended on credit from those nations. Assuming these debts brought goodwill and prestige to the new government, and it set the stage for improving its credit worthiness.

Second, to strengthen that creditworthiness, again in opposition to Jefferson and Madison, Hamilton won the support of George Washington and Congress to establish the First Bank of the United States in 1791, a predecessor to today's Federal Reserve Bank. In Hamilton's own words, expressed in Federalist Paper No. 30 in 1787, "Money . . . is considered the vital principle of the body politic; as that which sustains its life and motion, and enables it to perform its most essential functions."[2] If that principle is so essential, the government should have a say in operating the central bank.

The third prong in Hamilton's plan was not only to provide strong government support for agriculture, widely believed to be the preeminent source of income and wealth, but also to give even greater emphasis to manufacturing. To Hamilton, while agriculture has a "strong claim to pre-eminence over every other kind of industry," it should have no exclusive claim to that status.[3] Manufacturing, among other industries, had the capacity to increase the division of labor and specialized skills, offer employment to the nation (including women and children), attract skilled labor through immigration, substitute domestically manufactured goods for imports, contribute to technological progress, cultivate greater diversity of talents, and increase demand for surplus from agriculture. In short, manufacturing could create a nation that offers the amplest opportunities to "stimulate the activity of the human mind, by multiplying the objects of enterprise . . . [and expanding the means] by which the wealth of a nation can be promoted."[4]

Again, Hamilton won this third feature of his plan in part because on its success depended both the ascendancy of manufacturing and the repayment of the debt that the federal government had assumed. However, he knew that manufacturing could never succeed on the scale he had envisioned without considerable help from the federal government. This task could not be left to private-sector initiative. Given the underdevelopment of the United States compared with that of Europe, "the United States cannot exchange with Europe on equal terms"; the absence of "reciprocity" would make the new nation "the victim of a system which would induce them to confine their views to agriculture and refrain from manufactures."[5]

Over the years, the mercantilist orientation became embedded in the country's political economy. Like China and India today and the Global South in general, Hamilton did not want to be confined, technologically or otherwise. He knew, as did members of Congress, that impoverishment awaited the United States if it allowed the advantages of manufacturing to remain with Europe. In his view, "It was for the U.S. to consider what means it could devise to render itself the least dependent" on European manufacture.[6]

The means were many, as Hamilton proposed to Congress, and the country followed. These included protective duties (tariffs) on foreign goods rivalling domestic products, prohibitions on imports of manufactures deemed critical and that could undermine U.S. producers,[7] subsidies that could encourage advantage in domestic and foreign markets, specific rewards or bonuses (in the form of premiums) for "some particular excellence or superiority, some extraordinary exertion or skill," exempting manufactured goods from duties, encouraging new inventions by monetary rewards or exclusive privileges, creating regulations to deal with fraud, and facilitating the circulation of money to ensure timely payments and investments.[8] Most of the themes and emphases associated with Hamilton's plan have continued—the power of the federal government, migration, deficit spending, the U.S. credit, tariffs, finance, and subsidies.

Consistent with the mercantilist model, the government decides on economic strategy—whether to transition from agriculture to manufacturing, to protect a particular industry through a variety of tactics, to expand the labor market, and to protect infant industries, which mercantilists such as Friedrich List were advancing in Germany, rejecting the more open market that the United Kingdom was advocating.[9] It is also the government, not the "invisible hand" of competition or private initiative in a self-regulating market, that best deals with the general or common good, and it is the government, often mocked as the site of unchanging habits in contrast to the individual, that is farseeing and sympathetic to change. Finally, and regrettably, except for getting more children and women in the labor market, little in mercantilism emphasizes social life and social development.

In an 1831 tribute to Hamilton, Daniel Webster, voicing the sentiments especially of the commercial and manufacturing classes, is claimed to have said, "He smote the rock of national resources, and streams of revenues gushed forth. He touched the dead corpse of public credit, and it sprung upon its feet. The fabled birth of Minerva from the brain of Jove was hardly more sudden or more perfect than the financial system of the United States as it burst forth from the conception of Alexander Hamilton."

To focus on tariffs, the United States initially imposed them primarily to collect revenue to help with the national debt. However, by 1816, Congress had begun to impose them to achieve a variety of ends but principally to protect manufacturing from foreign competition. Additional tariffs followed in 1828 and 1842, with the latter called the "Black Tariff" because it increased taxes from 20 to 40 percent and expanded its application from 50 to 85 percent of dutiable goods. The Morrill Tariff of 1861 pushed tariffs even higher—so high that a furious United Kingdom joined causes with the South in the Civil War. The Morrill Tariff, which lasted until 1913, had three goals: increase revenues for the war effort, protect manufacturing (the South saw this differently), and boost improvements in wages and employment.

The most important tariff to follow, the Smoot–Hawley Tariff of 1930, raised tariffs by as much as 60 percent for over twenty-thousand imported items, including agricultural and manufactured goods. Combined with the earlier 1922 Fordney–McCumber Tariff, Smoot–Hawley conspired with economic difficulties in Europe to help bring on and aggravate the Great Depression in 1929.

The mercantilist outlook induced a number of initiatives supportive of the country's physical, commercial, educational, and scientific infrastructure. Among these were two 1862 acts. The Railroad Act provided federal subsidies in the form of land and loans to build a transcontinental railroad, thus helping unite the country's eastern and western parts by 1867. The Morrill Act granted federally owned land to states for them to sell and thereby raise funds to establish and endow colleges focused on agriculture, science (including the military sciences), and engineering, among other areas. Colleges with these emphases were understood to contrast with liberal arts colleges, where learning was abstract. Over the years, the 104 land-grant public colleges and two private colleges (MIT and Tuskegee University) established under this legislation have played a powerful role in the nation's rise to worldwide dominance in agricultural trade and its ascendency to industrial predominance. These institutions helped support the emergence and development of the corporate era in this country as well as the spread of technology-oriented society through advances in steam engines, telephones and telegraphy, internal combustion engines, and electricity. The goods and services provided by the corporate sector, which itself depended on credit for its operation, began to meld with an increasingly consumerist society that also began operating on credit (deficit spending of sorts).

As the United States sought to protect the domestic market, which grew as the nation's population rose from 3.9 million in 1790 to 123.1 million in 1930, it also sought to expand its market abroad. In 1846, the United States went to war with Mexico and, when the conflict ended two years later, acquired an area that today encompasses Arizona, California, New Mexico, Texas, and parts of Colorado, Nevada, Utah, and Wyoming—over 50 percent of Mexico's territory. Through the Spanish–American War of 1898, the United States acquired Cuba, Puerto Rico, Guam, and the Philippines, and it annexed Hawaii that same year. To further expand its international markets, the United States insisted on the Open Door Policy for China, seeking to keep that nation's treaty ports open to the trade of all nations, especially latecomers such as the United States, rather than giving the "early birds" (mostly European countries and Russia) a monopoly of trading privileges on those ports and the interior they served.

These developments moved the United States further toward international economic and political primacy, which it effectively achieved in 1916, the year it became a creditor nation. The responsibilities attached to that status also increased, although the United States, at the time, was not disposed to assume them given the sacrifices entailed in replacing the United Kingdom as the world's banker.

Further, tariffs and financial issues and constraints on U.S. economic expansion played a role in the United States' refusal to join the League of Nations, thus largely occasioning the moral, legal, and political demise of that international organization. President Wilson's Fourteen Points, proposed as part of his advocacy for joining the league, called for removing "economic barriers" (including tariffs) and instituting an "equality of trade conditions." Article 23 of the league's covenant translated this principle into requiring states to "secure and maintain . . . equitable treatment for the commerce of all members of the League" and to give special consideration to the "necessities of the regions devastated by during the war of 1914–1918."[10] "Equitable treatment" would mean removing many of the trade barriers the United States had used in directing its economic ascendency. Looking toward the future, joining the league was seen as a restraint on the United States because the post–World War I psychology of Europe was to reconstruct much of the "old order," with the United Kingdom reassuming the lead role.

However, the United States was focused on an apparently unlimited future, using its own sociopolitical model as a foundation. As a result, far from giving special consideration to regions "devastated during the war," the United States demanded repayment of its wartime loans to Europe. Worse, it demanded those payments in gold or dollars, which the Europeans needed to stabilize their own finances. Given their meager supply of gold and dollars, repaying the loans in either would undermine their own economies. To compound the problem, the 1922 Fordney–McCumber Tariff severely limited Europe's capacity to earn dollars or gold to finance their loans by selling goods to the United States.[11] Also, the Smoot–Hawley Tariff simply worsened socioeconomic conditions in the United States, Europe, and the world and deepened the Great Depression. In 1933 alone, four thousand U.S. banks failed, family income fell by 40 percent and industrial production by 50 percent, and unemployment grew to 25 percent. In Germany, a comparably disastrous economy paved the way for Adolf Hitler's rise to power and the hardening of positions on arms limitation.

The Liberal Model: 1930–1971

The mercantilist period represented a continuing battle for negative freedom—freedom *from*. However, the Great Depression deeply humiliated Americans, and it embarrassed corporations and industrial leaders who had preached the ability of limited government and self-regulating markets to deal with all challenges. It laid bare the weaknesses of the mercantilist march in the United States, which almost uncritically accepted the view that social policy should be left to the market. [12] Even more importantly, the Great Depression brought into question the idea that the economic realm can operate independently of the social realm—whether any economic system could succeed outside the principles of reciprocity or redistribution.[13] It also questioned the operational effectiveness of a philosophy that overlooked the primacy of labor in creating value, something David Ricardo, Adam Smith, and Abraham Lincoln, all friends of capitalism, had so effectively taught and Karl Marx, though unfriendly to capitalism, had so forcefully reaffirmed and advocated.[14]

Although industrial leaders and ideological proponents of negative freedom put forth a plethora of excuses for the Great Depression, especially blaming it on government interference in the economy, the Roosevelt administration, between 1932 and 1938, led efforts to transform the U.S. economic system. The goal was not to shift away from capitalism but to focus less on negative freedom and more on positive freedom, with a turn toward the social issues that mercantilism had long neglected. In other words, the Roosevelt administration vouched for "freedom to" or positive freedom, and the policies that this liberal model would put in place provided a framework that enabled the U.S. political economy to evolve with fewer social privations, even while rejecting the view that the economic must be embedded in the social.[15]

Characteristic of the new liberal model, the Federal Emergency Relief Administration (FERA), created in 1933, distributed federal relief to the states, which used the resources to support unemployed families during the crisis. The Civil Works Administration, part of FERA, created public works jobs such as digging drainages, maintaining parks, and repairing roads. The Public Works Administration, also created in 1933, focused on larger-scale projects: building bridges, dams, airports, and hospitals. The Civilian Conservation Corps addressed the concerns of the youth, particularly for employment. (The depression years were especially hard on young people.)

The National Recovery Administration (NRA), created in 1933, sought to intervene directly in the market to stabilize it through wage and price agreements, but the Supreme Court declared the NRA unconstitutional. More successful and supportive of both bank depositors and banks, which needed to regain public trust, was the creation in 1933 of the Federal Deposit Insurance Corporation (FDIC). The FDIC has insured bank deposits since then. Capping 1933's flurry of liberal legislation, the Glass–Steagall Act required commercial banks, where customers deposit money and secure loans, to separate those activities from investment and securities business.

The Social Security Act, enacted in 1935, provides not only income and an old-age pension but also, among other things, aid to the blind and to dependent children. Other new federal bodies helped farmers, artists, inventors, and others. In particular, throughout the nineteenth century and the early decades of the twentieth century, government had largely joined industry in seeking to destroy labor unions, but now workers had a partner in government. In 1936, the National Labor Relations Act created the National Labor Relations Board to enforce the right of workers to form unions, and the act specifies procedures under which workers can select collective bargaining agents. The 1938 Fair Labor Standard Act sets standards for minimum wages, maximum working hours, overtime pay, youth labor, and recordkeeping in the private sector and by federal, state, and local governments.

The socioeconomic changes introduced by the Roosevelt administration underline the enabling role played by positive freedom under liberalism. They also reflect important themes: the idea of the regulatory state, the socially conscious or committed state, the group-and-individual–empowering state (as distinct from the individual-empowering state that conservatives delight in), and the fundamental fairness state. Roosevelt sought to embrace parts of all these ideas, and they would remain part of the U.S. political economy at least until the 1970s.

There is also a theme of limits; each of the three models of political economy is self-limiting. Under mercantilism, the unrestrained use of tariffs by the United States occasioned much suffering. In 1934, Congress passed the Reciprocal Tariff Act, authorizing presidents to negotiate with foreign nations to reduce their tariffs in return for reductions in U.S. tariffs. This liberal effort to open up trade for mutual benefit would find its way into the liberal vision behind the creation of international institutions after World War II. Before touching on those institutions, bear in mind a statement by the first President Roosevelt. His 1910 "New Nationalism" speech is very much in the tradition of the "great nation" aspirations of George Washington:

> Our country, the great Republic, means nothing less than the triumph of democracy, the triumph of popular government and, in the long run, of an economic system under which each man shall be guaranteed the opportunity to be the best that there is of him. This is why the history of America is now the central feature of the history of the world; for the world has set its face toward democracy; and, O my fellow citizens, each one of you carries on your shoulders not only the burden of doing well for the sake of your own country but the burden of doing well and seeing to it that the nation does well for the sake of mankind.[16]

Whether the world of 1910 was turning to the United States and what Pres. Theodore Roosevelt had claimed it represented may be questioned, but such was largely the case in the West as the end of World War II approached, especially in face of deep dissatisfaction about socioeconomic conditions. This was the case particularly in Europe as well as the rest of the world, including for people living under varying degrees of political subordination. Until 1989, the Soviet Union and the People's Republic of China, along with Eastern Europe, represented a social system that seemed to threaten—but never directly engage in—war with the U.S.-led West.

The threat also affected postwar international institutions, beginning with the UN itself and its mission in part to "employ international machinery for the promotion of the economic and social advancement of all peoples" to ensure "social progress and better standards of life in larger freedom," not simply negative liberty.[17] The UN's mission included saving succeeding generations from the scourge of war and affirming belief in and giving support to fundamental human rights as well as the dignity and worth of all human beings.[18] It extended

Roosevelt's positive-freedom domestic emphasis to the global system—a sort of "global New Deal."

Article 56 of the UN Charter refined the purposes further and requires members to "pledge themselves to take to take *joint and separate action* [emphasis added] in co-operation" with the UN to ensure the promotion of higher standards of living, full employment, and economic and social development; solutions to international economic, social, health, and related problems as well as international educational and cultural cooperation; and universal respect for and observance of human rights and fundamental freedoms for all.

To translate these abstract ideas into concrete actions, a number of institutions, including some specialized agencies, emerged or became part of the UN family. The purpose of the International Bank for Reconstruction and Development (IBRD, popularly known as the World Bank) was not only to help reconstruct societies after World War II but also to help provide long-term investments supportive of economic development. The International Monetary Fund (IMF) was to provide short-term monetary advances to states so that they could pursue full employment without fear of currency speculation that would invite austerity. The General Agreement on Tariff and Trade (GATT) would preside over the progressive lowering of tariff barriers and promote free trade among nations. The United Nations Educational, Scientific, and Cultural Organization (UNESCO) would further collaboration in education and culture. The World Health Organization (WHO) would focus on international cooperation in the field of health. The International Labor Organization (ILO), incorporated into the UN family from the League of Nations, would champion the rights and concerns of labor throughout the world. This worldwide socioeconomic framework was based on the psychology of Theodore Roosevelt's "Great Republic" as well as on U.S. economic supremacy. Washington's status as creditor nation was firm; it held 80 percent of the world's reserve (gold), and the dollar served as the system's key currency.[19]

Countering the worldwide structure of liberalism, with its primacy of capital within socioeconomic systems, was another orientation. Called communism and led by the Soviet Union, it espoused the first place of labor and social class in the experience and understanding of human history. Each of the two opposing ideological systems claimed to possess historical truth, making their respective stances quite rigid. The "truth" that the U.S.-led effort represented was the movement of social evolution toward freedom, culminating in the worldwide victory of liberal democracy. The "truth" of the Soviet-led effort was that the laws of social evolution were leading to the replacement of class-riddled societies by classless ones, led by workers.

No sooner had the liberal structure become dominant after World War II than it came under pressure from social and political crises in Greece, Turkey,

25

and Western Europe. These perceived threats of "communist subversion" invited U.S. intervention, which came in the form of the Marshall Plan, officially called the European Recovery Program. The Marshall Plan, in turn, followed from the Truman Doctrine, a March 1947 offer by the U.S. president to support any country threatened by Soviet communism. Secretary as State George Marshall explained the plan bearing his name in a speech at Harvard University:

> In considering the requirements for the rehabilitation of Europe, the physical loss of life, the visible destruction of cities, factories, mines, and railroads was correctly estimated, but it has become obvious during recent months that the visible destruction was probably less serious than the destruction of the entire fabric of European economy , , , Long-standing commercial ties, private institutions, banks, insurance companies, and shipping companies disappeared . . . The town and city industries are not producing adequate goods to exchange with the food-producing farmer. Raw materials and fuel are in short supply. Machinery is lacking or worn out . . . [S]he must have substantial additional help or face economic, social, and political destruction of a very grave character.[20]

The conditions that Marshall detailed list precisely where the World Bank should have directed its attention. In fact, Marshall went on to indicate that while the plan was armed against "hunger, poverty, desperation, and chaos,"[21] in Europe (and against the feared further penetration of the area by communism), its central purpose was "the revival of a working economy in the world so as to permit the emergence of political and social conditions in which free institutions can exist."[22] This is reconstruction and development—the very name of the World Bank.

Going around the World Bank with the $12 billion Marshall Plan (over $100 billion in 2016 dollars) affected the fledgling institution in several respects. Besides weakening its influence and authority, it forced the bank to deal with a Europe more closely aligned with U.S. foreign policy. It also played into the stance of Moscow, which depicted the Marshall Plan as an effort to weaken the Soviet Union and its influence in Eastern Europe. Moscow responded with the Molotov Plan for Eastern Europe, announced in late 1947.

For the United States, the Marshall Plan represented an important institutional step to manage the economies of the noncommunist world. The Organization for European Economic Co-operation (OEEC) was created in 1948 to administer the Marshall Plan. With eighteen European countries as the original OEEC members but no Soviet bloc nations, it was hard to maintain the idea of a world bank as opposed to an institution closely linked to Western interests.

In later years, similar liberal principles governed tariffs and promises to remove trade barriers. The Kennedy administration, under authority granted by the Trade Expansion Act of 1962, initiated what has come to be called the Kennedy Round of tariffs, negotiated between 1964 and 1967 within the overall framework of the GATT. These included adopting an antidumping code, reducing nonagricultural dutiable imports by over 30 percent, and creating a "trade and development" addition to the GATT, in part to protect certain goods from less developed countries (LDCs), just as the United States had sought to protect its infant industries. The Kennedy Round also brought the United States into closer alignment with Western Europe, which had formed a common market (predecessor to the European Union) and become wealthier because of its tariff policies, inducing the United States to accept lower tariffs.

The IMF, a central pillar of the international financial order, moved far from pursuing its founders' original goal of supporting full employment. Increasingly, it joined with the World Bank in accepting and espousing the policies of the United States and its economic allies within the Organization for Economic Co-operation and Development (OECD), successor to the OEEC, with Canada and the United States and later others joining as members. However, as early as 1959, questions began arising concerning the "reserve capacity" of the United States— its capacity to support the world's monetary needs while ensuring international monetary stability and, hence, economic stability. To be asked to supply enough dollars to support global economic transactions runs the risk, the argument went, of continuing threats of inflation, a run on the dollar (and thus a decrease in gold reserves), and increased debt for all countries that borrow in dollars.[23]

During the 1960s, internal social and political challenges led the United States to expand some areas of rights, primarily civil and political rights. It also led the Johnson administration to focus on a few social and economic issues, such as health, education, housing, and poverty relief, especially as these affected minorities and women. Internationally, to give effect to certain terms of the UN Charter and the norms of the Universal Declaration of Human Rights, adopted by the UN General Assembly in 1948, the United States signed (but did not yet ratify) the ICCPR, but Washington refused to accept or offer support for the ICESCR.

In concrete terms, every U.S. president from Harry S. Truman to Lyndon Johnson opposed the implementation of economic, social, and cultural *rights* as distinct from social relief—as evidenced in the many examples of U.S. intervention abroad, from China (1946–1949) and Iran (1953) to Guatemala (1953–1954) and Zaire (1963–1964) to Vietnam, among others.[24] In every case, local nationalist groups, claiming social rights, led a broad-based popular mobilization for basic needs against entrenched local interests, often tied to international groups, and the United States intervened to reverse that mobilization. It is true that each case involved minerals (e.g., cobalt, diamonds, tin, oil), "strategic" investments, or an expanded market, and the U.S. feared that local communist groups might exploit popular sentiments to gain political power. However, the central truth is that the mobilizations sought primarily social rights: the rights to agrarian reform, education, housing, health care, and labor mobilization. Such rights, once introduced, become not only part of the increased cost of government but also grounds for expanding the government's role in the economy. They can also invite increased regulation, reduce profits, and lead to higher taxes to pay for the social rights. Just as important, they can stabilize governments and make them less vulnerable to external interference.

Neoliberalism: 1972–Present

Mercantilism (and its mix with and transition into liberalism) gave little recognition to social rights, and their denial contributed to the harshness of the Great Depression and the associated difficulties of reconstituting society. The New Deal's introduction of domestic social programs (but not social rights) came into being within the context of the extended social emergency created by the economic devastation, and the "New Society" added a few other programs during the 1960s. At the international level, little or no progress in this area occurred except through WHO, UNESCO, and the ILO. In the United States, these agencies were regarded not so much as helping confer rights but as engaging in a form of international "welfare," a mostly negative term in U.S. politics—a sort of giveaway to the lazy and undeserving who distorted markets.

At the same time, the extension of social services and programs augmented the role of the government in society, with broadening regulation expressive of that augmentation—so much so that many neoliberals and conservatives came to denigrate the United States as the "regulated state." Neoliberalism has sought to dismantle these regulations, to remove what it considers obstacles to the full flowering of the laissez-faire economy based on the self-regulating or free market, at home and abroad. The removal actions, from 1968 to the present, have encountered four major challenges: the global push, especially strong in the Middle East, to restore Islam to greatness; the emerging voice of the Global South and its LDCs; the rise of neo-Confucianism; and a reordering of the international monetary system. All four have represented broad contextual challenges for the United States, in addition to the strategic competition with the former Soviet Union until 1989 over whether Moscow or Washington would embody the course of historical truth.

The first challenge, conflict in the Middle East (or West Asia), especially since 1967, has intensified a nineteenth-century movement in Islam to reconstitute itself.[25] Among that movement's features has been the restoration of *ummah*, a supranational community bound by Muslim religious ideals and superseding the nation-state as the most important actor in world affairs. In other words, a Muslim's highest loyalty, except for loyalty to Allah, is not to the nation-state but to *ummah*. That loyalty requires nations to promote the well-being of *ummah*, especially the social rights of members constituting the community. Indeed, governments, far from deferring to the self-regulating market, have a duty to control activities in economic life to protect those social rights.

By 1964, the Global South had transformed the UN from a predominantly Western institution into one with a numerical majority of LDCs. In that year, this led to the creation of the United Nations Conference on Trade and Development (UNCTAD) as part of the UN Secretariat, giving voice to LDCs' collective disaffection with the operation of the World Bank, the IMF, and other Bretton Woods institutions.[26] Also in that year, a sort of coalition called the "Group of 77" (its numbers later growing to 134) came together to help negotiate on behalf of LDCs' collective interest.

UNCTAD and the Group of 77 soon took stances resembling the mercantilism of Alexander Hamilton when the United States was developing. For example, they argued that the rules and operations of the World Bank and the IMF confined LDCs to producing primary commodities (e.g., bauxite, crude oil, rice, nuts, fruits) that commanded cheap prices on the international market. In turn, they had to purchase manufactured goods (usually not of the most sophisticated kind) at high prices. The earnings from the cheap commodities could never equal the expenditures for the expensive manufactured goods, LDCs argued, condemning them to a debt trap, always borrowing to make up the difference between earnings and expenditures, compounded by the enjoyment of little or no chance for full development.

Unlike the time of Alexander Hamilton, however, when the global economy was much less interlinked, LDCs could not move to a full-fledged mercantilist orientation that looked primarily inward. They had to deal with the international system. Thus, in 1974, the Global South, led by the Group of 77, issued a three-part proposal for an NIEO: the Declaration on the Establishment of a New International Economic Order, the Charter on the Economic Rights and Duties of States, and the Program of Action.[27] LDCs wanted sovereign control over their national resources; the right of each country, in pursuit of the common international interest, to choose its own economic and social system; the right to collaborate freely with other states and work jointly toward correcting socioeconomic inequalities; and the right to redress existing injustices, including the "widening gaps between developed and developing countries . . . and ensure steadily accelerating development and peace . . . for present and future generations."[28] The plan of action included reforming the IMF and the World Bank.

In the third challenge, an emerging Confucian economic culture had begun making itself known. It is understood to be compatible with capitalism through the impressive experiences of Singapore, South Korea, Taiwan, and Japan. The culture, a "this-worldly ascetic," is grounded on disciplined work, savings, education, and limited personal consumption. It is transmitted through the family while assuming and demanding a central role for the state, very much in the tradition of Alexander Hamilton. The success of the Confucian cultural outlook has challenged neoliberalism since the 1980s, intensifying with China's emergence as a major international economic power.

Finally, the challenge of the global financial order, which has been based on the U.S. dollar since 1945, actually began as early as the late 1950s and became clearer during the 1960s. The gold-backed dollar began to pose problems for Washington because the United States, especially as a result of the Vietnam War, began experiencing increasingly unfavorable balances of trade and payments. Countries began to turn in dollars for gold as they saw the United States earning less than it was spending. Consistent with the requirements of the financial system, the United States exchanged more of its gold for turned-in dollars, depleting its gold reserve and making holders of dollars even more nervous. With more and more dollars turned in and less and less gold to support dollars held by other governments, in 1971, the United States unilaterally indicated that it would no longer link the dollar to gold. In other words, it crashed the heart of the Bretton Woods system without giving the world an opportunity to adjust.[29]

The neoliberal order emerged within the context of these four challenges (plus the strategic confrontation with the Soviet Union), and it has been sustained in the United States and throughout the world since then. Leaders from the Republican and Democratic Parties have taken turns in implementing its terms with few modifications.

Some Lost Opportunities

A dollar crisis in 1972 provided the first test of the neoliberal order. Faced with international financial confusion and instability following the U.S. decision to discontinue the gold-backed dollar (a decision that included devaluing the dollar), the IMF's executive directors urged phasing out the dollar as the principal reserve currency and replacing it with special drawing rights (SDRs) of the fund. Specifically, all dollars held by foreign banks would be transferred into the IMF; in return, the banks would receive SDRs. The United States would then pay off the dollars within an agreed-on period, and the SDR would become the world's reserve currency.[30]

The United States did not agree to the proposal, even though it would have removed the burden of maintaining the world reserve currency and provided greater stability for the global financial system. It would have also limited the ability of the United States to spend beyond its means, especially in support of the military dominance it sought to maintain and expand. The proposal would have also eliminated what the French called the "exorbitant privilege" that the United States enjoyed: the ability to pay for its international debt by printing its own currency. Additionally, neoliberals believed that the SDR proposal would invite unacceptable IMF interference. Moreover, the United States wanted to retain another exorbitant privilege: the ability to use its dollar holdings to control the behavior of other nations and other transnational actors such as multinational corporations.

Two examples are illustrative. In the late 1970s, inflation caused by U.S. spending and the escalating price of oil created a crisis. With extraordinary arrogance, the United States unilaterally increased its prime interest rate to 19 percent by 1981. This increased the interest rate for every country that owed debts in dollars or that were likely to borrow in dollars. The burdens and crises for LDCs were many, as they were for U.S. citizens. To the Reagan administration, however, this was what "the market" demanded. More recently, in 2018, the Trump administration decided to withdraw from an agreement negotiated with Iran by the United States, Russia, China, France, the United Kingdom, and Germany. All other parties wished to abide by the agreement, but Washington imposed a penalty on all banks and other companies that did so. A U.S. embargo on Iran now covers almost all companies that do business in Europe and elsewhere, using dollars to facilitate their transactions.

The demands of LDCs through their proposed NIEO fared no better than the urged change in reserve currency. The Carter administration, seeking to improve relations with the Global South, took no definite stance on the NIEO proposals and even exhibited a willingness to discuss matters further. However, when President Reagan took office in 1981, he and British Prime Minister Margaret Thatcher collaborated to reject the proposals, in part because they were said to require government intervention in the economy and involved social rights that, if accepted, would change the liberal order.[31] Reagan and Thatcher also felt that the NIEO proposals, if implemented, would benefit the Soviet Union.

There were additional reasons for rejecting the NIEO proposals. As part of the Global South's efforts to gain greater say in the international economic system, members of the Group of 77 and UNCTAD had called for a new world information and communication order. They felt that the West controlled existing information and communication systems and was poised to continue doing so for the foreseeable future given the role of emerging technologies for controlling the development, organization, storage, transborder transfer, and distribution of information. Moreover, the West strongly influenced the International Telecommunication Union (ITU), the international body responsible for allocating and managing the international radio frequency spectrum and geostationary orbits for communications satellites.[32] Both the ITU and the international radio frequency spectrum answer to UNESCO.

The United States took the position that the NIEO threatened its commitments and those of the West in general to the free flow of information everywhere in the world. LDCs contended that what the West—and the United States, in particular—called "free flow" was, in fact, a one-way flow from the West to the Global South. To address the controversy, UNESCO organized a commission in 1977, chaired by Nobel Laureate Sean MacBride, to study and report on the issues. The resulting MacBride report sought to bridge the gap in the positions of the West and LDCs, as suggested by its subtitle's reference to a "more just and efficient" order—"just" to satisfy LDCs and "efficient" to satisfy the West, especially the United States.[33] Neither side was satisfied.

Washington withdrew from UNESCO in 1984, followed a year later by the United Kingdom, grounded on conclusions reached by the U.S. Office of Technology Assessment for the Senate Committee on Commerce, Science, and Transportation:

> The world has changed. There are scores of new, independent poor nations participating in international regulatory and administrative organizations. They seek to change the existing allocation of benefits and privileges, which are lopsidedly in favor of a few industrialized states and the most powerful users in those countries. The United States is not only unwilling to make those concessions but, in fact, seeks to obtain a greater share of scarce global resources to meet the needs of its transnational enterprises and its global military force.[34]

In short, the NIEO appeared to threaten the U.S. share of international resources, such as the radio frequency spectrum and the orbits for communications satellites, as well as its economic ascendency and, perhaps most important, its global military reach.

At the very time of rejecting the NIEO, the United States was undertaking an unprecedented peacetime military buildup that, in the minds of many, was designed to bankrupt Moscow. Washington would not entertain any reduction of its international privileges and instead sought to expand them. Further, the SDI envisioned a space-based antimissile system that would, for example, depend on communications satellites. The United States would not accept the reallocation and regulatory efforts of the Global South, which had begun to dominate UNESCO.

The NIEO's final international challenge to neoliberalism came with calls to reform the IMF itself. Far from supporting this call, the West made the IMF a force for dismantling social programs in the Global South, which depended deeply on that institution. Taking its direction from Washington, the IMF would impose "conditionality" on countries seeking its help (whether through a loan, debt relief, or financial aid), a form of structural adjustment requiring drastic reductions in government subsidies for food, health care, housing, and education as part of overall reductions in public spending. Conditionality would also require the increased privatization of public services, among other things, and, in many cases, the opening up of a state's capital account to private speculation, all in the name of free market economics.[35]

The regulatory focus on taking neoliberalism worldwide has had its expression domestically. In the United States, it aimed directly at reducing or eliminating government regulations and other interventions into the market. More indirectly, neoliberal ideas guided reductions in public spending, "starving the beast" called the government. Of the two tax cuts under President Reagan, the second, in 1986, reduced taxes on the top 1 to 2 percent of earners from 70 percent in 1980 to 28 percent. The 2017 tax cut under President Trump reduced corporate taxes from 35 percent to 20 percent and exempted the first $11 million from estate taxes. The George W. Bush administration and that of Barack Obama reduced taxes as well.[36] In a way, starving-the-beast logic was also behind reducing U.S. contributions to UNESCO before the United States withdrew from that agency entirely.

The Reagan administration led in the direct removal of regulations or reducing support for government agencies responsible for delivering services, including community development block grant programs, Medicaid, food stamps, and aid to education. For his part, President Clinton signed off on legislation repealing the 1933 regulation forcing banks to separate their investment activities from their commercial ones. Clinton also supported reduced requirements for mortgage eligibility, fueling speculation in the mortgage market. George W. Bush and Trump engaged in similar deregulation, especially the latter as he has moved neoliberalism into reversals in such areas as clean water, national parks, health care, environmental protection, and banking.

In the area of privatization, the history of Conrail offers an early example. The government created Conrail in 1976 to take over bankrupt freight railways in the northeast. Eventually, it was making a profit and was privatized in 1999. Similarly, Pres. George W. Bush, through an executive order, facilitated the rental or sale of public facilities such as housing projects, roads, and sewage treatment. The United States also outsourced a great deal of military work to contractors, with contracted workers in Iraq outnumbering U.S. military personnel there. Other proposed areas for privatization have included low-income housing, federal loan programs, traffic control, the postal service, prisons, Medicare, and urban mass transit.[37] The publicly stated rationale for privatizations has been to reduce government spending, generate income to help deal with deficits, and improve efficiency, but these have rarely resulted.[38]

Challenges and Lost Opportunities Continued

Three other areas of concern remain here: Islamic and Confucian cultures and their challenge to neoliberalism; tariffs and their prominence for the U.S. political economy; and the question of historical truth.

The Islamic de-emphasis of national borders within a nation-state system poses problems that neoliberalism's focus on the individual has yet to cope with successfully. Take oil. For whose benefit is it produced and sold? Focusing on the nation-state, Islamic culture invites thinking about *ummah*; the same follows for the occupation or alienation of land, whether seemingly against or in favor of one nation-state. Within Islam, these issues affect the entire community, leading to today's difficulties in dealing with conflicts and claimed or projected solutions in the Middle East. For example, Osama bin Laden and his followers saw U.S. military bases in Saudi Arabia as a form of occupation, and hence, they alienated lands belonging to *ummah*. Neoliberalism's focus (and that of capitalism in general) on individual responsibility—in business, for example—confronts shared responsibility and risks under Islamic finance. Thus, capitalism has never penetrated a Muslim society in an orderly way; neoliberalism, in its effort to constitute the world in its own image, finds this frustrating.

The Confucian outlook in political economy furnished a parallel experience when Japan, embracing a mercantilist model, challenged the United States during the 1980s.[39] Some U.S. policy makers suggested that Tokyo would pose less of an economic challenge if it spent more on defense.[40] At first, Washington convinced Tokyo to increase military spending (something that Article 9 of Japan's constitution had carefully limited). Japan also agreed to purchase more agricultural products from the United States and to share some of its military and other technologies. Secretary of State Shultz, several years after leaving office, listed some of those technologies: "robotics, lasers, large-scale integrated circuits, and other components for weapons, fiber optics for communication, next-generation computers, and many high-quality . . . conventional products."[41] Other concessions followed, but then the United States accused Tokyo of some Hamiltonian practices, such as subsidizing domestic companies, discriminating against foreign suppliers in government contracts, stealing Western technology, manipulating its currency to keep exports cheap, and employing high tariffs. Japan rejected some of these claims and pointed to weaknesses in the U.S. model of political economy.[42] U.S. negotiators never took Japan's claims seriously; neoliberalism was superior, so Japan must be cheating if its economy was outdistancing that of the United States.

Tokyo had to be careful, however. Despite its growing economic might, its security depended on the United States, and the Reagan–Gorbachev negotiations on arms limitation made the Japanese anxious. Could Japan retain U.S. security commitments if Washington thought Tokyo sought world economic domination?

By 1988, with the United States facing an annual trade deficit of about $120 billion and Japan enjoying a surplus of $80 billion, criticisms of and threats toward Tokyo dominated U.S. economic discourse. When a Japanese company bought Rockefeller Center a year later, it was felt that Japan's efforts to deal with its trade surplus by purchasing American properties signaled a course of action designed to take over this country. James Fallows summed up the psychology of public elites, suggesting that they could not imagine why any country would want to challenge Washington's economic supremacy other than from diabolical motives, including those of a Marxist. Why, the elites asked, was Japan unable or unwilling to restrain the "destructive" expansion of its economic power?[43]

Today U.S. policy makers and pundits level the same charge against China, with a self-described "socialist market" economy but one that actually pursues the mercantilist model followed by Japan in the 1980s and before, by Singapore today, and by South Korea and Taiwan on their paths to development. In fact, the United States did not criticize post-1945 Japan until that nation was felt to threaten U.S. economic supremacy. Moreover, accusations centering on the Japanese government's involvement in shaping economic development (for example, through its Ministry of Industry and International Trade) ignored similarities in many respects to the role of the Defense Advanced Research Project Agency (DARPA) in the United States. Instructive here is DARPA's 1987 creation of SEMATECH, a consortium of semiconductor industry leaders to augment U.S. competitive capacity.

In any event, the United States forced Japan to open its markets further and engage in what is called voluntary trade restraint by limiting exports and increasing imports. The Japanese economy has yet to regain its 1980s dynamism. Neoliberalism won the immediate battle but without proving that its model is the best for economic development through open competition. It showed success only when the United States applied superior economic and military power to pressure Japan to change. The Confucian cultural model, like Islam's, is likely to continue challenging the neoliberal model.

In the matter of tariffs, two major international rounds of negotiation have occurred since neoliberalism came to dominate U.S. policy and thinking: the Uruguay Round of Tariffs (1986–1994) and the Doha Development Round, which began in 2011. Some 123 states participated in the Uruguay Round, removing a great many barriers to trade. The round created the World Trade Organization (WTO), making the GATT and its many achievements integral to the newly created organization. Negotiators also went into areas, such as agriculture and its associated broad subsidies, that nations had been reluctant to touch, and they agreed on reductions in subsidies. It also began the process of opening trade in banking, insurance, and other services. Finally, the round tackled the protection of intellectual property, increasing the WTO's ability to decide disputes between and among nations. Significantly, neoliberalism has some skepticism about this area, which connotes a degree of global centralization of governmental power.

The Doha negotiations are ongoing, largely because further agreements in certain areas—agricultural subsidies, for example—remain challenging. In the meantime, a reaction against neoliberalism's espousal of free trade has developed. Ironically, this is especially evident in the United States, which has not only rejected a proposed Trans-Pacific Partnership (TPP) designed to contain China and solidify U.S. status as a Pacific power but also acted outside the WTO's hard-won multilateral framework for trade negotiations to pursue bilateral agreements.[44] China, accused of every charge leveled against Japan during the 1980s, faces tariffs declared unilaterally by the United States. Beijing has retaliated, and Western Europe has reengaged in negotiations in a number of areas, including agriculture.[45]

At this juncture, a question arises on whether communism, with its focus on social class and the class struggle, or liberalism, with its emphasis on liberty, will be revealed as the bearer of the historical truth about human social destiny. By the 1980s, the ideology of each side had lost much of its animating passion, especially in the case of communism. The confrontation between ideologies had given way to more of a military struggle. The U.S.-led West, for example, began to make moral distinctions between so-called authoritarian and totalitarian states, with the latter, mostly communist regimes, considered the greater danger to liberty and demanding opposition. The United States found authoritarian states less objectionable if only because they generally accepted the market forces espoused by neoliberalism.

In 1989 and 1990, as reforms sponsored by Gorbachev led to the dismantling of the Soviet Union, the West interpreted that development as a victory for and vindication of liberal democracy and its economic expression, neoliberalism. So overwhelming was the euphoria that Francis Fukuyama summed up much of contemporary sentiment among U.S. elites in *The End of History and the Last Man*.[46] Fukuyama contended that the historical struggles that human beings have faced regardless of their disparate cultural backgrounds would converge in or move toward a capitalist liberal democracy. The liberal democracy type of human being would be the peak of human social and political development.

By December 1991, the Soviet Union, which could have been saved with more economic aid and less self-regarding advice from the West, collapsed. Its successor, Russia under Pres. Boris Yeltsin, opened itself to some of the most exploitative features of neoliberalism, including the wholesale privatization of major economic sectors. Only Albania, China, Cuba, North Korea, and Vietnam maintained even a pretense of commitment to communism, although China was on its way to its own chosen model—a socialist market economy. The West, believing that Beijing would eventually join the triumph of neoliberalism, admitted it as a member of the WTO in December 2001 following years of negotiations.[47]

With the claimed triumph of liberalism, U.S. political elites saw less cause to be concerned about social rights, which they had been when viewing communism as a threat. In fact, the United States cut social programs, and military spending suffered few cutbacks, even though Russia was but a shell of the former Soviet Union. NATO's incorporation of former Warsaw Pact members was cited as justification for increases in military spending, as was a search for new fields of play.

Madeleine Albright, secretary of state from 1991 to 2001, was especially persuasive in articulating those new fields of play. In a commencement address at Harvard University in 1997 (fifty years after George Marshall had appeared there), she outlined her view of the international state of affairs, including challenges and where the United States and the world should go:

> [I]t is not enough to say communism has failed. We too must heed the lessons of the past, accept responsibility, and lead . . . [W]e cannot limit our focus, as Marshall did in his speech to the devastated battleground of a prior war. Our vision must encompass not one but every continent . . . Today I say that no nation in the world need be left out of the global system we are constructing. And every nation that seeks to participate and is willing to do all it can to help itself will have America's help in finding the right path . . . NATO is a defensive alliance . . . It does not regard any state as its adversary, certainly not a democratic and reforming Russia that is intent on integrating with the West and with which it has forged an historic partnership, signed in Paris . . . Since George Marshall's time, the United States has played a leading role within the international system . . . as pathfinder—as the nation able to show the way when others cannot . . . We are doers. We have a responsibility . . . to shape history, a responsibility to fill the role of pathfinder and build with others a global network of purpose and law that will protect our citizens, defend our interests, preserve our values, and bequeath to future generations a legacy as proud as the one we honor today.[48]

Albright spelled out the special place of the United States, as had George Washington when he called the young nation a pathfinder, presaging other names to follow, such as "indispensable nation," "exceptional nation," the "lone superpower," and the "greatest nation on earth." This nation would accept responsibility—without indicating from whom the United States accepted this responsibility or on whose behalf it would give it—to construct a global system involving every continent. This system, according to Albright, would include Russia, which was privatizing enough state-owned assets and was, favorably enough, disposed to neoliberalism to become a member of what was being called the Euro-Atlantic community. Even Africa came in for praise from Albright as a potential part of the global system, with its riches, "both in human and material resources," and its "best new leaders . . . pursuing reforms that are helping private enterprise and democratic institutions gain a foothold."[49]

Albright said nothing about sharing contending ideas, even those of Gorbachev, with whom so many discussions had taken place concerning the social democratic order from which, he thought, Russia and the world would benefit. No deference was made to India, which had resisted the idea that using the government to reduce inequality distorted the efficacy of the market. Neither, despite Albright's frequent reference to democracy, did she convey an awareness of any body of other ideas on political economy, including those coming from the NIEO proposal, neo-Confucianism, or Islam. A preferential option for the poor, coming out of the liberation theology of Latin America, received no better treatment. In the case of Islam, Iraq was the focus as the United States reviewed plans to determine how the Middle East, for example, could become more accepting of U.S. values. Notably, the Middle East was the only area Albright had excluded from regions she deemed likely to contribute to the contemplated international system or the "new world order," as former president George W. Bush would call it.

About eight months after her Harvard speech, Albright, facing close questioning by Matt Lauer on NBC-TV's *The Today Show*, explained how she might respond to American parents whose sons and daughters "may soon be asked to go into harm's way," especially in light of the obvious reluctance of other countries to become involved in U.S.-led foreign wars. She responded that the United States would do all it could to avoid the use of force, "[b]ut if we have to use force, it is because we are America. We are the indispensable nation. We stand tall, and we can see further than other countries into the future, and we see danger . . . to all of us."[50]

Beginning in 2003, the Iraq War, presented as necessary to get rid of Iraqi nuclear weapons, was supposed to last less than a month and cost less than $50 billion (for which Iraqi oil would pay). In reality, the war launched an effort to open the Middle East to liberal democracy.[51] It did not end officially until 2011, cost the United States over $2 trillion and the Iraqi people hundreds of thousands of lives, and brought no semblance of liberal democracy.[52]

In the meantime, the war at home contributed to a progressive erosion of social support, the removal of regulations designed to protect society and groups within it, the weakening of the countervailing power that unions provided to the overwhelming power of business corporations,[53] a disregard for the "least among us,"[54] growing disparities in the distribution of wealth and income, and the devastating impact of tax cuts on the capacity of government to deal with social ills. Worse, the moral spirit of the country began a steep decline—and understandably so when, as former secretary of labor Robert Reich recently wrote, "the richest four hundred Americans have more wealth than the bottom 50 percent of Americans put together; the wealthiest 1 percent own over 42 percent of the nation's private assets; and the share of wealth held by the lower half of households has fallen from 3 percent in 1989 to 1 percent today."[55] This is a moral scandal of epic proportions, not a model inviting emulation. It is a model not of global order but of global disorder.

The United States entered an economic recession in 2007 largely as a result of the neoliberal model. The "new world order," calculated to ensure American global preeminence, became a victim of the model. Homeowners lost trillions of dollars as home values declined and bankruptcies multiplied; Americans lost trillions more in the stock market, with retirement savings declining precipitously or evaporating and small businesses disappearing. As well, hundreds of billions in public funds had to be spent to save private financial institutions, many of which had helped precipitate the crisis. With unemployment reaching 10 percent and the recession's social consequences too dire to capture, people began wondering about the neoliberal model, especially when its proponents did so little for those most seriously affected by the recession, except for enacting a health-care bill that advocates of negative liberty later gutted. Indeed, the misdistribution of wealth and income continued increasing with the nation's slow recovery from recession.[56] Further, to continue the recovery, the Trump administration's neoliberals enacted a $1.5 trillion tax cut that overwhelmingly favored the top 5 percent of the population, simultaneously increasing the government's operating deficit and the national debt, further "starving the beast."

Other areas of the world—especially those like India, Latin America, and especially China—that sought to limit neoliberalism's penetration began to show some results. For example, twelve South American countries, constituting 420 million people and a GDP of $6.5 trillion, formed the Union of South American Nations, aspiring to develop—at least in part, as the European Union has—with a unified passport, parliament, and, eventually, single currency. Its principal goals are improving public health, with considerable government intervention, and defense. The treaty came into force in 2011.[57]

India had led the nonaligned movement within the Group of 77, especially during the most troubled times of the Cold War and with the proposals for an NIEO. Since then, it has carefully built up certain areas of its national infrastructure and pursued development by way of government-led and financed initiatives. Today, because the United States refused to negotiate issues raised under the NIEO, especially those dealing with information and communication, New Delhi is creating problems for Facebook, Google, Amazon, and other technology giants, taking the stand that data gathered in India must be stored there and opposing the use of this data to profit outside India with little return to the country where data is collected.[58]

China's "market socialism," a form of mercantilism, began about when neoliberalism began its national policy expressions in the United States. However, repression of the Tiananmen Square demonstrations of 1989 stimulated strong pressures from Washington, on human rights and other grounds, to effect some internal changes in exchange for "normal" relations. Not only did China reject the U.S. position, finding external pressure unacceptable, but also, it asserted that the United States had human rights problems of its own.[59] Beijing indicates an interest in relations based on mutual benefits and mutual respect—meaning, in part, mutual compromises and relations based on equality, not domination. Among the compromises China has sought is treatment consistent with its rising international socioeconomic status.

When China felt that it was accorded such respect—for example, voting power in the World Bank and the IMF—it began the process of seeking, with others, to build new institutions. With Brazil, Russia, India, and South Africa, Beijing created the New Development Bank in 2014, with equal shares for the founding nations in contrast to the U.S.-dominated World Bank. In 2016, China founded the Asian Infrastructure Investment Bank and contributed $100 billion to its capital. Despite Washington's opposition, many of the closest U.S. allies (except Japan) joined the bank, giving it sixty-eight members as of mid-2019.[60] Both these institutions indicate that China will not accept an international system shaped solely by the United States, however indispensable or farseeing Washington understands itself to be. Beijing is interested in a system that accords with broader interests. The two institutions also signify China's interest in helping organize a multipolar world.[61]

As China expands its trade and investment reach into Africa, Asia, and Latin America, areas dominated by the United States at least since the 1950s, Washington has begun to see those activities as a challenge to its international economic primacy.[62] Nor has the Belt and Road Initiative linking China and other Asian countries with European and African nations gone unnoticed by Washington. This estimated $4 trillion project, including funds from the Asian Infrastructure Investment Bank, could transform the infrastructure linking the three continents in unprecedented ways.

The United States is striking back, pressuring China with unilaterally declared tariffs and insisting that China open its markets in such a way that its industries (more fully developed than their U.S. competitors) cannot enjoy any advantage. In other words, Beijing should give up its mercantilist model—one the United States, by and large, had embraced until 1929. Washington also wants China to forego the pursuit of certain technological developments in areas ranging from artificial intelligence and information technology to robotics, aeronautics, and advanced manufacturing, all of which are part of Beijing's plans for forging ahead industrially by 2025 and competing more effectively internationally. China's actions have even begun to induce the Trump administration to reverse recent U.S. positions on reducing foreign aid by some $3 billion, creating in 2018 what the *New York Times* describes as "a new foreign aid agency—the United States International Development Finance Corporation—and giving it authority, $60 billion in loans, loan guarantees . . . and insurance to companies willing to do business in developing nations."[63] This bankrolling will take place in Africa, Asia, and Latin America, all to help build infrastructure—the very thing China is doing on the three continents. Further, the U.S. effort is governmental, not private; the new agency will even pay to insure U.S. firms against the risks they incur.

Many quarters of U.S. society blame U.S. deficits on China (along with Europe), but some observers, reflecting on historical transatlantic ties, hope to enlist Europe in pursuing an effective stance against China, as the ill-fated TPP had been designed to do.[64] More compelling as a strategy, embedded in the new NAFTA (now called the United States–Mexico–Canada Agreement or USMCA) is a provision making it difficult for Canada and Mexico to deal with "nonmarket" economies, such as China's.[65]

Cautionary Note

The United States will not resolve its domestic troubles in the areas of deficits, recessions, and national debt via tariffs or broad unilateral actions such as those pursued by the Trump administration. However, more domestic savings, a greater focus on education, reduced inequities in income and wealth distribution, and a change in the burden of the world's key currency plus a change in election financing could make a major impact.

The United States—and the world—could have avoided all the threats, unfriendly maneuverings, and wars detailed here if it had taken steps earlier to forego its claim to and pursuit of global supremacy, if it had accepted a truly global currency in the 1970s, if it had pursued increased savings rather than a culture of consumption and an indulgence in expenditures for military domination, if it had made alternative investments—in the environment, for example—with savings derived from reduced military spending.

A new anti-globalism could have been avoided if Washington had not summarily rejected the NIEO and instead been willing to modify the global economic order, if Washington had foregone its broad disregard for and destruction of social rights, a course of action that now haunts the global social and economic system, including its role in the rise of racial and religious discrimination of the most offensive kind.[66] Even now, a new cold war can be avoided by some willingness to reflect on why China, during the relatively few years of neoliberalism, has been able to grow so spectacularly, enough to challenge the United States. What in China's model has enabled it to bring half a billion people out of poverty, a development virtually without precedent? What of South Korea, which, amid almost overwhelming challenges during the 1970s and 1980s, succeeded in a wholesale transformation of its society?

The United States could become more willing, consistent with its avowed commitment to liberty, to allow the flowering of different approaches to economic development instead of maintaining a blind adherence to liberalism and neoliberalism. The United States might even focus on strengthening the UN in ways beneficial to this nation and to others.

3

RACE AND CLASS: THEIR
BEARING ON SOCIAL RIGHTS

Groups of people form societies partly to improve their opportunities in life—to gain security or improve their social well-being, for example. However, supposed differences within societies play important roles in limiting or augmenting life chances, sometimes to the detriment of society itself and certainly to the disadvantage of certain groups or individuals. Among those differences are race and class.[1]

Race, which refers to certain observable physical differences, is generally used as grounds to define and distribute claims to inferior or superior status and rights. The result is unequal treatment—in society and in life chances. Class, broadly understood, refers to a person's status in society based on income, wealth, and education. Therefore, it affects access to other resources that society offers its members.

Race and class are peculiarly connected in the United States, serving the ends of white elites. This connection has diminished social rights at home and abroad, fed corporate profits, and sown social and political discord. It also endangers society and could further harm the United States and the world over the long term. A prime example is the intersection in the area of immigration.

Race and class are not inevitably connected. In the evolution from tribal to pre-capitalist societies, individual economic interest was rarely, if ever, paramount. Until the emergence of the modern state, accepted codes of social honor, generosity, reciprocity, and redistribution protected all members of a community against starvation unless the community as a whole faced starvation. A given society could come under the domination of another, rendering changes in those codes, but even then, the most suffering did not come from the disintegration of the accustomed economic life of the dominated. Rather, their weakened social status, position, and roles produced a sense of inferiority, injuring the institutions in which social life is embedded. In short, the social element—the social good—took priority until the emergence of capitalism as the economic system.[2]

With the emergence of capitalism and the modern state, social commitments attached to cities and towns folded into the role of the nation-state. Those commitments were attached to individuals by virtue of their membership in the state regardless of their social class. Societies that emerged through deliberate, time-defined political and social contracts rather than a gradually evolved, normative practice—the United States, for example—used terms like "the common good" or "the general welfare" to label those commitments. Such societies spoke in terms of civil, political, and social rights to ensure the preservation of values rather than in terms of reciprocity, honor, or the shaping of character.[3]

Civil rights range from rights to own property, exercise free speech, and enter into contracts to freedom of thought, conscience, and faith as well as to liberty of person and what is generally called the right to justice, which is the right to defend other rights. Political rights link to having a share in political power as a member of the state. These include the rights to vote, serve on a jury, and run for political office. Social rights, as British sociologist T. H. Marshall wrote, extend "from the right to a modicum of economic welfare and security to the right to share in the full range of social heritage to social life . . . according to the standards prevailing in the society."[4]

Seen in terms of these rights and, by extension, the obligations of government, the state is less an arrangement of offices than an ethical association for achieving certain ends.[5] In the United States, James Madison, for example, saw the state as an institution to remove obstacles to the ability of individuals and private groups to achieve specific ends.[6] His view, along with that of Alexander Hamilton, who felt that Congress had the power to assure the general welfare, have helped define both negative and positive liberty in the United States.

The idea of social rights assumes a sense of community associated with a shared ideal. Thus, the framers of the U.S. Constitution spoke of commonwealth. However, in terms of social rights, the moral wound of race burdened the very birth of the United States. The community did not, in fact, include certain human beings as members and denied their civil, political, and social rights. Until the Civil War, the U.S. Constitution regarded a slave as three-fifths of a person in calculations for representation in Congress and the electoral college. This accounting mechanism, the so-called Three-Fifths Compromise, related to balancing wealth and political power between the North and the South; it did nothing to recognize slaves as members of the newly created community.[7] Thus, the issue of race was implicated in the nation's development, domestically and internationally, from the launching of the new community. Even so, Alexander

Hamilton's economic model complicated matters, especially as he saw migrants as critical to its development.[8]

Turning to a broader discussion of race and class, the new nation denied blacks a claim to civil, political, or social rights. After the Civil War and the abolition of slavery, they gained the right to citizenship and the right to vote through the Fourteenth Amendment, adopted in 1868, and the Fifteenth Amendment, adopted in 1870. However, this did not change the attitudes of white Americans toward people of color, whom they continued to regard as inferior and dangerous, whether they were Africans, Asians, or other.

The character of Joanna Burden in William Faulkner's novel *Light in August* captures such attitudes:

> I had seen and known negroes since I could remember. I just looked at them as I did at rain or furniture . . . not as people but as a thing, a shadow in which I lived, we lived, all white people, all other people. I thought of all the children coming forever and ever into the world, white, with the black shadow already falling upon them before they drew breath . . . And it seemed like the white babies were struggling, even before they drew breath, to escape from the shadow that was not only upon them but beneath them too.[9]

The meanings contained in that quote are many, but central to this discussion is the idea of a "shadow," a specter, that whites saw blacks as casting on society, including the just-born infant and even the unborn, "coming forever and ever into the world."[10]

People of color reacted to that shadow in multiple ways as they sought an equal place in U.S. society after the Civil War. Their actions are instructive, particularly when examining official behavior before and after the war, as exhibited by judicial decisions, beginning in 1857 with *Dred Scott v. Sanford*. The issue before the Supreme Court was whether "a negro, whose ancestors were imported into the country and sold as slaves, [could] become a member of the political community formed and brought into existence by the Constitution of the United States and as such become entitled to all the rights and privileges . . . guaranteed by that instrument to the citizen."[11] In other words, does the community include blacks? The court said no—"They are not included and were never intended to be included."[12] The court went further, contending that for those who drafted and adopted the U.S. Constitution and became citizens of the new polity, it was "for them and their posterity but no one else." Further, the political rights and privileges guaranteed to citizens "were intended to embrace those only who were members . . . or who afterward, by birthright or otherwise, become members"

45

according to the "provisions of the Constitution and the principles on which it was founded."[13]

In other words, the United States was founded by and for a particular group of people, and it was intended to remain for that group and its posterity by birthright or others who might become members according to the U.S. Constitution. The *Dred Scott* decision went on to say that neither changes in public opinion nor feelings in relation to blacks, in the United States or elsewhere, would induce the court "to give to words of the Constitution a more liberal construction in their [blacks'] favor than they were intended to bear when the instrument was formed and adopted."[14] That idea continues to have a hold on significant sectors of U.S. society, resonating strongly with the alt-right and some other conservatives. Among the most important lessons they draw from *Dred Scott* is that the framers never intended blacks or any people of color to be members of the community called the United States. They were, in the court's words, altogether "unfit to associate with the white race, either in social or political relations," and so inferior that they had no rights "the white man was bound to respect."[15]

In 1896, in *Plessy v. Ferguson*, and two years later, in *United States v. Wong Kim Ark*, the court tested the meaning of the Fourteenth Amendment, with these two cases pointing in opposite directions. Homer Plessy, a man of "one-eighth negro blood," refused to vacate a seat in the white compartment of a train, which, by law, had separate compartments for whites and nonwhites. The question before the court was whether requiring separate compartments for whites and nonwhites violated the Fourteenth Amendment's protection clause, which forbids states to "deny to any persons within its jurisdiction the equal protection of the laws." Taking its cue from an 1849 Massachusetts decision, the court ruled that the Fourteenth Amendment was not intended to eliminate distinctions.[16] The equal protection clause could never "have been intended to abolish distinctions based on color or to enforce social as distinguished from political equality or a commingling of two races upon terms unsatisfactory to either." Supporting the separate compartments, the court went on to say that if "the civil and political rights of both races are equal, one cannot be inferior to the other civilly or politically," and if, on the other hand, one race is inferior to the other socially, the U.S. Constitution cannot put them on the same plane.[17] The specter of social rights continued.

Wong Kim Ark was born in the United States, but his parents, like anyone born in China, were ineligible for citizenship under the Chinese Exclusion Act of 1882.[18] Could a person born in the United States of parents who were ineligible for citizenship be a citizen? A "yes" answer would jeopardize the "posterity" view of citizenship, the idea that the framers did not intend the U.S. community to mean that people could become citizens by an "accident" of where they were born. In this case, the Supreme Court said the Fourteenth Amendment states that "all persons born or naturalized in the United States and subject" to its jurisdiction are "citizens of the United States."[19] Wong Kim Ark, born in the United States and subject to its jurisdiction, was a U.S. citizen.[20]

However, *Plessy* rather than *Wong Kim Ark* guided the legal and moral vision of the United States for some sixty years, a vision reinforced with the court's 1923 decision in *United States v. Bhagat Singh Thind*.[21] An Indian Sikh, Thind contended that genetically, he was white despite the color of his skin. He belonged, he argued, to the Caucasians, the Northern Indian, high-caste Aryan group out of which came the Indo-European peoples. As such, he was eligible for naturalized citizenship under legislation that excluded Indians but included "free white persons."

The Supreme Court declined to accept the genetic argument despite a history, including *Plessy v. Ferguson,* of decisions grounded on supposed genetic factors. Arguing culturally and sociologically, the court said that *Aryan* is a linguistic term but that the words "free white persons" are common speech to be construed in accordance with the understanding of common people. "Free white people" refers to the children of English, French, German, Italian, Scandinavian, or other European parentage—those who were part of the original contract, the U.S. Constitution, and those who were intended, by parentage, to become a part of it.[22] The court went on to note that people of such parents could merge quickly into the population, unlike a Hindu, who would remain readily distinguishable.[23]

The *Bhagat Singh Thind* decision illustrates how perceptions of the "other," including non-nationals, can determine rights under the law. It may also be seen, as sociologist Philip Krestsedemas has noted, that the court, by and large, "made it clear that the race [of which] Thind appeared to be in the eyes of the average American citizen was of greater significance than any evidence he could produce about his biological lineage."[24] In addition, wrote Krestsedemas, the decision reflected the view that the socialized sense of community membership should be maintained and that ordinary people should have a stake in the definition of that membership.

Immigration, the Other, and Whiteness

Turning to the relation of race to the movement of peoples across national borders more generally, immigration has significantly defined the identity of the United States. During successive waves of immigration, that identity, viewed rather fluidly, has been a means of conferring power and privilege on some groups and denying them to others.

The first wave of immigration to the new nation largely encompassed Catholics coming to a predominantly Protestant country, led by people claiming to trace their ancestry mostly to England. These migrants came mainly from Southern

Ireland (as distinguished from "Scottish Irish" from the North). According to historian Nell Irvin Painter, they were "white enough to hold themselves above black and Chinese people in the name of whiteness. As Celts, however, the poor Irish could also be judged racially different enough to be oppressed, ugly enough to be compared with apes, and poor enough to be paired with black people."[25] Other migrants came from Germany and, of course, the United Kingdom, but debate focused on Catholics and the poverty that seemed to define them.

By the time of the Civil War, another wave of migrants, this time overwhelmingly from Western Europe and including their children, enlarged the country's white population but not without raising concerns. Racists sought to distinguish among those of Teutonic and Alpine (Celtic) heritage from Mediterranean immigrants, viewing the latter as generally "darker." In the 1890s, anxieties began to be expressed about racial success and "reproductive vigor," with a strong emphasis on the special place of Anglo-Saxons.[26] In the 1920s, amid concerns about the discovery of "degenerate families" among the white population and clamors to sterilize or test the intelligence of immigrants, whiteness was exposed to a third wave of immigration, this time from Eastern Europe and including Jews. This ethnic mixture triggered more anxieties. A fourth wave in the 1960s, with immigration primarily from the Global South, coincided with the first attempts of the United States to deal seriously with certain civil and political rights of African Americans.[27] In general, all immigrants admitted to citizenship gained civil and political rights despite any reservations that self-described Anglo-Saxons may have felt about the broader implications of their presence in the United States.[28] However, for many years, third- and fourth-wave immigrants were denied social rights and, in general, not viewed as equals.

What arose before World War I was a racial linkage: whiteness became associated with universal dominance. As the philosopher Linda Martín Alcoff describes regarding this position, there is "a facticity of whiteness, whether or not it factors into a person's self-ascription. Whiteness is lived and not merely represented. It is a prominent feature of one's way of being in the world, of how one navigates that world and how one is navigated around by others."[29] The level of prominence varies, sometimes even ruling. It can, in part, be expressed in what Bruce Norris in his 2010 play *Clybourne Park* so aptly captured about the assumptions of whites in the United States: they are entitled to all public space and to inhabit and move into whatever neighborhoods they desire.[30]

Alternatively, whiteness may be viewed, as did Joseph Conrad in *The Heart of Darkness* in the 1890s, as European imperialism in Africa, with its broader implications. "The conquest of the earth," Conrad observed, "which mostly means taking away from those who have a different complexion or slightly flatter noses,"[31] was the existing way of life. That taking was justified in the minds of Europeans. Indeed, some of that justification was on the grounds that much of the "earth" being conquered was *res nullius*—it belonged to nobody, although people lived and had their being there.

Many of the immigrants to the United States had little consciousness of being white.[32] After all, they could just as well have constituted a class given commonalities in their backgrounds. Most had fled some feared condition: poverty; religious, political, racial, or other persecution; actual or threatened famine; compromising minority status; loss of property. Also, most encountered atrocious working conditions in the United States. They did not constitute a class because they either became white, part of a dominant group,[33] or would be lumped with the powerless and frowned-on people of color: blacks, the Chinese, Hispanics, and Native Americans. For whites, there was also the chance to eliminate, especially in comparison with the powerless, such self-ascriptions as German, Greek, Irish, Italian, Jew, and Pole. In exchange for electing race over class as the dominant communal identity, the various European ethnic groups would all share in the material and other returns joined to or connected with whiteness.

For a variety of reasons, some immigrants welcomed the chance to sever their identity from the countries they had left and found the prospect of the new racial identity agreeable.[34] However, given the many temptations to class formation (exacerbated by the Russian Revolution in 1917), whiteness had to continue delivering a social return, a proof of white ethnics' membership in a common racial community. With nonwhites excluded from that community, appropriate, measurable distinctions had to be made—and made continuously—if betrayal were not to become an issue.

Just before, during, and after the third wave in what Painter calls the "expansion of whiteness," proof came in President Wilson's domestic and international public policy pursuits.[35] Domestically, his administration resegregated federal employment, beginning with Department of the Treasury and the Post Office Department in 1913 and expanding to the Department of State and other agencies. Then in 1915, Wilson sought to prevent the comingling of races (a preoccupation of *Plessy*) by criminalizing interracial marriage in the District of Columbia. This was eight years before the *Thind* decision gave the average white citizen a stake in emphasizing the cultural basis for white identity over genetic identity. Internationally, Wilson discontinued the practice of having black diplomats represent the United States in Haiti and the Dominican Republic, and he blocked Japan's request to include a clause on racial equality in the Treaty of Versailles, the most important of several treaties ending World War I.

In the years between the world wars, a limited expression of social community came into being under Pres. Franklin D. Roosevelt, who is intimately associated with the New Deal and its social programs. However, many of his domestic policies made distinctions. For example, at least since the 1917 Russian Revolution, Washington had touted housing as a means to inculcate patriotism, but it largely aimed efforts to expand homeownership for white Americans, giving them a stake in society and helping inoculate them against the attractions of socialism.[36] The New Deal's Federal Housing Administration (FHA) sought to help uproot the country from the Great Depression by insuring mortgages, but the new Home Owners' Loan Corporation designed color-coded "area maps" to designate levels of risk for insuring mortgages. Green areas were the safest; red areas, where minorities lived, were the riskiest. The FHA would not insure loans to risky areas, and banks would not offer mortgages without insurance.[37]

The same differentiation appeared in the workings of the new Social Security Board (later renamed the Social Security Administration) and the Fair Labor Standard Act, established to monitor and enforce minimum wages, hours of labor, and prohibitions against child labor. Social Security did not cover agriculture and domestic service, occupations where minorities (especially blacks) predominated. The pattern was repeated in other agencies. Economist Richard Rothstein has described the case of the NRA, established during the New Deal's first year. The NRA, until the Supreme Court struck it down, created "industry-by-industry minimum wage, maximum hours, and product prices . . . [but it] did not cover canning, citrus packing, and cotton-ginning . . . so [blacks who dominated these areas of work] were denied NRA's wage and labor standards."[38] The armed forces largely confined minorities to support roles that put black lives at risk but did not make them eligible for the mortgage subsidies white servicemen enjoyed.[39] (In 1896, Massachusetts senator Henry Cabot Lodge had contemptuously described many of those servicemen—Italians, Russians, Poles, Greeks, Hungarians, among others—as "paupers, convicts, and diseased persons" who were a threat to "the original stocks of the 13 colonies.")[40]

World War II's appalling demonstrations of what racism could occasion did not modify in any substantive way the attitudes of U.S. leaders; nor did wartime clamor at home about human rights. Doing so could disturb the delicate race–class balance at home and, in turn, create problems abroad, especially in regard to colonial countries.[41] Nevertheless, the United States could not easily dismiss the question. What the Japanese unsuccessfully sought at Versailles in 1919—a statement of principle on racial equality—China raised during negotiations on the UN Charter, with broad support from Latin American and Caribbean countries as well as Japan and some countries from the Global South. Additionally, the deliberations succeeded in including, among the UN's ends, the "promotion of the economic and social advancement of all peoples," the solution "of international economic, social, health and related problems," higher standards of living, full employment, and conditions of economic and social progress, and "universal respect for and observance of human rights and fundamental freedoms for all without distinctions as to race, sex, language, or religion."[42] All these principles are laudable, especially in affirming social rights, and racial equality might be deduced from them. However, no agreement could be reached on an explicit principle of racial equality.[43]

After World War II, the United States had a strategy for balancing race–class issues at home, the rising push toward racial equality at home and abroad, and the challenges of global leadership when faced with an ideologically oriented opponent preaching class solidarity. That strategy reflects the views of Edgar Gardner Murphy, an Episcopal priest and social and educational leader who was prominent in the Progressive Movement at the beginning of the twentieth century. Like other Progressives—from William James and Theodore Roosevelt to Brooks Adams and those who sought to idealize their alma mater in "Fair Harvard"—Rev. Murphy was deeply committed to the ascendency of Anglo-Saxons, but he sought some accommodations with inferior peoples. He thought he saw the following:

> [E]verywhere, the former coalition of weaker groups is being broken up, and the inferior peoples are being . . . reorganized . . . [into] stronger aggregates and . . . the co-existence of whites and non-whites under such conditions posed problems of the strong living with the weak . . . so living as to assure peace without afflicting desolation, as to preserve order without defeating justice, as to uphold a state which will express the life of the higher group without enfeebling or destroying that waiting manhood of . . . weaker peoples.[44]

Therefore, he believed, the United States should pursue a form of racial *noblesse oblige*, assume a noble responsibility toward the racially inferior, doing so to ensure peace and order but without impairing the nation's vigor and superior capacity and without accommodating the "waiting manhood" of the weak and inferior.

Murphy's Spirit

The spirit (if not always the conception) of Rev. Murphy's view found its way into every area of the post-1945 international order, especially the moral order. At the heart of his accommodation has been the International Bill of Human Rights, with the formation of a body of basic norms and principles for global governance: the Universal Declaration of Human Rights (1948), the ICESCR (1966), and the ICCPR (1968).

The first of the three, the Universal Declaration of Human Rights, includes social, economic, and cultural rights as well as civil and political rights. However, it only became binding as part of international and treaty law in 1976, when the two international covenants came into effect and incorporated its terms. Still, the declaration has had moral clout throughout its life. Like the UN Charter itself, it refers to rights "for all without distinction as to race, sex, language, or religion," the rights of "everyone," and "the inherent dignity and . . . equality and inalienable rights of all." These rights had to be respected and dealt with.

The United States followed several tactics in responding to this view within a broader *noblesse oblige* strategy begun in 1898 in relation to Cuba, Hawaii, Puerto Rico, the Philippines, and Guam. First, Washington and the United Kingdom led an effort to include the "domestic jurisdiction clause" within the UN Charter; as a result, Article 2, Section 7, forbids the UN from intervening in matters that are essentially within the domestic jurisdiction of states.[45] This shelters the United States from international intervention in racial matters within its borders. Second, the United States manipulated language, such as attributing different meanings to such expressions as *nondiscrimination*, without distinction, and *equality*. None of the three key international agreements refers to the equality of races, instead including the sovereign equality of states and the moral equality of individuals. Third, echoing *Plessy v. Ferguson*, Washington emphasized civil and political rights while excluding as much as possible references to economic, social, and cultural rights, such as the right to food, housing, health care, education, or equal wages for equal work. Such rights would apply to all, eliminating the distinction in social returns to whites in contrast to racial minorities. Maintaining the incentive to whiteness or white identity rather than class identity could become unsustainable; bitter cries of betrayal would be the basis for social disorder.

Henry Wallace's third-party presidential campaign in 1948, including his opposition to the Cold War and admiration for European-style socialism, combined with the perceived communist threat to endanger the U.S. liberal and, later, neoliberal thrust. In response—and against the wishes of President Truman—Sen. Hubert Humphrey convinced the Democratic Party to adopt a platform plank advocating civil and political rights. His view was to give every citizen a stake "in the emergence of the United States as leader of the free world."[46] Indeed, a focus on civil and political rights served the Democratic Party into the 1960s and 1970s as the civil rights agenda became more and more demanding, even if it would eventually become clear that the United States was unprepared for a multiracial society at home or abroad.

In 1948, President Truman, going the civil and political rights route, signed an order legally integrating the armed forces, although they remained de facto segregated as late as the Vietnam War, as detailed by Robert McNamara in 1968, the year he ended his seven years as secretary of defense.[47] A number of court decisions showed a similar pattern of partial steps forward, including the 1954 *Brown v. Board of Education* case reversing the "separate but equal" doctrine of *Plessy v. Ferguson*, even if public education for minorities would remain largely inherently inferior because of the property tax basis of school financing.

The civil rights movement of the 1960s did gain legislative and sometimes judicial affirmation and protection of the right to vote as well as outlawed racial discrimination in employment. Further, the Fair Housing Act of 1968 instituted some safeguards against discrimination in the sale, rental, and financing of housing regardless of race, religion, national origin, or sex. After fifty-plus years, though, the attitudes that informed discrimination in the first place have limited the implementation of concepts formulated to eliminate those attitudes.[48]

Pres. Lyndon Johnson's Great Society initiative introduced a variety of social programs in food, housing, health care, and other areas, some of which continued New Deal efforts. However, some of its opponents and even supporters termed Johnson's initiatives as "welfare" programs—that is, they offered subsidies to the poor. Far from expressing a focus on community and the common good, *welfare* became a pejorative term, thus deemphasizing class and prioritizing whiteness. Those who benefited from welfare could be depicted as intellectually, socially, and morally incapable of securing an independent existence. Generations on welfare, it was said, constituted a form of pathology, and its recipients parasitically exploited the rest of society. Further, with the collusion of the press and popular literature, it was made to appear that welfare programs were for minorities, even though poor whites constituted most of the beneficiaries. Psychologically, poor whites could separate themselves from "welfare queens" and other nonwhite beneficiaries, and they could vote against such programs, just as many poor whites opposed letting nonwhites join labor unions.[49]

Murphy's Spirit Continued

Abroad, the United States did not simply follow its earlier *noblesse oblige* patterns. Rather, from Iran and Guatemala to the Congo (Zaire) and Vietnam, its initiatives overthrew governments seeking to introduce significant social reforms. In contrast yet equally noteworthy were the formation of the nonaligned group in 1955, the creation of the UNCTAD and the Group of 77 in 1964, and the body of basic norms and principles for global governance noted earlier.

Following World War II, a bipolar political and military system defined the Cold War, with the major states grouped around the two powers dominating international relations. To resist pressure to choose between these two coalitions, each defining itself with rigid ideological positions, African and Asian countries at a 1955 meeting in Bandung, Indonesia, took the first steps toward forming the Non-Aligned Movement (NAM), establishing it as an organization in 1961.

For the United States, mired in Rev. Murphy's anxiety that the weaker races might challenge Anglo-Saxon primacy, the NAM was anti-white, and the events leading up to it provoked a panic of sorts.[50] According to the political scientist Robert Vitalis, President Eisenhower was advised, among other things, to create a public relations counter-narrative by appointing a "Negro Ambassador to a large and important country such as France."[51] Also, when a future NAM leader, Gamal Abdul Nasser of Egypt, nationalized the Suez Canal in 1956, the United States refused to support the efforts of its allies (France, Israel, and the United Kingdom) to retake it, in part to limit the propaganda benefits to the former Soviet Union but most importantly, Vitalis writes, to contain what was perceived as the "personified and emotional demands of the people of the area . . . for slapping the white man down."[52]

However, the NAM would have its own objectives. As seen by India's Jawaharlal Nehru, the NAM could provide political, economic, and moral alternatives to what the two Cold War blocs offered, including moving peoples under colonial rule more rapidly to independence. These were countries informed by doubts (shared by blacks, among others in the United States) about moral-sounding ideas emanating from the Western powers, including statements like the Atlantic Charter, which Churchill and others had indicated did not apply to people of color.[53] NAM nations were also concerned about the nature and degree of material sharing that the existing international order would allow.

By 1962, UN membership had more than doubled from the original 51 nations to 110. With the help of the NAM, most of the new members came from Africa, Asia, and the Caribbean. Three years earlier, President Eisenhower, speaking with French president Charles de Gaulle, had expressed the complaints of certain U.S. elites about such developments: "Many of these people were attempting to make the leap from savagery to the degree of civilization of a country like France in perhaps ten years without realizing that it took thousands of years to develop the civilization which we know."[54]

If the formation of the NAM upset the United States, UNCTAD and the Group of 77 could only add to U.S. concerns. The two bodies emerged in part over frustration in the Global South regarding the projected timing of independence for colonial peoples. (Estimates ranged from fifty to seventy-five years after World War II for "selected" groups that were seen as unlikely to be ready for independence for many years.[55]) Moreover, UNCTAD and the Group of 77 focused on social rights that emphasized race rather than class, an emphasis the United States firmly opposed.

In 1964, the Global South used its majority in the UN to influence the creation of UNCTAD, which would report to the UN Secretariat, a worldwide body operating outside the U.S.-dominated World Bank, the IMF, and the GATT. The new organization immediately began working to persuade the GATT to find ways to improve exports from the Global South. By 1974, many UNCTAD members had also joined the Group of 77 (now with a membership of 134 countries) to propose an NIEO designed to protect LDCs' natural and other resources. The idea of the NIEO was to equalize terms of trade and investment among countries while advancing a broad social agenda employing the machinery of governments and international organizations to bring about more equitable social and economic outcomes for individuals and peoples.

To the extent that the NIEO agenda of social justice and social rights applied to everyone, it would remove the material and cultural advantages that the average white person would enjoy over nonwhites. This ran counter to the U.S. emphasis on race over class, and it flew in the face of the neoliberal focus on limited government. Moreover, the agenda would promote loose alignments of less-developed nations with the democratic socialists of Western Europe and, to an extent, the socialism or communism coming out of the Soviet Union and Eastern Europe.

To compound U.S. difficulties, the international human rights instruments on civil and political rights and on economic, social, and cultural rights came into effect. By 1976, they had become part of international law when adopted by enough countries. Earlier, the United States could escape censorship for its own human rights violation by saying that the terms of the Universal Declaration of Human Rights were "aspirational." Now those provisions were binding. Throughout the negotiations on creating the ICCPR, no issue was more important for Washington than Articles 26 and 27. Although not conceding racial equality, Article 26 would guarantee protection to *all* regardless of supposed differences "on any grounds such as race, color, sex, language, religion, political, or other opinion, national or social origin, property, birth, or other status."[56] Article 27, dealing with minorities, is phrased in such a way that it is inapplicable to the United States: "[In] those states in which ethnic, religious, or linguistic minorities exist, persons belonging to minorities shall not be denied the right in community with other members of their group to enjoy their own cultures . . . or their own language." Since the United States grouped all ethnic whites together, no U.S. whites belonged to an ethnic minority group; with respect to blacks, Hispanics, and Asians, among others, the United States saw them more in racial terms not covered by Article 27. Indeed, the term "in those states" was intended to refer to Eastern European countries; the United States did not like the idea of group rights either, and it saw the phrase "in community with other members of their group" as going beyond the rights of individuals.

The ICESCR seeks to give the rights it covers the same legal standing as their civil and political counterparts. Like the right to free speech and/or the right to freedom of conscience and religion, they could not then be repealed.[57] Economic, social, and cultural rights—such as the right to food, equal pay for equal work, health care and housing, and education and to share in society's cultural and scientific advancement and a standard of living supportive of a family—require a certain minimum amount of government support for all persons, a sort of reciprocity, mutual help, and redistribution system.

At the time the covenants came into force and the NIEO was proposed, the United States was under a great deal of economic and political stress. It had gone off the gold standard in 1971, faced high oil and other commodity prices, felt the psychological effects of defeat in the Vietnam War, suffered an increasingly adverse balance of trade and the highest interest rates in its history, and experienced continued, if diminished, student rebellions—not to mention the effort to impeach President Nixon. Moreover, the United States was embarrassed by government changes in the Global South—in Indonesia, Iran, and Chile, for example—while facing what seemed to be a more formidable Soviet Union. Jimmy Carter, seeking to regain some international moral influence for the United States, turned to human rights, and he became the first president to place those rights at the center of U.S. foreign policy.[58] His administration still focused on civil and political rights, but it applied a hint of the social (uniting families) under the 1975 Helsinki Accords with the Soviet Union.[59] The United States did not ratify the ICCPR, despite the Carter administration's efforts, until 1992—and only after the reservation was attached indicating that the rights provided in that covenant could not add to those specified in the U.S. Constitution. Congress has never discussed, let alone ratified, the ICESCR, and the Reagan administration rejected proposals for a NIEO at a North–South conference held in Cancun, Mexico, in 1981.

With neoliberalism holding sway from the 1970s to the present, the United States gutted social programs through deregulation, the weakening of unions, huge tax cuts, privatization, and the glorification of the self-regulating market, especially after the fall of the Soviet Union had removed the perceived international class threat.[60] Lowered tariffs and IMF adjustment programs invariably forced nations to cut subsidies to food, housing, education, and health care, among other things, furthering a global de-emphasis on big government. Globalization and the fourth wave of migration to the United State combined to effect additional changes in national and local society. Globalization has been producing unimagined wealth, with individuals and institutions (e.g., businesses, nongovernmental organizations, governments) operating on a global scale. Global exports expanded from $58 billion in 1948 to $16 trillion in 2016. However, little of that new wealth has been shared broadly across national societies, and within the United States, one in five children lives in poverty, and one in five goes to bed hungry.[61] The top 1 percent of the U.S. population owns more than 40 percent of the nation's wealth.[62]

Things Change — Can They Remain the Same?

The 1965 Immigration Act stimulated the fourth wave of immigration to the United States. Consistent with the civil rights movement and the international human rights focus on equality, the act removed racial quotas that had been in effect for most of the twentieth century, opening the door to a broad flow of immigrants from Africa, Asia, the Caribbean, and Latin America. By the 1980s, nonwhites dominated immigration to the United States.[63] Those who wanted to "leap from savagery . . . to civilization" were no longer mostly abroad; many more were now within the United States, even if not fully a part of it.

Immigrants in the fourth wave, unlike those in the first three, could not become white, as clearly shown in the case of Bhagat Singh Thind, so they could not serve the quest to mask and contain class. They would have to remain nonwhite, and many came from societies that advocated the NIEO and the international covenants and were victims of IMF adjustment programs. Thus, fourth-wave immigrants would potentially support more, not fewer, social rights as well as provide a lever for emphasizing class over race.[64] Most importantly, the new immigrants contribute to a demographic transformation that will make whites a numerical minority in the United States. As Alcoff has observed, "Whiteness will continue to exist after it loses its majority, but it will be living in a country it can no longer easily dominate."[65]

This future has engendered wide and deep anxieties in the United States and, to almost a like extent, in Europe, which has had increases in immigration to deal with its aging population and, of late, to cope with shared responsibilities toward refugees. The United Kingdom and Australia also face challenges. Huge tax cuts for the rich, cutbacks in social programs, and displacement caused by globalization have, together, disordered what Michael Omi and Howard Winant, in *Racial Formation in the United States,* term a "racial project"[66]—a "race-based distribution of resources" organized to "ensure the continuation of what is actually an oligarchy" into which immigrant whites as a whole bought and committed themselves to defend the status quo if the distribution favored them, even a little, over nonwhites.[67] Whites began to experience being left behind, overlooked, disregarded, disrespected, and lied to as well as a precipitous decline in their socioeconomic standing.[68] This has set the stage for broad, if sometimes disguised, discussions, and popular resentments have induced behaviors that threaten to escalate outside normative control—the rise of the Tea Party, for example.

One of the most forceful intellectual engagements on these issues is the late Samuel P. Huntington's 1993 article in *Foreign Affairs,* "The Clash of Civilizations?"[69] Huntington implied here what he explicitly stated in later works: Anglo-Saxon cultural norms will no longer exclusively define U.S. national values. Blacks, he argued, had largely incorporated the English language, were by and large Protestants, and had exhibited low fertility rates. On the other hand, assimilation was unlikely for Hispanics and other groups. Focusing on culture (rather than biology or territory as grounds for national identity), he sought to retain U.S. national and racial ascendency but within a more expansive cultural setting called civilization, which he defined as "the highest cultural grouping of people and the broadest level of cultural identity people have short of that which distinguishes humans from other species."[70] He identified seven civilizations, with a possible eighth—Western, Confucian, Japanese, Islamic, Hindu, Slavic-Orthodox, and Latin American and possibly African.

In the same 1993 article, Huntington, focusing on "the West and the Rest," outlines the unprecedented power and influence of the West (especially with the disintegration of the Soviet Union) and indicated that the term *world community* is but a euphemistic collective noun (replacing *free world*) "to give legitimacy to actions reflecting the interests of the United States and other western powers."[71] According to this article, "[t]he West, in effect, is using international institutions, military power, and economic resources to run the world *in ways that will maintain Western dominance* [emphasis added], protect Western interests, and promote Western political and economic values."[72]

This is part of why the United States could not accept the proposed NIEO, why it saw the Iraqi War of 2003 in part as a clash of civilizations, and why the U.S. battle (in civilizational terms) against social rights will continue to protect the ascendency of white identity, even as demographic changes make this more and more difficult. This is also why much of President Trump's seemingly incoherent postures on race conceal an underlying continuity and logic. The Trump administration's efforts to "de-territorialize" citizenship are consistent with Huntington's focus on de-territorializing nationhood and nationality/citizenship. In this view, a child born in the United States to Nigerian parents or Korean citizens should not be a U.S. citizen—or, by extension, part of Western civilization. Likewise, a child born in Germany or Brazil of U.S. parents would not only be a U.S. citizen but also part of the American nation and Western civilization. On the other hand, a territorial-based system of citizenship and nationality, as specified in the Fourteenth Amendment, would threaten the United States, a view illustrated in President Trump's imagery of "invading caravans" of undesirables. Congressman Steve King, from Iowa, furthered that same view in 2018 when he brought into the public sphere aspects of Faulkner's image of nonwhite children casting a shadow over white ones. According to Representative King, the United States "can't restore our civilization with somebody else's babies."[73] In short, he seeks both a cultural and a biological solution, which immigrants from the Global South cannot provide.

Given the historical emphasis of race over class, the raw accentuation of race in public life should not be surprising.[74] Recall the Willie Horton affair during the presidential campaign of George H. W. Bush, the "Southern strategy" of Richard Nixon, and the "you know where I stand" messages of opponents of school desegregation in Boston, the supposed seat of national cultural enlightenment.

Thus, it is unfair to accuse President Trump of dividing the country with his public preference for whiteness. Race has divided the county for over four hundred years, and despite some significant efforts, it has failed to wrestle with its cultural penetration of our lives because race subconsciously serves the ends of whiteness. Any national debate on the subject often turns into mutual recrimination and "both sides of the issue" television or radio exchanges. Instead of serious discussion, the pundits wordsmith, substituting *culture* or *civilization* for *race*, *cultural heritage* for *racial heredity*, and *centuries of racial experience* or *centuries of tradition* for *racial instincts*.[75] In the service of whiteness, the nation has deliberately deemphasized social class, often condemning many poor whites to poverty and indignity, and despite the experienced horrors of World War II, it has fought all efforts to promote racial equality as distinct from nondiscrimination in matters of race.

The 2018 murder of eleven Jewish congregants at Pittsburgh's Tree of Life Synagogue by a man who saw Jews as facilitating immigration is only a recent expression of a national moral pathology. So too was the 2015 killing of nine black people as they worshipped at the Emanuel African Methodist Episcopal Church in Charleston, South Carolina. The twenty-one-year-old killer felt he had to do it because blacks had "raped our women and are taking over our country [and therefore] have to go." A 2017 Charlottesville, Virginia, demonstration centered on protecting a statue of Confederate general Robert Lee became a riot, with attacks against blacks and Jews. The cry that "Jews will not replace us" expressed not only fear and bitter anger but also hatred rooted in the concept "us" and "our," including "our country"—not theirs.[76] Even Stephen Bannon's efforts, as a one-time advisor to President Trump and since, to forge ties with white supremacists in Western and Eastern Europe should not shock anyone. His views about preserving a certain biological and cultural heritage are not unlike those of Ralph Waldo Emerson (who wrote his dissertation on the special place of Anglo-Saxons), Henry Cabot Lodge, Samuel Huntington, Rep. Steve King, or President Trump. They also accord with the words of the Harvard University alma mater until its 2017 revision: it spoke in terms of being the "herald of light and the bearers of love" until the "stock of the Puritans die."[77]

Globalism has produced immense wealth, but abundance has not trickled down to the least advantaged anywhere. Few countries have managed to escape fifty years of neoliberalism in ways that would ensure effective redistribution. Even when national governments attempt redistribution, international society has no central authority that would hinder the supremacy of capital. Within the United States, the successes of the strategy to deemphasize class—giving social, psychological, and assumed moral space to the continuing domination of race—was based on the promise to whites of a "shared privilege," assumed to be an indefinite commitment. The neoliberal order—with its privatizations, deregulations, and gutted social programs—has shattered that promise, in part resulting in and aggravating the recession of 2007–2008 and then requiring taxpayers to bail out the very institutions and leaders of the tragedy.

Keep in mind that the term *neoliberalism* specifies neither Republicans nor Democrats. It is a world-encompassing socioeconomic ideology that embraces and is embraced by both parties, as evidenced, for example, by the Clinton administration's (1993–2000) actions undermining social programs and deregulating markets during the 1990s.[78] Neither should the impact of this ideology be measured primarily in economic terms.[79] The primary impact is social: people feel disregarded, stepped on, injured, deprived, undignified, and powerless. The crushing of self-esteem is fundamental, calling into question personal identity.

Neuroscience suggests that "hate speech" affects a site in the brain that, like starvation, can have long-lasting, corrosive consequences.[80] When a felt rejection and its associated injuries couple with rapid demographic change and when those who have enjoyed the privileges of whiteness find themselves in the same social circumstances as racial inferiors, the brew is ready for social and political explosion.[81] Social elites, largely sheltered, do not feel this, yet the United States will not deal effectively with the nexus of race and class, so long neglected, without serious, extended national debate. Indeed, the nation must prepare to deal with the issues of social rights for all on a global scale.

4

Education: Political and Popular Culture

Every human institution—by inherited practice, conscious design, or chance—seeks to perpetuate itself. Such a temporal extension of anything, rendering it permanent or assigning it attributes of "foreverness," requires defining the thing itself, giving it an identity.

In the modern political lexicon, the principal sociopolitical identity into which human societies shape themselves is the *nation* or the *nation-state*, terms used interchangeably here despite some differences. This institution, which came into being in the West during the seventeenth century, has become universal (although not without facing some contest). As with other sociopolitical institutions, its perpetuation has been principally through education—abstract education about the nature of the self and the ends it seeks as well as practical education through the teaching of values and principles and an essentially unconscious imbibing of common practices. These modes of learning through abstract instruction and common practices are particularly appropriate for understanding the sociopolitical being because the political too is both abstract and practical.

Nation, Self, and Uniqueness

The idea of a nation is expressed by the ideology of nationalism, which describes and furnishes a justification for the nation-state.[1] That ideology contends that the people constituting a nation—those who share a common past, defined by joint and common exertions, including sufferings and triumphs, and who have conscious aspirations for a common future—have the right to self-determination. Thus, George Washington, in his farewell address, reminded Americans of the coveted shared status they had achieved: "With slight shades of differences, you have the same religion, manners, habits, and political principles. You have in a common cause fought and triumphed together. The independence and liberty you possess are the work of joint councils and joint effort—of common dangers, sufferings, and successes."

The ideology of nationalism has further argued that self-determination is best experienced through the attachment of sovereign status to the nation—this is to say, becoming a nation-state. Further, the only good state is a nation-state because humanity divides itself into nations *naturally*.[2] As well, the nation-state is the ideal form of political organization, especially in that it offers social justice, identity, and, of utmost importance, security against "unlike others" who always pose a potential military threat. In the psychological sense, the nation-state offers security domestically and through a common belonging. Other segments of the national community will, by reason of their character and affiliation, be moved to help any segment that needs it through a kind of moral and social contract. Additionally, the nation-state, by virtue of its sovereignty, confers on its nationals or citizens equality with all the members of other nation-states. In view of these benefits, nationals or citizens owe their highest loyalty to their respective nation-states. As the late British historian Arnold Toynbee observed, nationalism gradually became a secular religion through which people began and continue to worship the nation-state.[3]

In the United States, people (especially the young) learn that their nation is unlike any other. In the words of writer William Pfaff, the United States "accepts no comparison with others, and so it has been the most nationalistic of all major nations. Not only politicians and public men but people themselves constantly assert its superiority over all others [in a way that suggests that] the virtue of its Constitution were proof of permanent national success."[4] The U.S. Constitution incorporates certain principles Americans see as universally valid and applicable: the separation of powers, with an independent judiciary; a republican structure as opposed to the monarchical orientation that dominated at the time of the constitution's adoption; and limited government in the sense of the protection of property, the sacred nature of contract, and the first ten amendments to the constitution.

Nowhere do these principles or Washington's farewell address refer to the fact that the liberty for which the 1776 revolution was fought had its roots in liberty to pursue certain ends. Doing so would soil the moral luster of the principles and sow confusion concerning whether moral norms supersede commercial interests. Neither do the principles indicate the fact, cited by historian Andrew Serwer and his colleagues, that in 1860, "the capital in slaves equaled three times the dollar amount that the North and the South had financed in manufacturing, seven times that invested in banks, and forty-eight times the amount of U.S. government expenditures."[5] Popular education largely overlooks the role of property in the thirteen colonies in 1776 and in the South's desire for independence in 1861 or the question of how much a single nation existed at either of these two historical junctures.

American nationalism, which Lincoln used so well to avert the dissolution of the republic, reflected the spirit of Washington's farewell address, which spoke of the "national Union" as the source of "collective and individual happiness," something about which citizens

> [s]hould cherish cordial, habitual, and immovable attachment . . . accustoming [themselves] to think and speak of it as the palladium of [their] political safety and prosperity, watching for its preservation with jealous anxiety, discountenancing whatever may suggest even a suspicion that it can be abandoned, and indignantly frowning upon the first dawning of every attempt to alienate any portion of our country from the rest or enfeeble the sacred ties which now link together its various parts.

As Lincoln imposed federal supremacy on the South immediately after the Civil War, he was indeed fulfilling the sentiments of Washington and other Founding Fathers. The South, using code words like *states' rights* to continue resisting federal authority, employed similar words to indicate its refusal to accept that blacks and other nonwhites were ever part of the nation. Nor is it clear that Washington ever intended that blacks and other nonwhites would or should be part of his own definition of a nation. In this sense, the Southern view may be closer to that of Washington than the supposed positions of the North and Lincoln. This ambiguity continues to define attitudes in many quarters—attitudes learned in part through court decisions but more so by social practice in the form of subtle and not-so-subtle discrimination as well as the aggregate of images fashioned by culture.[6]

Stronger national impulses arose after the Civil War, finding expression in a major push into the U.S. West. The doctrine of "Manifest Destiny," which had begun taking hold of the public in the 1840s, drove U.S. territorial expansion during the nineteenth century and later. It held that this nation, because of the special virtues of its people and their institutions, was chosen to expand and spread its way of life all across North America. Thus, settlers, in part fueled by post–Civil War immigration, moved across the United States and, by the 1890s, with the West Coast secured, continued abroad to Cuba, Puerto Rico, Guam, the Philippines, and Hawaii, all but the last taken during the 1898 war with Spain. In 1903, writes Pfaff, the United States invented the country of Panama "to make possible a canal construction, under U.S. authority, in that new and allegedly sovereign territory. The canal was opened in 1914."[7]

None of these international activities make reference to imperialism; the United States did not see itself as imperialistic (or even nationalistic), and young people today still largely learn about the actions of the U.S. government much as President McKinley characterized them in 1898 to Congress: "The grounds justifying [the war with Spain over Cuba] were the interests of humanity, the duty to protect the life and property of our citizens in Cuba, the right to check injury to our commerce and people."[8]

At about the time of the Spanish–American War, a focus on trade in China made linking the Pacific and the Atlantic by way of a canal in Panama, the annexation of Hawaii, and taking control of the Philippines seemingly important strategic steps to ensure great-power status for the United States for an indefinite future. Some—such as President McKinley and Elihu Root, secretary of war from 1899 to 1904, suggested that the U.S. Constitution, brought into being on the moral ground of the consent of the governed, should be amended to accommodate U.S. expansion, but few took such voices seriously.[9] Instead, the idea began to grow that the radical document called the U.S. Constitution had placed the stamp of a felt and asserted uniqueness on the republic. "The United States was, in a fundamental sense, fulfilled at its start," Pfaff wrote. "Nothing that followed has been thought to augment or alter the order created by the ratification of the . . . Constitution."[10]

This sense of perfection, however much imperialism contradicted it, sprang from a Puritan outlook that saw the republic, the nation, as a "new beginning for [hu]mankind." It had been ordained by God in what was then, as now, a corrupt world.[11] That corruption, for most of the twentieth century, was seen (and taught) through selected examinations of World War I, World War II, and their offspring, including the 1917 Bolshevik Revolution in Russia.

In the case of World War I, the United States, after remaining neutral for two years, decided to enter not just to save democracy, President Wilson declared, but also to end all wars. In negotiations at the war's end, the nation appeared to act— and saw itself as acting—as the only impartial participant, seeking no territory or other tainted special advantage such as indemnities. On the contrary, it sought a just peace for all. Wilson even went around national leaders in Italy and other countries to appeal directly to their people on proposed peace settlements on the grounds that politicians may not truly represent their people. In his proposed Fourteen Points to effect a just peace, Wilson called for, among other things, self-determination, disarmament, the elimination of trade barriers, and the creation of a general, international association of nations to maintain peace.

World War II, in the minds of most Americans, represented the same ideas as World War I. The United States did not want to go to war. Without provocation, Japan attacked, and the United States had to defend itself as well as Europe, the world, and democracy against dictatorships (Nazism and fascism, specifically). The postwar orders (the League of Nations after World War I and the UN after World War II) were U.S. efforts to create and extend "new beginnings" that it claimed to represent and embody to the rest of an undemocratic, corrupt world, especially Europe, from which the Pilgrims had fled to establish the new nation.

Self and Some Challenges

The new international liberal order, created after World War II, faced a challenge that had begun with the Bolshevik Revolution. With the decline of Europe's old power centers after 1945, that challenge confronted the United States directly as Soviet influence became worldwide, with communist regimes in the Soviet Union, Eastern Europe, China, Vietnam, and Cuba as well as strong communist parties in France, India, Italy, and Japan. The challenge to the United States and its largely capitalist allies was not so much the actual number of communist regimes—although that was important—but rather the ideological force that communism claimed to represent. That ideology, wrote Pfaff, threatened to do "nothing less than [effect] the displacement of the United States from the vanguard of history."[12]

Displacement would happen by countering U.S. self-definition by proving the following: communism, not liberalism, represented the way of the future, with social equality for all; the very laws of history grounded this representation rather than some mystical sentiment about being chosen by God; those laws promised to dismantle certain oppressive economic structures, the most important of which was social class; and the elimination of social class would pave the way for integrating all human interests throughout the world. Outside of a few academics and intellectuals from Europe, the United States confronted the Soviet Union, communism, or their challenges in ideological terms almost exclusively by promoting private property. More home ownership, for example, would elicit patriotism from those who gained a stake in society and would protect it to defend their property. For the most part, U.S. propaganda, which served as the basis for instruction in schools, rather effectively short-circuited ideological debate and discussion from 1946 until the Soviet Union disintegrated in 1989.

Washington contended that the Russian Revolution was not, in fact, a revolution at all and thus not comparable to the American Revolution. Instead, the Russian Revolution represented a false claim put forth by a radical, godless group that had usurped a true democratic revolution through deceit, coercion, and propaganda. This conspiratorial minority sought not the liberation of human beings, their equality, and property protection but the hidden self-interest that included the confiscation of property, the imposition of atheistic materialism, and control under the dictatorship of the Communist Party.

The images of materialism, dictatorship, propaganda, conspiracy, confiscation, usurpation, coercion, godlessness, and atheism—education would weld all these to contrast with the United States, which it defined as open, democratic, God-fearing, truth seeking, and property protecting, with free elections and majority rule. Further, popular culture conflated communism with socialism without distinguishing between the two. Even today, almost no U.S. politician wishes to be identified with socialism. In the twenty-first century, the most advanced industrial state is incapable of discussing socialism and yet claims to be open and democratic. This is frightening.

The United States had also led in teaching the world that the West constituted the "free world" in a life-and-death global struggle with the unfree world under the direction of the Soviet Union. As countries in the Global South sought independence from colonial subjugation, this simplistic dichotomy viewed them as just as likely to join the free world (even though its most prominent members included the former colonial masters) as the world piloted by the Soviet Union. When many nations in the Global South overwhelmingly elected instead to form a nonaligned group, the United States was not pleased. During the height of decolonization, political leaders, including secretaries of state John Foster Dulles (1953–1959) and Dean Rusk (1961–1969) as well as their diplomatic teams deployed around the world, considered new nation-states irresponsible when they failed to choose good (the free world) over evil (the unfree world). The United States regarded the Global South with suspicion, supporting or opposing their governments to the extent that they appeared to lean toward either of the two competing blocs.

As globalization expanded during the last third of the twentieth century and communism collapsed in 1989, the U.S. position was not only that the West had won but also that liberal democracy, with capitalism embedded in it, had won, vindicating values that this nation embodied. Further, these winning values included certain universal norms such as democracy, principally in the form pursued by the United States, and the free market.[13] The association of democracy with free-market, laissez-faire capitalism became open and unapologetic, and it heightened the emphasis on the individual.[14] The individual was at the ideological roots of the commercial freedom (or liberty) for which the American Revolution was fought; that freedom (even when not admitted explicitly) has remained the dominant animating feature of democratic freedom about which the United States speaks and to which its actions demonstrably committed it. The very idea of progress as espoused by liberal democracy links to the free market, and every citizen is socialized into so believing.

Taught also is that the individual, at the core of the laissez-faire system, is the self-disciplined, self- making person whose productive and reproductive labor was, in Puritan thinking, linked to the idea of stewardship on behalf of the public good. This stewardship would find its crowning expression as a "city upon a hill," an exemplary community where the individual would find happiness and the public would serve as "the emulative model for the rest of the world."[15] While laissez-faire capitalism inherited this view, it gradually transposed the idea of the individual into a person disjoined from any consideration of the public good. This modern individual—impelled by self-interest grounded in the perpetual, restless desire to satisfy needs—rationally calculates how to employ material and nonmaterial resources to improve her or his condition.

The individual becomes the best judge of what is most personally advantageous, and the act of judging and realizing advantageous (rational) outcomes becomes a major source of self-realization, development, and happiness. Therefore, the virtues of liberty, autonomy, and responsibility should be understood as private. Society properly considered should aggregate self-actualizing subjects with the welfare of society coextensive with the aggregation of individual well-being. This view transforms a person from a *social* being into an *economic* animal, with every individual pursuing their own private, material self-interests. From the standpoint of Adam Smith and his disciples, there is little need for government intervention because the material welfare of society can be assured through the self-chosen economic paths of all citizens dealing with competition and clashing interests— hence the idea of the free market, free from government regulation.[16]

The public discourse has emphasized individualism, free markets, and liberty, which includes the space for wounding social failures. Such failures, the discourse claims and teaches, reflect individual efforts and judgments within the context of self-regulating markets, limited government, competition, and the so-called invisible hand of self-regulation that guides competition so that its returns result in social and political harmony for society. This view fits well with James Madison's view of factions (not individuals but individual groups) that are many and native to all societies. Government, he argued, could not be free and prevent these factions. At best, it can limit their adverse consequences by allowing the self-interest of one faction to check the self-interest of another.

Corporation, Society, and Culture

Among the organized factions within modern societies are what we have come to call corporations. The principal institutional representative of capitalism, the corporation has developed to its highest levels in the United States and exists under many names, including *firm*, *company*, *business*, and *trust*, among others. Formally, it is a group of people legally authorized to act as a single entity, recognized as such locally, nationally, and globally. That recognition comes in part in the form of rights that the corporate artificial person may exercise, whether seeking and gaining access to courts, hiring and firing employees, entering into contracts, owning and disposing of assets, or claiming and exerting a right to speak.

Unlike a natural person, these private artificial counterparts can take financial risks without endangering their owners' (shareholders') personal assets. Very much like a natural person, on the other hand, corporations act on self-interest, and like natural individuals under capitalism, they pursue interests on behalf of their owners with little concern for the common good. According to the ideology of capitalism, competition among corporations within free markets benefits society. Like natural individuals, again, capitalism portrays corporate decisions as rational ones that, left alone, will occasion material plenty.

This worldview also teaches about corporate culture, routinely viewing it in terms of setting goals, shaping structures, forming strategies, pursuing customers, and making investments to realize defined outcomes. That culture entails the desire to expand market share, undersell competitors, and, less emphasized, keep wages and benefits as low as possible, limiting labor unions and sometimes destroying them. As well, corporate culture denotes a powerful force composed of private individuals and groups striving for success and producing results by virtue of created advantages in efficiency, professionalism, or technology. It is a "me first" culture, feeding into the exchanges between natural and artificial persons, including the nation-state, in international relations, and it has ripened into President Trump's "America First" mantra, along with his expectation that leaders of other nation-states will take matching stances.

U.S. corporations affect many people and effect many changes, both at home and abroad. For example, in careers and professions, they may require professional degrees and licenses for accountants, architects, designers, engineers, lawyers, physicians, nurses, and social workers, among many others. In this way, corporations are associated with employment, salaries, family stability, and social mobility, often in terms linked to the social marker of ascending the corporate ladder. That ladder has suggested career advancement, encompassing the officially promoted understanding that through discipline and hard work, a person can progress from the entry level to the upper rungs of social and employment hierarchies. Additionally, children do not have to follow the occupational lines of their parents or elder siblings; they can choose their own professions, and with the arrival of the automobile, they can move on wheels across the borders of states.

Corporations, as children and others are informally taught, have come to be associated with freedom, liberty, and progress; even the social disasters of the 1930s Great Depression and 2007's Great Recession provided little by way of lasting, coherent counter-instruction. Within the context of corporate culture, the consumer era merged into the communications age at the beginning of this century, with deficit spending by individuals to maintain the "affluent society" lifestyle matching government deficits to deal with national security and its associated worldwide body of alliances. As the number and duration of wars (or threats of war) increased, collaborations between government and business also increased, so much so that each began to parrot the language and discourse of the other, with emphasis on advertising or advertising-financed news influencing consumers. Less and less thought centered on citizens or citizenship. A focus on the family as the primary unit of consumption left little space to bring the mind to bear on the common good. Instead, as one heard and saw, resources would be concentrated on finding "knowledge workers," the overwhelming number of whom would have to pay for their education. As popular culture and official ideology contended, education moved toward becoming a personal and private matter.

Beginning essentially in the 1960s, the dominance of television and other communications mass media took hold. Living rooms became the center of TV's attention, and even children's programming mixed seamlessly with advertising, grounded on socializing children into the role of future consumer.[17] However, the broadcast frequencies used by TV giants—not only CBS, NBC, and ABC but also Fox and CNN—are ostensibly public spaces, and the government ostensibly allows these private corporations to use them to benefit the "common good." Hence, the Federal Communications Commission (FCC) regulates them, but it has consistently favored private profits and power over the concerns of the common good—and no wonder. In part, industry personnel are all too often recruited to be FCC decision makers, but the penetration of corporate culture is just as important.

The political culture of individualism and private property has become all-pervasive in the United States. Thus, Washington has rejected any international movements or initiatives that come to the forefront on grounds that they concern and involve too much government intervention. This was the case, for example, when the Group of 77 proposed the NIEO in the 1970s and when the United States resisted a report of the Independent Commission on International Development Issues under the late Wily Brandt of Germany during the 1980s and world conferences on women encompassing the 1970s, 1980s, and 1990s.[18]

A major part of corporate life and the corporate environment, especially when government and research universities form partnerships, has been technology—often the path-breaking technologies that enable the United States to enjoy industrial primacy among highly developed countries. The term *technology* in this context includes *the idea of technology*. Since the beginnings of human culture, that idea, separate from individuals, is that technology not only can correct human limits and deficiencies but also is virtually unlimited. José Ortega y Gasset called this "technologism."[19] U.S. society has embraced it more than has any other, creating new frontiers for the United States.[20] Companies at the forefront of technology can often see the next steps, leaving others to try to catch up. For example, Intel, IBM, and Microsoft initially dominated in the Information Age, with Amazon, Apple, and Facebook moving to share that leadership. A few Chinese companies today can offer strong competition and catch up; other countries are more limited in their capabilities.

The point here is that the technologism of U.S. corporations, especially those in alliances with research universities and the government, preserve a sense of progress, of the capacity to confront and solve any problem—whatever can be imagined can be done. The Human Genome Project, explorations of outer space, inquiries into neuroscience, artificial intelligence, and the colonization of Mars all express the idea of technology. Because these efforts depend on immense corporations as well as support from public coffers, a focus on the joint, the common, and the social might be recognized; instead, the emphasis has been on individuals.

The learning that helps shape this overall political culture comes from the media, in general, and the press, in particular. The First Amendment to the U.S. Constitution prohibits Congress and all states as subdivisions of the federation from enacting any law abridging the freedom of speech or the press; it establishes a fundamental commitment to this freedom as critical for democracy. The underlying thinking is that a free marketplace of ideas will help provide the environment for individuals and society to learn, develop critical faculties, and examine the work of government. The amendment also suggests that human beings are intelligent moral actors, and that shared information is important to their decision making. In other words, the amendment is less concerned with the individual alone than with the individual, society, and the common good.[21] This deeper meaning is rarely taught and is often lost.

The Media, Advertising, and Culture

The U.S. news media, now globally dominant, developed along with the nation, expanding after World War I and World War II. Previously, the U.S. press centered on Western Europe news agencies: Reuters (the United Kingdom), Havas (France), and Wolff (Germany). Together, they partitioned the world, and newspapers of the United States and other countries depended on them for news of goings-on not only throughout the world but frequently even within their own nations.[22] The Associated Press (AP), voicing sentiments then common in the United States, complained that the European agencies and bureaus disparaged the United States—focusing on race riots, criminal activities, railroad accidents, Indians, and the safety of travel—and that each agency portrayed its own country most favorably without fear of contradiction.[23] If U.S. news outlets were allowed to compete, they would not engage in propaganda, the AP claimed; rather, the U.S. press would, on behalf of the people of the world, ensure that the news would be truthful and unbiased.[24]

With considerable international efforts, including some government subsidies,

U.S. media grew to dominance after World War II. The United States would not admit to using propaganda, and it claimed that it created Voice of America and Radio Free Europe, for example, to convey unbiased information. However, at home, the Fourth Estate depended on advertising revenue from businesses, and their codependence gradually became more and more pronounced. Businesses create goods or produce services. Through their programs or platforms, the media—including TV, radio, newspapers, magazines, films, Facebook, and other social media—aggregate audiences for "sale" as potential consumers of those goods or services. Advertising, an industry in itself, induces prospective purchasers to take note, gain knowledge, and buy, and the industry leaders earned the title, wrote historian Stuart Ewen, of "captains of consciousness."[25] Today social media companies can, with a great deal of specificity, enable advertisers to target individuals and groups through constructed profiles, grounded on information accumulated about audience preferences.

The mass production generated by industrial societies must be complemented by mass consumption, which began evolving in the seventeenth century. Even then, the objective was not simply to consume goods and services but—in the case of "exotic" goods, such as pepper, sugar, tea, and cotton—to purchase social status and embody certain values, such as gentility, masculinity, respectability, and femininity.[26] Within the United States, especially after World War II, advertisers used studies in psychology and social psychology as part of a concentrated effort to harness drives, instincts, and passions that economists and political theorists identified with being human. The goal was to define society by "gratified spectatorship"—a largely passive life for individuals whom advertising would transform from citizens embodying the virtues of discipline, denial, and thrift into indulgent nonconformists who sought satisfaction in material fulfilment and were disposed to spend. At the same time, modern industry needs predictability on the part of workers and consumers, so advertisers simulate self-determination and nonconformity within the context of predictability. Today consumer predictability is ever more specific, with personal identity data widely gathered, stored, and shared.

Various agents achieved this simulation of self-determination by elaborating a sense of dynamism, choice, and change within society. Thus, fashion serves as an instrument of change, as does climbing the corporate ladder or being part of new possibilities created by science and technology. Branding as well as annual changes in cars, sneakers, telephones, or the tastes or preferences of each generation (labeled baby boomers, Generation X, millennials) offer some of the sense of change. The "conception of consumption as an alternative to other modes of change," in Ewen's words,[27] includes the idea of *marginal utility*, a popular term in both economics and consumer culture. In economics, marginal utility measures how much of a given item a consumer is likely to purchase. In consumer culture, it denotes the *additional* satisfaction a consumer gains from buying and using goods or services. Ewen asks, does it add to one's sense of style—a refinement of taste, actual or presumed? Does it answer to a range of aesthetic values—comfort, symmetry, balance, ease, or fit? Does it speak to visible membership in a social class? Does it accommodate political values of pluralism? Does it extend markets for all kinds of goods, thus satisfying the broader ideological values of greater freedom of choice?[28]

As political as the effort to establish brand loyalty, the repeated buying (or rejecting) of goods is even more so. The decision of whether to purchase something is a form of popular participation in the solvency or insolvency of an economy, industry, or company, and the act of purchasing—or refusing to purchase—is the equivalent of electing or rejecting a government that consistently satisfies or fails to satisfy the needs and desires of its participants. It is a democratic process but one that, in part, allows for turning the political realm away from traditional government and governing.[29] This emphasis on consumer choice, when the choices are those offered by the producers, is often lost.

The media's ties to advertising income links them to the industries paying for the advertising, and often those industries own the media. The idea of a free press or unbiased media is unpersuasive even if popular culture by and large accepts it, notwithstanding recent clamors about "fake news." This is evident when media critiques, to the extent that they exist, vary minimally from frameworks created by the economic system and its consumer orientation. The increasing ties among businesses, media companies, advertisers (image makers in general), and the government often create a form of embeddedness reminiscent of the Iraqi War, when some six hundred news reporters lived and traveled alongside U.S. military units—they traveled with soldiers, saw what they saw, and were under fire when and if the units were.[30] The reporters discovered the limits this embedding entailed as they were entirely dependent on the armed forces and had to offer them fealty and trust in return. One result was that the public heard too few critical evaluations of the war until it was too late.

Embeddedness is not just an event of war; it persists in the transformation of news reporters as individuals into commentators, consultants, and experts, speaking to one another in all these roles. As well, the techniques used to manipulate the consumer (who has largely replaced the citizen) reflect those used in politics, especially in elections, viewing voters as consumers of information, including political information. Of course, the elections themselves are now aspects of business and a major source of income for the media, with profiles of voters used to help those voters choose among issues framed for them.

Critical in this context has been the selling of personal information data to third parties (as Facebook and others have done) and the uses of this data, as with Russian attempts to influence the 2016 presidential election. Despite condemnations of Russia's activities, the technique is much admired and widely used in varying forms by media experts as well as by other nations and players. For example, the Center for Election Systems, based at Georgia's Kennesaw State University, wielded Moscow-like techniques in Georgia's state elections.[31] In the meantime, trivia divert voters, cultural life is redefined as a perpetual round of entertainment (including shopping, especially during "special days"), and what passes for public conversation is but a form of baby talk rather than a major source of information. People become but audiences, little aware as the public sphere progressively shrinks along with the discourse it had represented and nurtured. Public universities and civic culture are endangered, privacy is virtually nonexistent, and the monopolization of society, including the media, proceeds with but superficial attention.[32]

The monopolization of the media is but a logical extension of the business landscape, with ready responses for the few naive questions that arise. We live in a globalized world; we have to face the Chinese, the Japanese, and the Koreans, all of whom are coming at us as equals. Yes, we should focus on equality at home, but we should be careful about how we go about it. Little is said about how the interests of the people who live, move, and have their being in the United States might diverge from the interests of global corporations, some of which even decline to repatriate profits. Indeed, does any coincidence of interests remain given how inequitably material prosperity has been shared since 1970?[33]

The Academy, Religious Institutions, and Public Intellectuals

Universities and religious institutions have played a significant role in U.S. education and in generating the resulting political culture. While public universities are endangered, as are public schools in general, curricular construction is subverted in the interest not only of preparing future consumers but also of further whittling away the public sphere. Thus, Apple, Microsoft, and Google, among many others, covet control of once-public institutions of learning.

The early leaders of the republic conceived formal academic schooling as a public trust.[34] The Puritans, even when endorsing the establishment of private academic institutions (usually affiliated with religious institutions in a broader Christian community), insisted on that public trust and the pursuit of the common good. However, capitalism's focus on the individual at the expense of the community and the private over the public gradually associated education too with the individual and the private. Today the free market and its affiliated consumer culture seek to make every aspect of education a commercial commodity. As such, it would deserve little or no public support, and as the price of an education rose and individual or family capacity to purchase it declined, educational institutions would come to depend more on market financing and be less inclined to minister to the common good. Charter schools, whatever their virtues, are part of the broader assault on public education.

Religious institutions too have influenced U.S. political culture, with some of the nation's most distinguished academic institutions emerging from religious roots—Harvard, Yale, Brown, Columbia, Princeton, and Boston University, for example—and the recent influence of born-again Christianity on the political culture is immense.[35]

No one has better described the effect of combining religious teachings with largely secular philosophical discourse than the late Protestant theologian, ethicist, and political theorist Karl P. Reinhold Niebuhr.[36] His expositions on "political realism" gave the country an intellectual grounding for its foreign policy, and thinkers from Henry Kissinger to Barack Obama have emulated at least portions of it. As laid out by Niebuhr, political realism rests on the view that national self-interest, national egoism, aggression, the arbitrary exercise of power, and little if any moral restraint define international relations. Political realism, therefore, means endorsing a balance-of-power system—a managed anarchy characterized by competing national interests, not unlike Madisonian factions in domestic politics.

Niebuhr's reasoning largely goes as follows. Large sociopolitical collectivities such as nation-states have too few direct or face-to-face interactions to gain an accurate perspective of one another's needs or invite sympathy. Unlike individual human beings, these groups have no conscience. In any event, ethical action is a product of self-criticism, but nation-states discourage such criticism, especially when it is most needed, because it would undermine unity and collective action. Often nation-states and their leaders view criticism as treasonous. What is of utmost importance is that nationalism transforms individual selfishness as an ideal into national egoism.[37] Ordinary people's search for power, prestige, and significance is vicariously realized through the success of a leader or the nation. This transformed selfishness has made for much of the nation-state's history of aggression and arbitrary exercises of power.[38]

An attribute underlying the weakness of individuals and groups (the nation-state, in particular) is hypocrisy—insincerity, deceitfulness, duplicitousness. In the international system, this leads to an inescapable insecurity. Niebuhr, in one of his most enabling positions, claimed that the "paradise of our domestic security is suspended in a hell of global insecurity."[39] In other words, political realism casts the United States, with its self-claimed virtues, into an immoral world where it must act not only to ensure national survival but also to achieve its special mission of extending its way of life to the rest of the world. How can the United States claim to be virtuous given assertions that nation-states have no consciences, that societies are immoral, and that ethical action is impossible without criticism? Niebuhr did not answer this explicitly, but he generally implied that the United

States is the most open and self-critical society and, therefore, the most ethically oriented one. This view is part of U.S. exceptionalism.

Despite a widespread belief in a "paradise of domestic security" in the United States, domestic life has rarely, if ever, been secure for Native Americans, women, racial minorities, religious minorities, socialists, communists, or small farmers, among others. Even the democracy that implicitly offers security has had but limited support from the nation's leaders, as documented in a little discussed 1973 study by Michel Grozier, Samuel P. Huntington, and Joji Watanuke, *The Crisis of Democracy: On the Governability of Democracies*.[40] These authors saw the tumult of the 1960s, a time when many Americans opposed the Vietnam War and supported civil rights, as responsible for a declining trust in the government. That decline "had its roots in the expansion of political participation in the late 1950s and early 1960s."[41] In this light, is it surprising to see ongoing attempts to limit the electoral franchise or limit who may become citizens or President Trump's efforts to undermine democratic institutions?

What about self-criticism as a kind of moral "inner check?" It is often superficial, faked, or confined within the existing framework of accepted values about ourselves. Americans were shocked and dismayed when Alexander Solzhenitsyn and Andrei Sakharov, celebrated as critics of the Soviet Union, turned critical eyes on U.S. society. Solzhenitsyn, whose criticism of the Soviet Union led him to take refuge in the United States, directed his attention to what he described as America's "inability to prevent the growth of organized crime or check unrestrained profiteering at the expense of public morality," confusion of truth with majority rule, a "materialistic twentieth century [that] has all too long kept us in a subhuman state," and gratuitous detailed offerings in the Western press about a "former British Prime Minister who had undergone surgery on one testicle, about the kind of blanket Jacqueline Kennedy uses, or about the favorite drink of some female pop star."[42] Sakharov, milder in his criticism, focused on U.S. businesses and the priority they gave to commercial interests rather than freedom, including the freedom to choose one's country of residence.[43] Sakharov further invoked norms from the Universal Declaration of Human Rights to support his claim that the freedom to choose one's country of residence should have moral and psychological ascendancy, in time and place, over commercial concerns.[44]

That additional feature of the claim to exceptionalism is a kind of inner moral exercise or justification for foreign policy actions (or inactions). In the case of U.S. foreign policy, Niebuhr found that it reflected a certain naiveté, a kind of innocence of idealism and good intentions, along with insufficient appreciation for the complexity of human history. All nations, of course, are, in their own way, innocent or immature; they cannot fully grasp or assess all or even most of the likely consequences of their actions, let alone the impact of those actions on the ideals they espouse. The Bolsheviks may be said to have been innocent in their thinking about or expectations of a general uprising of Europe's industrial proletariat. China could be said to have been immature in supposing an uprising of peasants in the Global South. There is no objective reason to think that the United States enjoys any special innocence in this area, as the socializing institutions claim, believe, and teach. On the contrary, the United States is well practiced in espousing high-minded ideals in its pursuit of strategic and commercial interests, from the Declaration of Independence, the Monroe Doctrine, and President McKinley's justification for the War of 1898 to the Open-Door Policy on China, containment of Soviet influence after World War II, and Operation Enduring Freedom, the official name for the "war on terrorism" since 2001.

The claim of innocence allows Niebuhr to suggest that if the United States became conscious of its power and gained the inner moral checks of moderation and restraint, it could, with a commitment to justice, lead in creating a community of world dimensions.[45] Indeed, the United States has long envisioned one day exercising leadership in organizing and directing the global community. Although the Cold War, to some extent, restrained this project of extending U.S. identity, the disintegration of the Soviet Union brought the prospect within range, but it would come with a culture of consumerism that Niebuhr would not have endorsed. The liberal order within which U.S. consumer culture has developed seeks nothing less than the transformation of countries from market or socialist economies to market societies. A transformation of that sort would imply the total commercial domination of society, as compellingly described by the political philosopher Michael J. Sandel.[46]

The extension of consumer culture takes place with only limited moral consciousness, generating in its wake some of America's difficulties with Japan in the 1980s, with Islam over the years, and with China today. This amoral culture is part of what both Solzhenitsyn and Sakharov condemned, inviting such strong reactions. Significantly, though, President Carter criticized the Soviet Union's human rights record after deciding to make human rights a cornerstone of U.S. foreign policy.

What is taught is that the United States is morally self-sufficient. There is no need to invoke normative principles outside U.S. laws and values. Such norms, it is said, are embedded in a "higher law" that the United States embodies. Therefore, when dealing with questions about whether the United States engaged in torture in Iraq or at Guantanamo, the U.S. media overwhelmingly sought to determine what leading Democrats or the late Republican senator John McCain thought. For those who do not know better—most Americans—the leaders determine when matters breach norms, exercising that authority based on their experiences or abstract learning.[47]

Thus, the idea of "America First," as espoused by President Trump, is not new. It simply has a wider and deeper meaning than he ascribes to it. Supreme

Court Justice Stephen Breyer, for one, would give some attention to law beyond the United States, but he has been criticized by some, including fellow judges, for doing so.[48] The United States even finds it difficult to promote the teaching of foreign languages except for defense purposes; many people—including presidents of colleges, state legislators, boards of trustees, and students—see it as unnecessary for human and societal development. In this view, conceding the need for other languages, even for those whose second language is English, would mean accepting that English is insufficient.

Members of religious and academic institutions as well as public intellectuals have expressed concerns about the liberal order.[49] The social inequality with which liberalism historically aligns itself should invite anxiety.[50] Accusations from the Right about bureaucracy, identity politics, tax burdens, and the erosion of the family and sense of community or from the Left about lax regulation, discrimination, gerrymandering, and unfair tax structures miss the point. As long as they continue to do so, neither of these essentially liberal stances will offer solutions appropriate to society's ills, which derive from a virtually forgotten feature of liberalism: the nature of the American Republican order and the pairing of that order with an economic philosophy that does not and cannot work as envisioned.

Ironically, liberalism actually emerged when the world of learning, influenced by developments in the physical and chemical sciences, focused on standards of evidence that, through debate and discourse, would lead to a significant degree of agreement among experts. This type of agreement, however broad, was tentative and could change with new, experiential evidence. In contrast to the pre-Copernican period, an appeal to Aristotle and Saint Augustine could not justify conclusions.[51] Empirical evidence was required, and that line of reasoning applies to the insufficiency of appeals to the U.S. Constitution and Founding Fathers over concrete evidence. This is part and parcel of the First Amendment as well as the U.S. Constitution's Speech and Debate Clause, and it is part of the rationale for the protection offered to tenured faculty. Implicit in this order is the idea of an educated public that could appeal to expert legislators, judges, and presidents and vice versa. Absent the opportunity for such appeals, complex issues, especially during challenging times, would come under the control of the dogmatists who offer simple solutions and the appearance of coherence.

Americans seem to have forgotten this attribute of liberalism despite paying it lip service by claiming to consider two sides of an issue, as if all complex issues could be reduced to two sides, but advertising propagandizes the nation, overtly and covertly. Conclusions from others short-circuit individual thinking, even if those conclusions partake in a certain logic that distorts beliefs, attitudes, and actions.[52] Propaganda, being continuous, exceeds individual capacities for critical attention or adaptation based on reasoning. Eventually, the ability to resist weakens, especially in the absence of outside frames of reference to suggest bases for comparison. Further, the manipulation of symbols, closely linked to psychological attributes—fear, anger, embarrassment, humiliation, hope, and status-based identity, among others—can be so precisely calculated that, as in the case of political campaigns, people crave for spontaneity, something different. The propagandist is aware of this.

With society's increasing complexity, all but a few individuals are overwhelmed and come to depend on platitudes, slogans, adages, catchphrases, and stereotypes to help them cope with information. (Advertisers are notably adept at exploring stereotypes.) There is a disconnect between the accountable individual, able and willing to assess evidence and form judgments, and what the individual receives largely from propaganda and imparts to others.

All politics, including election campaigns, are, with limited exceptions, forms of advertising. Instead of speaking of character, we speak of credibility; instead of speaking of facts or truth, we think of what is credible. Karl Popper, warning about the evils of totalitarianism in *The Open Society and Its Enemies*, did not seriously analyze the consumer societies and the role of advertising.[53] Neither did he face the emerging market society. His advocacy for a democratic liberalism, the true liberal order, has been forgotten as we now face its twilight—the dogma of neoliberalism.

As Niebuhr and other have noted, the idea of the American Republic includes a notion of its being ordained by God, partaking of a certain perfection. The American Revolution has been seen, consistent with a conceptual category identified by Albert Camus as a "historical revolution,"[54] as guided by some assumed knowledge about and preparation for the end of history. This idea was part of the Russian Revolution as well. Such revolutions can and often do make light of, disregard, or even deny the existence of the present and its values depending on whether they see such values as contributing to the assumed ends of history. In addition, in their claims to originality and uniqueness, historical revolutions, like that of the United States in general, deny much connection to the past, yet most of the claimed or assumed unique features of the United States can be found in the United Kingdom by the time of the Glorious Revolution in 1688.

Niebuhr and others have noted the gap between the better aspirations of the United States and its actual behavior, something he also finds in other nations, because all human beings need ideals to guide them. Even though Niebuhr had doubts about the possibility of a universal community, the American Republic has never sidestepped the possibility that it could lead such a community. U.S. business groups have always sought for the nation to assume that role, and technology has invited many to speak on behalf of its possibility. In 1990, Nobel Laureate V. S. Naipaul spoke on "Our Universal Civilization," suggesting that the United States embodies values of tolerance, equality, liberty, and individualism as well as the pursuit of happiness.[55] These values, he argued, have become universal. He spent much time on the pursuit of happiness, although he did not examine its association with aesthetic categories such as suitability, fit, restraint, and taste, attributes much lacking in public life. He did not note how little material things contribute to happiness or its pursuit.

Important here is that consumer culture has no fundamental interest in or commitment to these values and their realization. However, it is interested in using them to reach material ends. So business views the idea of a U.S.-led universal civilization as usable; to non-businesspeople as well as to many Christian churches, this is an end to be sought because it would facilitate the spreading of the Gospel to the world. Politically, liberalism also desires a U.S.-led universal civilization, even though the market economy's worldwide operation has worked poorly for so many people and it refuses, in claiming some degree of perfection, to correct its flaws, many of which Karl Polanyi so meticulously described.[56]

At issue is whether the ideal of common fellowship on a universal scale, using values touched upon here, represents too great a leap in relation to actual experiences.[57] Just as important, as French philosopher Jacques Maritain has observed (and Niebuhr and others failed to note), is whether humanity (including Americans) should continue to "suffer from the cleavage between the ideal which constitutes its reason for living and acting and for which it continues to fight and the inner cast of mind which exists in people and which implies in reality doubt and mental insecurity about this ideal."[58] That insecurity cannot continue indefinitely. Socialization, as understood by the Republican ideal, was to create a form of social organization based on individual self-government rooted in internalized norms. Extremes in wealth and poverty, among other things, would make that governance problematic because they overtly and continuingly contradict a sense of fairness and invite moral and social outrage.

The people of the United States—and people everywhere—seek to be part of a community defined by social justice, not one controlled by consumer culture, even when contesting who should be members of that community and what social justice may look like. Thus, deep questioning appears in many phases of social life, often informed by what social scientist James C. Scott terms the "hidden transcripts" of groups—contained in songs, jokes, frowns, silences, tales of humiliation and shame, felt repression, self-rejection, and fears, fear of even self-expression in the company of those who are seen as dominating the culture.[59] Many are confused about their status, their future, and their children's future. They have few external frameworks to draw upon to contradict, coherently, the culture's dominant themes.

What they are certain about is that they are unfulfilled, they are anxious, and they seek relief. That relief, in some form, could come in a variety of expressions. One is through routine, commonplace collaboration with evil—the "banality of evil," as Hannah Arendt so agonizingly documented.[60] For example, "decent people" will die in the absence of a health-care system that provides for all rather than allow taxes to help blacks, Hispanics, and Muslims; these decent people are potential collaborators with repressive regimes. Also, false relief could come through coalitions hinged to perceived threats to national security from immigrants and their unpatriotic supporters at home and abroad.

On the other hand, relief could come through a class-conscious dawning among "hyphenated Americans," in general, of their deeper claim to social resources. Armed with this consciousness, like Walter in *A Raisin in the Sun*, they could remind us that their fathers and mothers "brick by brick" earned those benefits, and they could assert that they will, without seeking to court trouble, break social barriers to avail themselves of them.[61] It could also come by way of demographic changes, along with "social media" appeals to the young, airing new voices that lessen the appeal of accustomed explanations for difficult questions. These voices could overthrow past patterns, upending supposedly settled truths, such as the idea of a frontier that ignores racism, the Puritan ethic whose supposed purity informed our irreproachable institutions, or the economic royalism that has represented (like the divine rights of kings) a single family of ideas for more than two centuries: mercantilism, liberalism, and neoliberalism.[62]

Relief may come as more and more people see through their cultural conditioning, refusing to be blindly driven by the idea that a good life consists of comfort or non-thinking ease or that ease and comfort derive from consumption. Liberated by such insights, they will ask further questions about the purpose of life and living, about how to organize a society to protect a frontier spirit, competition, shared risks, and fundamental fairness, all toward serving that purpose.

Perhaps a combination of these paths will be the operating mechanism. Regardless, one thing is certain. To earn and sustain legitimacy, the United States must recreate its origins and history and its knowledge of who have been part of its origins and history. The nation's future cannot be defined by a Christian civilization or a market one, and those considered "others," at home and abroad, must co-construct the future. For example, the people of Asia—Bangladeshi, Chinese, Indian, Indonesian, Japanese, Korean, and Vietnamese—are not knowable as variants of an oriental culture; English will not be the default language. Everything is, in fact, connected; thus, many of the immigrants who seek refuge in the United States today are a consequence of U.S. failures for three decades to lead in the effort to halt and respond to climate change.

5

THE ENVIRONMENT: OUR
HOME AND OURSELVES

On April 1, 2016, the United States and China, which then emitted 40 percent of global carbon emissions, jointly committed themselves to signing the Paris Climate Agreement, joining 174 other nations and the group of countries in the European Union. This agreement is an accord within the United Nations Framework Convention on Climate Change (UNFCCC), which was adopted in 1992 and became legally binding on countries in 1994; today it has 197 ratifications. Its principal aim is to mitigate emissions of greenhouse gas emissions beginning in 2020.

In June 2017, however, the United States gave notice of its withdrawal from the Paris Agreement. President Trump's announcement, while a shock to the world, was only unusual for the drama accompanying his action. Earlier U.S. presidents—of both political parties—had equally disappointed the world at important junctures in global efforts to deal with the degradation of the earth's environment and, in particular, to deal with climate change.

A brief history of the evolving consciousness concerning the environment provides a clearer understanding of the true nature of threats to it and to human beings—a necessary step toward removing or mitigating the likely impacts of those threats. In that history, the disappointing role of the United States underlies the lack of emphasis on cultural components that should be part of efforts to remove or limit the threats. The meaning of this insufficiency for humankind reveals the positive role that the United States can still play, beginning with adhering to the Paris Agreement.

Early History

Within the United States, the rise of the environmental movement traces back to the 1960s, when the public became more aware of environmental issues as it confronted certain immediate dangers, such as oil spills, radioactive fallout from nuclear weapons tests in the atmosphere, and the improper and excessive use of insecticides. Several books played an important role in launching the movement. Rachel Carsen's *Silent Spring* (1962) revealed the effects of DDT, which endangers animals, from bees and birds to domestic pets, and plants, with broad implications for agriculture. Paul Ehrlich's *The Population Bomb* (1968) urged the U.S. government to lead efforts to curb global population growth, seeing that the earth was incapable of sustaining current growth rates. The Club of Rome's *The Limits to Growth* (1972) reinforced Ehrlich's population views but moved the focus to the relationship of population to rates of economic growth. These and other works helped induce individuals and groups to agitate for and secure change.[1] In 1963, for example, the Soviet Union, the United Kingdom, and the United States signed the Treaty Banning Nuclear Weapons Tests in the Atmosphere, in Outer Space, and Under Water (also known as the Partial Test Ban Treaty), with 123 nations later signing on. The treaty bans all nuclear weapons tests except those conducted underground.

Further, responding to domestic and international pressure as well as a felt need to exhibit international leadership in protecting the environment, the United States enacted the Clean Air Act in 1970 and created the Environmental Protection Agency (EPA) to consolidate a number of federal research-focused, standard-setting, monitoring, and enforcement activities. The Clean Water Act followed in 1972. Internationally, Washington helped create the United Nations Environment Program (UNEP) in 1972. On December 28, 1973, consistent with the International Convention on International Trade in Endangered Species of Wild Fauna and Flora adopted earlier that year, the United States enacted the Endangered Species Act to protect imperiled domestic species from extinction.[2]

No development for the United States or the world was more significant than a worldwide conference on the environment, along with a body of socioeconomic demands from the Global South and a scientific breakthrough, all during the 1970s. Together, they helped further a broader, deeper understanding of and commitment to the need to protect the environment. In June 1972, representatives of 114 countries, along with a large number of nongovernmental organizations, attended the Stockholm Conference on the Human Environment. For the first time in history, the global community as a whole met to take action on a variety of environmental issues. They achieved many things, including the Stockholm Declaration and its action plan, the first global-scale agreement on protecting and managing the environment. The plan defined appropriate standards for living within the human environment, standards that include the need for adequate food and water, sewage and waste disposal systems, housing, living and working conditions, and complementary technologies. Moreover, the conference led to the creation of new institutions to promote collective and individual action, including the UNEP—which would preside over issues involving the ozone layer, biodiversity, hazardous chemicals, and waste—and the Stockholm Declaration, with its twenty-six principles that have served as guidelines by which all states can work toward common and separate goals.[3]

The Stockholm Declaration begins by presenting the following fundamental rights and principles:

1. Man has the fundamental right to freedom, equality, and adequate conditions of life in an environment of a quality that permits a life of dignity and well-being, and he bears a solemn responsibility to protect and improve the environment for present and future generations . . .
2. The natural resources of the earth—including the air, water, land, flora, and fauna and especially representative samples of natural ecosystems—must be safeguarded for the benefit of present and future generations through careful planning and management, as appropriate.[4]

The declaration laid a foundation for common and differentiated responsibilities that have developed in environmental policy and law. Principle 21, for example, seeks to reconcile the interests of the global community with claims of sovereignty under which nation-states reject external intervention in their domestic affairs. Principles 22 and 24 elaborate on multilateral cooperation to compensate for damage to humans, to the non-human environment, and to collaboration across borders.[5]

The further major development associated with the conference was the Global South's push during the 1970s, through the Group of 77, to reshape the international economic order in a manner that would make economic relations between developed countries and LDCs more equitable. Any idea that developed countries, as the principal culprits of environmental damage, did not bear primary responsibility for repairing that damage invited anger and could have undermined prospects for agreements in Stockholm. The 1972 conference, whose agenda did not initially consider development, sponsored enough collective learning that it accommodated such issues, along with the concept of common and differentiated responsibilities. Thus, Article 30 of the 1974 Charter of Economic Rights and Duties of States (at the core of the Group of 77's proposal that year for an NIEO) states that "the protection, preservation, and enhancement of the environment for present and future generations is the responsibility of all states."[6] LDCs were deeply interested in this concept, and it became central to future conferences.

The third associated development was new scientific insight into the rapid advance of environmental degradation. A 1974 scientific paper by Mario Molina and F. Sherwood Rowland at the University of California Irvine alerted the world to the destruction of the ozone layer, and the work later brought them a Nobel Prize for Chemistry. Molina and Rowland argued that this layer, which protects the earth from solar radiation, was being destroyed by a class of compounds, called chlorofluorocarbons (CFCs), used in refrigerants, aerosol sprays, and the making of plastic foams.[7] Significantly, they showed that a set of human industrial activities endangered not one country, continent, or region but the entire world.

The 1980s were a mixed period in the United States in terms of responding to environmental challenges, but remarkable developments took place internationally. Peoples and governments awoke to the nature and scope of the global threat not only to the ozone layer but to the environment in general—and how unsparing those threats were of any national, regional, or peoples' borders or preferences.

Within the United States, progress came with the Comprehensive Environmental Response, Compensation, and Liability Act (CERCLA) (1980), *Changing Climate: Report of the Carbon Dioxide Assessment Committee* (1983), and the Resource Conservation Act (1987). On the international level, the World Charter for Nature (1982), the Vienna Convention for the Protection of the Ozone Layer (1985, updated two years later by the Montreal Protocol on Substances That Deplete the Ozone Layer), and the report of the World Commission on Environment and Development (WCED) (1987) all represented major steps forward.[8]

Changing Climate resulted from the Carter administration's effort to gain a comprehensive assessment of carbon dioxide release, the impact of that release, and the likelihood of future increases in it. Acting under the Energy Security Act of 1980, the government tasked the National Academy of Sciences with conducting the study and producing a report, in part to help deal with the many conflicting views being presented to the U.S. government and people.[9] *Changing Climate* opens with a discouraging generalization claiming a broad class of problems that have no solutions and that, increasingly, "atmospheric CO_2 and its climatic consequences constitute such a problem."[10] On the other hand, the report clearly states that atmospheric CO_2 is an important determining factor for the earth's climate and that its increase "is primarily attributable to the burning of coal, oil, and gas."[11] The report goes on to say that "atmospheric CO_2 concentration will pass 600 ppm [parts per million] (the nominal doubling of the recent level) in the third quarter of the next century. We also estimate that there is a 1-in-20 chance that doubling will occur before 2035."[12]

Here is a recognition of the problem, along with its principal cause, yet also a willingness to downplay socioeconomic and environmental effects and to place doubts on the extent to which the problem is solvable. To the authors of *Changing*

Climate, the socioeconomic effects are "largely unpredictable" because human beings have lived in "almost all climate zones and move easily between them."[13]

> Viewed in terms of energy, global pollution, and environmental damages, the "CO_2 problem" appears intractable. Viewed as a problem of changes in local environmental factors—rainfall, river flow, sea-level [rise]—the myriad of individual incremental problems take their place among other stresses to which nations and individuals adapt. It is important to be flexible both in [the] definition of the issue, which is more climate change than CO_2, and maintaining a variety of alternative options.[14]

True, it makes sense to explore a variety of options in facing any problem, and climate change itself is due to many related factors, including overpopulation, ocean acidification, water pollution, genetic modifications, deforestation, and the decline in wetlands, among others. However, *Changing Climate* conveys a mistaken impression about the centrality of CO_2 and its place in human activities, masking the possibilities of reversing the problem. It also mischaracterizes the nature of and likely consequences of climate change, equating it with the different climate zones in which human beings have lived and moved. It further sought to highlight a myriad of "incremental problems" affecting different nations and regions, with their own stresses, rather than the common global problem demanding a collective response. Broadly speaking, *Changing Climate* identified the overall role of fossil fuels in climate change, but it often focused more attention on limiting the effects of the change than on removing the causes. It sought a solution but within the confines of the existing structure of energy arrangements.

Changing Climate provided the groundwork for different reactions by the American people and Congress, including the enactment of the Resource Conservation Act. Enacted by Congress in 1976 and amended in 1984 and 1986, the act has strengthened the EPA to better manage hazardous and nonhazardous waste. Today the agency oversees the generation, transportation, treatment, storage, and disposal of waste and oversees storage tanks for petroleum and other potentially hazardous substances. The local as well as the national and international public should be awakened to its augmented role in dealing with climate change. The creation of CERCLA (sometimes referred to as the Superfund) to deal with liabilities, compensation, and cleanup from waste should be kept in mind as well in examining the 1980s. All that said, President Reagan reduced the EPA's funding by 20 percent in 1982, thereby limiting its work during his administration.

Internationally, matters were more promising and less ambiguous. In 1982, the UN General Assembly adopted the World Charter for Nature, a step notable for many things. First, the use of the term *charter* suggested a special document, very much like the UN Charter, a constitution issued by a sovereign state—the sovereign people of the world, through their representatives in the UN—outlining conditions under which individuals, states, and other organizations may operate. The World Charter defines rights and privileges, along with responsibilities and immunities, including the immunities of nature. Further, unlike the 1972 Stockholm Declaration, the World Charter does not focus on the "human environment." Between 1972 and 1982, conceptions of the environment had evolved to understand more fully that human beings are part of nature and that any attempt to separate them from other parts of nature is not only ill-advised but also fundamentally dangerous. Finally, like the Stockholm Declaration but with greater insight into the complex interdependence of humanity and other areas of nature, the charter seeks action at the "national, international, individual and collective, and private and public levels to protect nature and promote international cooperation."[15]

A few quotations suggest how the charter inspired subsequent actions. It begins as follows:

> Mankind is part of nature and depends on the uninterrupted functioning of natural systems which ensure the supply of energy and nutrients.

Under its general principles, it continues as follows:

1. Nature shall be respected, and all its processes shall not be impaired.
2. The genetic viability of the earth shall not be compromised . . .
3. Ecosystems and organisms as well as the land, marine, and atmospheric resources that are utilized by man shall [be] managed to achieve and maintain optimum sustainable productivity but not in such a way as to endanger the integrity of those other life ecosystems or species with which they coexist.
4. Nature shall be secured against degradation by warfare or other hostile activities.

Under the area of "functions" the charter states the following:

> 10(a) Living resources shall not be utilized in excess of their natural capacity for regeneration.

> 11(a) Activities which are likely to cause irreversible damage to nature shall be avoided.

11(b) Activities which are likely to pose a significant risk to nature shall be preceded by an exhaustive examination; their proponents shall demonstrate that expected benefits outweigh potential damage to nature, and where potential adverse effects are not fully understood, the activities should not proceed.

The quotes are informative in many ways: the place of humans in nature, the precautionary rule (11b) that has become a major tool for activists everywhere, principles that confer certain immunities on nature, and a call for our individual and collective respect of nature.

The ozone layer is one of those features of nature threatened by human activities—activities referred to in the charter and, in 1985, the Vienna Convention for the Protection of the Ozone Layer. That convention, supported by the United States under strong leadership from Congress, provided a framework for sharing and exchanging data.[16] Two years later, the Montreal Protocol on Substances That Deplete the Ozone Layer amended the Vienna Convention, providing for specific and stringent measures to control prohibited ozone-depleting substances (ODS).[17]

The Montreal Protocol offers both short-term and long-term plans to address ODS, and it mandates phasing them out, coupled with the development of environmentally friendly substances or alternatives, the latter influenced by imposing limits on demand and supply. The protocol signals to users and producers alike that society will tolerate ODS only briefly, and it makes this position most persuasive by indicating that future investment decisions will reflect a limited timeframe. Consistent with lessons learned from the Stockholm conference and other research, it provided financing and technical assistance for the countries of the Global South so that their commitment to the protocol's terms would not be a discouraging economic burden.[18] Additionally, the protocol put in place "a dynamic [management] process, driven by science and technology, which allow[s] stringency and scope of controls to be adjusted in reference to current scientific understanding, environmental effects, technological capabilities, and economic conditions."[19]

The protocol achieved three other things worth mentioning here. It equipped humankind with an example of a usable trade-sanction tool, one that can deny access to the world's lucrative markets to those who undermine the environment.[20] It recognized and put in operation the principle of differentiated obligations or responsibilities suggested in the Stockholm Declaration, as evidenced in the responsibilities of countries from the North and the South. Finally, in deference to the interests of present and future generations and the continuing sustainability of nature, it put into practice the World Charter's precautionary principle: states and other entities should take proactive measures to abort environmental damage; potential errors must be measured in favor of environmental protection instead of waiting until the full seriousness of environmental threats are known. By 1995, many countries had discontinued producing certain types of ODS; others are scheduled to do so by 2020.

Another significant international development in the 1980s was the publication of *Our Common Future,* influenced by both the World Charter for Nature and the Montreal Protocol. The report was a product of the WCED, which was established and chaired by Gro Harlem Brundtland, prime minister of Norway, at the request of the UN secretary-general. The commission's mission—a global agenda for change—was to propose long-term environmental strategies for achieving sustainable development by the year 2000 and beyond, recommend ways to translate environmental concerns into greater international cooperation (especially among developed and developing countries), and consider how the international community could better protect the environment over the long term. It may be said that the 1983 creation of the WCED was a spiritual complement to the World Charter for Nature.

The WCED, seeking to move beyond the charter's majestic ideas, recommended a host of actions to embrace its spirit in the form of binding law. In the late 1980s and the 1990s, many WCED ideas were at least partially adopted.[21] Among these were steps to increase the voice and role of the scientific community and NGOs so that people and nations could make many better informed choices. Also adopted was a recommendation to establish a global assessment program to complement the work of the UNEP and provide "timely, objective, and authoritative assessments and public reports on critical threats and risks to the global community."[22] Steps have been taken to create legal rights and responsibilities, especially at the national level, with adequate enforcement as well as to collaborate with businesses on a universal declaration and convention on environmental protection and sustainable development. In 1988, the UN created the IPCC to do exactly what the WCED urged, and some U.S. activities, domestic and international, complemented some of the WCED's recommendations. Other recommendations were never dealt with—for example, to identify and establish an independent, worldwide source of funds to finance activities related to the environment, from the use of the global commons (such as seabed mining) to "parking charges" for communications satellites. Both would have avoided the power play of national governments and their private-sector supporters, particularly from the fossil fuel industries.

Thanks to pressure from the fossil fuel industry, the Reagan administration gave only limited support to environmental matters, but pressure from many members of Congress, the U.S. public, and the international community induced the United States to ratify the Montreal Protocol, join many of its key allies as WCED members, and participate in conferences pushing for worldwide action.[23] However, in 1988, a year after the WCED called for a comprehensive international convention to deal with issues of the environment, the U.S. Senate debated but failed to pass the National Energy Policy Act (NEPA), which would have called for a national energy plan, created an office of climate protection, promoted energy efficiency, supported research and development in the environmental field, advanced conservation, pursued renewable sources of energy, protected natural resources of energy, and invested in the basic sciences in climate and ecological research.[24] The NEPA would have urged the United States to offer subsidies to developing nations in the form of foreign aid, investments, and insurance to combat climate change. Mirroring WCED recommendations, the NEPA would have called for "an international meeting in the United States by the end of 1992 to adopt a global climate protection convention."[25]

In the late 1980s, general sentiment in the United States for action to deal with climate change very much began to resemble what was happening globally, as attested by the many meetings on the subject among countries and the public voices heard during U.S. national elections. Internationally, the Group of 7 and the Group of 77 led a series of meetings, culminating in a November 1989 conference of some sixty countries in Nordwijk, Holland.[26] That gathering called for a global summit, which the UN General Assembly authorized.[27] The UN General Assembly called on the UNEP and the IPCC to begin "preparations for negotiations on a framework convention on climate, taking into account the work of the IPCC."[28] Within the United States, popular sentiment became more supportive of protecting the environment, influenced in part by congressional testimony from Dr. James Hansen, director of NASA's Goddard Institute for Space Studies, as well as by political leaders, including senators Al Gore, Timothy Worth, and George Mitchell, among others. Vice Pres. George H. Bush, who had spent eight years supporting President Reagan, began to call himself an environmentalist.

The Earth Summit

Consistent with the inspiration of the World Charter for Nature, the lessons learned from and achievements of the Montreal Protocol, the WCED's recommendations, the NEPA vision, and the global desire to deal collectively with environmental problems, UNCED—the Earth Summit—took place in Rio de Janeiro, Brazil, on June 3–14, 1992. Representatives of 178 nations, including 117 heads of states, gathered in the largest gathering of world political leaders to date.

As the first major world conference after the Cold War ended, UNCED was a collective opportunity to set a global agenda reconciling social and human development with appropriate protection and nourishment of the environment. Among UNCED's most important results was the UNFCCC—the Global Warming Convention. This treaty became legally binding in 1994 after enough nations ratified or endorsed it. Its primary aim is to get nations to stabilize and then reduce discharges of carbon dioxide, methane, nitrous oxide, and other greenhouse gases that were recognized as responsible for global warming. Signatories must adopt national policies to this end and share, for purposes of transparency, the results. Unlike the Montreal Protocol, however, the convention did not set binding, enforceable targets, a weakness that the Kyoto Protocol partially remedied in 1997.

The Earth Summit is associated with the Declaration on Environment and Development (known as the Rio Declaration), which elaborates twenty-seven principles for effective environmental action.[29] Attendees also adopted the Statement of Principles on Forests, with the objective of monitoring and helping preserve rapidly disappearing tropical forests. The Global North and South had strong and complementary interests in these natural areas as the sites of the most diverse bodies of plants and animals.

Further, the Earth Summit attendees agreed on the remarkable Convention on Biological Diversity, a treaty for preserving biological "variability among living organisms from all sources, including . . . territorial, marine, and other aquatic ecosystems and the ecosystems of which they are a part; this includes diversity within species, between species, and of ecosystems."[30] Giving concrete voice to the World Charter for Nature, this convention, which came into force in 1993, has as its primary objectives the conservation of biological diversity, the sustainable use of species and ecosystems, and the equitable sharing of the benefits arising from using genetic resources from the conserved species. It includes appropriate access to the genetic resources as well as the proper transfer of relevant technologies.[31] Those last two objectives are especially important for the Global South, where most of these species are found but where technology lags far behind that of the Global North, which wants access to the genetic resources.

Finally, the Rio Conference adopted Agenda 21, a 350-page blueprint for the twenty-first century on strategies and actions to achieve global sustainable development. Parties to the UNFCCC were to meet, at agreed-upon times, to monitor progress on its terms. Like the other environmental agreements during this period, Agenda 21 required a degree of material, psychological, and critical support at levels unprecedented in international relations. The very planning, mutual education, and consciousness raising among member states, which began in 1989, was extraordinary.

Two major shortcomings undermined the optimism attending to the Earth Summit: the absence of enforceable targets for reducing greenhouse gas emissions (as was the case of the Montreal Protocol) and the lack of identifiable leadership for the worldwide movement. NGOs, the UN, and various other stakeholders recognized that most climate-changing emissions came from industrialized nations. In 1997, an international conference in Kyoto sought to remedy the lack of enforceable targets. The Kyoto Protocol, extending the Framework on

Climate Change, imposed targets on greenhouse gas emissions. It made the targets applicable in a manner that mirrored national and regional differences in emissions, wealth, and the capability (including the technical capacity) to make the reductions. Also, it set two five-year timeframes for fulfilling targets: 2008 to 2012 and 2012 to 2016.[32]

Global developments overtook the second period in the form of the 2015 Paris Conference, the twenty-first follow-up conference within the Framework on Climate Change. In the resulting Paris Agreement on Climate Change, 195 countries unanimously agreed to work toward limiting the rise in global temperature to below two degrees centigrade above preindustrial levels. Further, they set an aspirational goal of limiting the temperature increase to one and a half degrees centigrade to further reduce the risks and likely impacts of climate change. The participating countries also agreed to operationalize the goals by aiming to realize peak emissions as soon as possible and achieve global net-zero emissions by 2050. Using the best available science to help further their endeavors became a unanimous undertaking. Developed countries committed themselves to maintaining a goal they had set earlier of marshalling $100 billion per year, until 2025, to support the treaty's collective goals. New goals would be set after 2025. The countries also committed themselves to meeting every four years to set more ambitious goals if necessary and report to one another and the public about progress toward their respective targets. They agreed to work with the IPCC to monitor accountability, use the best science, and cooperate to support early warning systems, emergency preparedness, adaptation strategies, and risk insurance.[33]

The want of leadership, the second major shortcoming, was recognized by the mid-1980s. Especially in the area of climate change, the emerging environmental movement needed international leadership. By the time of the 1989 Nordwijk conference, the consensus was that the United States would assume that role. When George H. Bush, in his 1988 campaign for president, indicated that he had become an environmentalist, this statement appeared to support such a role and the understanding of 1989.[34] During a news conference at the 1992 Summit on the Environment, President Bush stated that the United States "fully intends to be the world's preeminent leader in protecting the global environment"[35] and that it accepted the Framework on Climate Change.

Maurice Strong, the Canadian who served as secretary-general of the Rio Conference, rightly saw that gathering as a historic moment. Through the hundreds of thousands of people who had gathered in Rio, humankind sought a global alternative to the narrow confines to which the Cold War had consigned it for almost fifty years. It was historic because almost 10,000 international journalists at the conference informed the world about its activities and because 2,400 representatives of NGOs, answering to activists throughout the world, were ready to be part of a coherent leadership in collaborations with governments, as *Our Common Future* had urged (and an additional 17,000 NGO representatives attending a parallel NGO forum were prepared to join). It was historic because the sharing and common learning that had begun in 1972 in Stockholm matured into common dreams.

The United States failed to embrace this historic moment. It never fully accepted the responsibility to lead. Not only did it dash international hopes around its promise of leadership, but also, its subsequent behavior often indicated that the United States might subvert progress that could be realized without Washington's leadership. For example, the United States has not joined the 196 nations that have ratified the Convention on Biological Diversity. Also, the United States, despite pleading by its industrial allies, has refused to ratify the Kyoto Protocol, which seeks to correct some weaknesses in the Framework on Climate Change. President Trump's withdrawal from the Paris Climate Agreement is consistent with this broader and longer history.

With the United States as the world's dominant power and greatest emitter of greenhouse gases, Washington could have used its technological and economic predominance to help build a physical and moral infrastructure that would protect nature and nurture sustainable socioeconomic development. Moreover, the United States could have helped link the effect of its joining those efforts with movement toward a more humane pattern of globalization. Instead, wrote UNEP executive director Klaus Topper in 1999, globalization has "led to the dismantling of local economies and communities, the decline of family farms, and the destruction or undermining of renewable energy [initiatives]" as well as furthered the advance of "climate change, [the] loss of biological diversity, [and] the pollution and exhaustion of water resources."[36] The social results are with us, including much of the climate change–induced transborder migration from Syria, Central America, and certain areas of Africa as well as popular political uprisings against that migration in Europe and the United States.

New Efforts, Increased Collaboration, New Dangers

Had the United States assumed leadership of the environmental movement, it could have accepted as well a transition from an ethic rooted in national security to one directed at human and planetary well-being, as embodied in the framework's orientation and as argued by Christiana Figueres, executive secretary of the Framework on Climate Change from 2010 to 2016.[37] Her view is supported by the burden imposed on all to shift toward a non-carbon energy system and away from the carbon-based system that has held sway since the beginning of the Industrial Revolution. It is also supported by events at UN headquarters in New York in 2015, even before the Paris meeting, when governments adopted the seventeen

Sustainable Development Goals. Ten of the goals—including universal primary education, gender equality, and the eradication of extreme poverty—were part of the fifteen-year Millennium Development Goals set by the UN in 2000.[38] They were also a component of the 2030 global partnership commitments between developed and developing countries that were a feature of the 1992 Framework Convention on Climate Change. Had the United States assumed the expected leadership, it would now have an opportunity to lead efforts to realize these common Global North–South goals.

Despite the lack of U.S. leadership, both the world and the United States, through the efforts of many of its fifty states, have made important strides forward on environmental issues, even if with mixed results. Within the United States, the Alliance on Climate Change, composed of sixteen states plus Puerto Rico, is committed to lowering carbon emission by 26 to 28 percent from 2005 levels by 2025, as the Paris Agreement requires.[39] In the wake of the 2018 U.S. elections, seven other states (Kansas, Maine, Michigan, Nevada, New Mexico, and Wisconsin) have elected Democratic governors who have indicated that climate change must be addressed, and the issue of the environment is an important part of the policy profile of every declared Democratic Party candidate for president in the 2020 election.

However, voters have soundly defeated several key climate policies on state ballots in 2018, including a carbon tax in Washington State. Arizona voters rejected an ambitious renewable power target that would have required utilities to get half their electricity from renewable sources by 2035. This defeat, thanks to the strong opposition of oil and gas companies and an ethic saying that the nation can deal with climate change with little sacrifice, has given some encouragement to climate change deniers.[40] In nearby Nevada, in contrast, voters approved a ballot measure, which they must vote on again in 2020, requiring electric utilities to secure 50 percent of their power from renewable sources.[41]

Throughout the world, wrote Brad Plummer, environmental reporter for the *New York Times*, "[w]ind and solar power are poised to become dominant sources of electricity."[42] California, with the support of the Union of Concerned Scientists and enlightened political leadership, has embarked on a "green rush"; Massachusetts and other states are following. Canadians and Europeans, who lead the United States in a number of areas, are adopting some of California's incentive-based approaches.[43] China, which burns nearly half of the world's coal, has invested heavily in wind, solar, and nuclear energy, and it expects renewables to succeed coal as its principal source of electricity in the 2030s. It could do so earlier because of success in the solar area. India, like China, relied on coal, the cheapest source of energy, in its rise out of poverty, and it too plans to move away from coal as renewables become more competitive. So too have even Saudi Arabia and some other oil producers in West Asia, and Western Europe has largely kept its commitments.

Relying on election cycles and hoping that cost structures will enable the energy transition are not enough, commendable as they are. While carbon-free sources of energy like wind, solar, and nuclear are growing quickly, it is impossible to accurately predict the pace of achievement after certain critical levels are realized, while growing demands for energy are outpacing the speed with which alternative or non-carbon sources can fulfill those demands. Thus, the use of fossil fuels keeps rising alongside economic growth and the defeat of incentives for alternative energy. Besides examples like the ballot defeat in Washington State, population increases, and the continuing dependence of the poor on coal, the oil and gas companies collude in wielding their powerful influence toward producing more fossil fuels in the name of national economic self-sufficiency and national security. As their lobbying seeks to lower prices on fossil fuels, alternative energy sources find it harder to compete, and the use of fossil fuels continues on the false hope of some miraculous rescue.

No such rescue will come, as the evidence since the 1980s teaches and as reinforced by new reports of the environmental challenge. The October 2018 IPCC Special Report, *Global Warming of 1.5°C,* indicated that the aspirational goal of the Paris Agreement should now replace the "well below" two-degree goal of that agreement. Moreover, the report noted that achieving the lower target, while likely reducing damage to ecosystems and human well-being, as well as moving forward on the overall task of achieving the UN Sustainable Development Goals would require far-reaching transformations in energy, buildings, land use, industry, and transportation and in cities and towns. It would also require substantial increases in renewable energy.[44]

About a month later, the congressionally mandated Fourth National Climate Assessment indicated that the global annual average surface air temperature had increased by about one degree centigrade between 1901 and 2016 and that the past three years had been the warmest on record for the globe.[45] The report warned of likely "extreme events" in areas such as physical infrastructure, agriculture, water quality and quantity, and natural ecosystems. Heavy rainfall will increase in intensity and frequency across the United States and the globe, record-setting "hot years" will occasion large forest fires in the Western United States and Alaska, and early spring melt will continue to affect water resources and cause hydrological drought with increasing duration—all predicted many years ago.[46] The report notes the likely impact on the U.S. economy, including a 10 percent reduction in international trade and investment.

Finally, a study led by biogeochemical oceanographer Dr. Laure Resplandy of Princeton University indicates that the IPCC may have underestimated the pace of ocean warming from 1991 to 2016. The report, published in *Nature,* argued that the world faced the possibility of even greater coastal flooding (and many cities and towns abut the ocean), food shortages (especially in protein from fish, on which so many of the world's poor depend), and mass die-off of coral reefs, among other damaging effects.[47]

Wasted Time, New Insights, New Efforts

Since 1992, the United States and the world could have avoided the exertions now needed to counter the threat of an irretrievable change in climate. The present crossroads allows little margin for error, and the alternatives are known. The United States can continue a carbon-based way of life, with high moral-sounding commitments to change but few actions commensurate with the crisis, including a collective willingness to accept necessary sacrifices. On the other hand, the nation can fulfill its commitments under the Framework for Climate Change and the Paris Agreement to do what the collective learning of nearly fifty years has made clear. Only deep, committed, worldwide collaboration and cooperation can save us.

The World Charter for Nature intimates something further: a cultural message must complement environmental actions, a message grounded on a set of insights provided by humanity's collective heritage. First, nature represents an order of which the earth, including humans, partakes. This order is fundamentally harmonious in the sense that its parts or segments consist of some uniqueness and are complementarily interdependent and interactive.[48]

Second, each part of nature, including all entities on earth, are subjects, not simply objects to be acted on. They are in constant communication with one another, even if human beings, at this stage in human evolution, do not recognize or understand the grammar and rhythm of this communication. In short, the earth is a community of subjects, as eloquently stated by the Catholic priest and cultural historian Thomas Berry.[49] In part, this may be grounds for the claim of mystery, waiting to be revealed. The Abrahamic tradition, especially Islam but also Judaism in Psalm 19, views nature as a text to be revered; the Native American tradition and the traditions of indigenous peoples, in general, have a similar view of nature.[50] To those less religiously inclined, Francis Bacon, in *Novum Organum*, claims that the human being "can do and understand so much only as he has observed in fact or in thought of the course of nature: beyond this, he neither knows anything nor can do anything."[51] As such, Bacon argued, we are but interpreters and servants of nature, whether we touch on the highest levels of scientific and technological inquiry or reflect on the inner state of our being and its relationship with the universe at large.

Third, understanding the relationships among the various interacting parts of nature is central to knowledge and understanding, which is something the

Confucian tradition insists upon. Human society, including the human economy, exists and develops as a derived category that irrefutably proceeds from and depends entirely on the earth's economy. The "either/or" ethic that says we cannot protect nature if we are to protect jobs or food for children is easily proven false. The Buddhist tradition tries to inform us that we do not produce anything; we merely reproduce what nature has produced.[52] The WCED reflected this view as it examined today's interlocking crises and the related changes they demand:

> These related changes have locked the global economy and global ecology together in new ways. We have, in the past, been concerned about the impact of economic growth upon the environment. We are now forced to concern ourselves with the impacts of ecological stress—degradation of soils, water regimes, atmosphere, and forests—upon economic prospects.[53]

Of course, this understanding is incomplete because the relationship is reciprocal, requiring attention to both the impact of actions on the environment (economic growth, for example) as well as the effect of the environment on the economy. Here, the cultural tradition of Hinduism is instructive: sustainable relationships depend on balancing relationships among the interacting parts.[54]

The fourth insight is the difficulty of understanding nature, the relationships and balance of interacting subjects, and the communication among subjects in all their minuteness and intimacy, creativity and complexity, intensity and linguistic nuances. Indeed, Bacon again offers supporting guidance. In his view, "[t]he subtlety of nature is greater many times over than the subtlety of [our] senses and understanding."[55] Human "knowledge and human power meet in one" in the sense that knowing causes makes it possible to produce many effects and to the extent that power derives from producing effects. We are called upon to be mindful and humble.

Contemporary humanity has not nurtured mindfulness as a virtue. The reverse has been the case, based on actual and supposed accomplishments in the sciences and technology, in the production of the goods and services that define our economic growth and development, in adventures to the moon and other celestial bodies, in probing molecular and subatomic worlds, and in daring into artificial intelligence and the nature of the mind itself. Despite many disclaimers, we are offspring of the "will to power," as Friedrich Nietzsche wrote. We seek command to make a dent, to have not just an effect, any effect or outcome, but a specific desired effect. We therefore seek command and, often, control.

"Nature to be commanded . . . must be obeyed," Bacon tells us.[56] In other words, a fifth insight is that the true character of command in nature entails obedience—obedience to the primacy of nature as the primary and reciprocal lawgiver, as primary economic corporation, as primary scientist and technologist, as primary healer, primary artist, primary pharmacist, primary university, and, above all, primary teacher. It is also the primary student who interacts with and responds to that which is communicated to her or him.

Despite the special place of human beings as nature's interpreters and stewards, we must accept a final insight: humility, gratefulness, and patience are virtues to cultivate in the quest for a common, sustainable future. This humility, gratefulness, and patience should encompass all we do, including the identities we hold dear: nation, state, race, ethnicity, social class, gender, language, birthplace, religion, socioeconomic ideology, civilization, and supposed or actual place in nature, among other things.

A focus on national security, with nuclear and other weapons of mass destruction, may not fit into that future. Capitalism in its current cultural form, including the greed it sponsors, along with its focus on the individual to the near exclusion of the community, may not fit. Claims to racial and civilizational preeminence may not fit. The rejection of science or the rightful place of the individual in society might not fit. The subjugation of women, the chief conservators of nature among us, may not fit. Lastly, the persistent overlooking of children and the poor may not fit.[57]

Today's misalignments delegitimize the sociopolitical system via the very crises it has brought about. If it is no longer legitimate, the updated Framework Convention on Climate Change points the way to an alternative, as does the Green New Deal proposal by Congresswoman Alexandria Ocasio-Cortez. In seeking to address climate change and, in so doing, deal with socioeconomic inequality, it represents an important step in the direction of the framework, notwithstanding the unmerited criticisms it has received. Combining the framework with the cultural narrative suggested here could help Washington look again at leading the global environmental movement.

6

THE WILL TO NATIONAL POWER OR GLOBAL LEADERSHIP?

Especially since 1945, the United States has taken the position that it is called upon to lead the world, particularly because communism, represented by the Soviet Union, threatened human freedom and well-being.[1] However, a careful reading of U.S. history discloses that what really has been at play is what Friedrich Nietzsche called the will to power. Nietzsche viewed the will to power as a driving force in human beings to reach the highest position or status as defined, imagined in, or suggested by cultural life. It combines the rational and the non-rational, with the latter dominating and the former but offering justification for this driving force. The late Erich Fromm, reflecting on the phenomenon through a framework of basic human needs, spoke of "effectiveness"—the gaining and preserving of a "sense of one's own will," of one's identity, of being able to avoid being an object, especially in the face of an overpowering world, the capacity to "make a dent."[2]

The will to power or the need to make a dent relates to both the individual and social collectivities such as the nation-state. The need to make a dent is but the general ground on which the will to power builds and is extended physically, socially, economically, politically, and, where it can make a plausible claim, morally. For example, a country may make a moral claim, with only a vague right to do so, when perfecting instruments of coercion to cross recognized borders in the quest to secure raw materials, dominate other people, control territory, subordinate national leaders, or exact tribute, such as taxes, access to markets, or investment possibilities.

Of interest here is the nature of the historical leadership of the United States within and outside its borders. Does the character of that leadership hold promise or even the possibility of helping both the nation and the world deal with *the primary challenges to humankind's collective future?* Among these challenges are the following: ongoing demographic changes; the transborder movements of peoples; the nature of the social compact that societies must embrace if they are to survive; the capacity of economic systems to accommodate that compact while generating promise for a complex political future; the acceptance of the place of humankind in the earth's ecology; the relationships among education, technology, and society; and the need for common security among peoples and nations, with attention to the role of law in gaining that security.

For over two hundred years, the United States' role in the world has focused on or expressed the will to national power and domination. This has been manifested from the time of U.S. independence, "expanding its power and influence in ever-widening arcs,"[3] in the words of conservative historian Robert Kagan. This expansion began in North America as the United States sought to remove, contain, or exclude competing centers of power and influence—the United Kingdom, Native Americans, Spain, and France. Then it moved into Latin America by way of the Monroe Doctrine and then Mexico and Russia (with the purchase of Alaska) and, with wider strategic reach, into the Pacific through the 1898 war with Spain and the Open Door Policy on China, along with the annexation of Hawaii and the creation of Panama to ensure the building of the Panama Canal. Wider U.S. maneuverings after World War II extended this push into Western Europe, Australia, New Zealand, and East Asia, with significant activities in the Middle East. With the end of the Cold War, the compass of U.S. influence and power incorporated Eastern Europe and the Baltic and began reaching into Central Asia.

Coupled with the spread of U.S. influence and interests has been the capacity to "project force to distant theaters,"[4] according to historian Paul Kennedy. This capacity expanded during the 1980s and the Gulf War of 2003, and it has largely continued during the Trump administration, defined in part by a web of fleets, air bases, and ground forces in every area considered strategically important as well as "a panoply of air-, land-, and sea-based missile systems," writes Kennedy, to deter any state or combination of states from attacking the United States or its allies. Further, U.S. armed services are technologically equipped to fight "smart" wars, with tools ranging from stealth bombers to night-fighting battlefield weapons that can identify and assess enemies and their actions through the use of satellites, early-warning aircraft, and oceanic acoustical detection systems.[5] Today an added frontier beckons as the Trump administration moves to create a U.S. Space Force.[6]

The United States has sought to gain and now enjoys mastery in all existing theaters—land, air, and sea—and seeks it in outer space. Barring an extraordinary change, the nation is unlikely to retreat from its current global reach, and no other nation comes near this status or the power and international standing it confers.

The American people take this status for granted; while some would like to reduce military expenditures and engagements, few are prepared to forego the status.

The immense expenditures supporting U.S. military dominance have not come without social consequences; nor has success come without resentments throughout the world. At home and abroad, social, ethnic, racial, gender, environmental, and other issues fester.[7] Serious social problems are evident almost everywhere in which the free-market economy (and its partner, consumerism) has gained sway, even in Western Europe, the most socially advanced region. On the other hand, military actions, especially since World War II, have proliferated.[8]

The international system and the people of the world are not more secure than they were fifty years ago. The advance of democracy, presented to justify the sacrifices societies have been called on to make, has neither demonstrated any refinement in its quality nor found more supportive adherents. In addition, the unprecedented material wealth of multilateral regimes led by Washington—in collaboration with multinational corporations espousing and promoting trade liberalization, open markets, and foreign direct investment—has occasioned a possibly unprecedented unequal distribution of wealth. The United States has never sought to support any institutional arrangement that would limit its claimed right to act unilaterally, whether in the area of disarmament or more generally. In the area of environmental stewardship, a global consensus calls on the United States to take the lead, but the nation has instead yielded to a narrow view of self-interest as defined by oil and gas interests.

From evidence of the U.S. will to power, it is clear that isolationist sentiments have never captured Washington. Nor has protecting democracy forced a reluctant nation into pursuing complex international military actions. Nor has the United States pursued idealist commitments to sovereign equality, self-determination, and collective security. It may have spoken moral-sounding words, but no reduction in U.S. military power followed the demise of the Soviet Union, along with its Communist Party and like parties in Eastern Europe. Rather, the sole remaining superpower has sought to augment its dominance. With the beginning of the twenty-first century, Secretary of Defense Ronald Rumsfeld began a "reform" of U.S. armed forces to ensure Washington's high-tech lead for long-term, international military advantage, and he began plans to consider the militarization of outer space.[9]

A Choice

The United States may continue on the path it has followed since 1945, seeking to serve, through multilateral regimes, its will to national power and worldwide domination. It could pursue the freedom to act unilaterally in the face of perceived strategic dangers because it alone has the capacity to do so while thwarting the development of such a capacity by others.[10] However, this drive is unlikely to succeed, barring the open flouting of everything the United States claims to believe in. For one thing, European skepticism is rising, especially since Washington's rejection of the nuclear weapons deal with Iran and its use of the dollar, as the world's key currency, to enforce that rejection against the European Union and other countries. Although developed in part with U.S. support to deal more effectively with the Soviet Union, the European Union has become increasingly concerned about the U.S. disposition to use force. It now seeks to lessen its dependency on the United States for certain security guarantees—for example, by considering the development of a European armed force. The United States has indicated its opposition to such a move, as it has the possibility that the euro might compete with the dollar as an international currency.

Moreover, countries like India and China are unlikely to accept the core tenets of the U.S.-created world order, unless that order changes radically to throw off U.S. dominance. Nor can Russia be counted out; returning to the heart of global diplomacy, it will take advantage of every opportunity to overcome the humiliation it suffered when the Soviet Union disintegrated. The opening up of the Arctic will only make Russia more formidable.

In short, the free market, as currently constituted and espoused, will find fewer and fewer takers, at home or abroad. The United States will face a crisis of legitimacy, and its capacity to use force will not ensure its continued domination.

There is an alternative. The United States could choose to exercise leadership in timely partnership with other states and on behalf of the world in areas where complementary interests are clear. This is part of the meaning of democracy.

Demographic Challenges

Demographic changes and the transborder movement of peoples affect almost every nation and region of the world. In some cases, as in Europe, the recent, current, and projected patterns are an overall decline in rates of organic population growth, corresponding increases in aging, and, among other things, declines in the working-age population. In the United States, immigration has accounted for population increases since the 1970s. Moving forward, much of the net increase in the global population will be from Africa, where increases between now and 2050 will be more than four times that of Asia and three and a half times that of South America. Southeast Asia will merely double.[11] On the whole, the population of the Global South will be much younger, while the Global North will be the principal site of older populations. Within the United States, Asians and Hispanics will likely continue to be the fastest growing population subgroups. Throughout the world, Muslims will continue as the fastest growing religious grouping. Women, in general, will continue to live longer than men, and in many societies, including the United States, their cultural opportunities will likely improve. Women will unsettle many of the patriarchy's vaunted claims, even as women's wages continue to lag substantially below those of men. Global urbanization will continue. By 2030, urban areas will contain more than 70 percent of the world's population, and the world's economy will likely be structured around megacities rather than traditionally understood nation-states.[12] Whether in Seoul, Shanghai, Tokyo, Jakarta, Mumbai, Cairo, Lagos, Sao Paulo, Los Angeles, Moscow, or Berlin, a complex communication network will link people together in ways the nation-state does not now allow.

The transborder movement of peoples parallels migration within national borders. The term *peoples* suggests that cultural differences will likely continue to be a major feature of this movement, constituted by groups escaping persecution, genocide, sexual slavery, wars, climate change, torture, or starvation as well as those simply seeking general improvement in their material circumstances.[13] In the Horn of Africa, the Middle East, the Balkans, the European Union, Central America, North America, Australia, and South Asia—including the Burmese–Bangladeshi–Assamese area, the Mediterranean, and the Caribbean—the movement of groups across borders causes anxiety, confusion, social dislocation, resentment, despair, and a disappearing sense of place for incoming and receiving peoples alike. Some groups, of course, settle appropriately, at least for a time, in their new nation. Just as often, the host populations turn to fear and sometimes hatred of the newcomers; even those who might see certain immigrants as co-ethnic, co-racial, co-religious, co-national, or co-linguistic groups begin feeling insecure. Why? The nation-state has been constructed and maintained on the "othering" of non-nationals or noncitizens, on false identities, so the newcomers are "less than," even within a given community based on identity. Poles find themselves treated as the other in the United Kingdom, and people of Japanese ancestry who were born in Brazil find themselves othered in Tokyo.

Historical and contemporary responses to the transborder movement of peoples have much to do with the very idea of borders based on claimed, ascribed, or supposed physical, social, and cultural identities. Those borders and the identities they purportedly represent may appear to constitute essences or inner truths rather than mere markers or labels created and recognized to help facilitate human social interactions. Thus, fears, expressed or concealed, arise respecting the capacity of groups to embody, represent, or assimilate a given cultural ancestry. Fears of multiculturalism and concerns about others belonging to larger cultural aggregates become commonplace. (In Germany, fascism and its followers felt that Jews had too much of a capacity to assimilate.)

How can the United States lead in this area? One step would be to join with UNESCO and similar global organizations, public and private, and teach about markers and labels, encourage examinations of larger identities to which human beings belong, and go beyond the abstract examination of that belonging to day-to-day enactments of its reality in our lives—"global citizenship" or "our country, the planet earth," for instance. The United States can join with other organizations to help teach that we all have many identities.[14] It is necessary to recognize as well the ways in which identities are consistent with our social nature and that identity can foster enriched human social and cultural interactions. This requires a new respect and encouragement for education, with undertakings to reorganize schools in a manner largely reflecting the medical school model, where field experience is central and evidence-based enquiry presides. The United States should also support UNESCO in establishing a global university focused on this type of education. At least initially, such an institution could lead in accepting and seeking the multiple identities that human beings have evolved into.

A focus on larger, more integrated identities will accomplish little without recasting historical studies to look at the world—indeed, the universe—as a whole. Some larger identities (race and civilization, among others) have been used to justify the brutalization and even elimination of groups of human beings. The term *the West* or *Western civilization* has been construed to attribute false "essences" to others—"Orientals," for instance. Of course, a look at the differences between the cultures of India and those of China may very well reveal, using Western categories, that the differences exceed those between the Occident and the Orient. Hence, it will be important to ground efforts to support larger integrative identities on careful, critical appraisals and to avoid fashioning them to subtly clothed prejudices.

In moving to a new type of education curriculum, policy makers should bear in mind that one cannot eliminate overnight emotional and psychological damage produced over centuries. Nor can transborder movements of peoples exceed the pace at which existing populations can socially and culturally adjust.[15] Therefore, global leadership in this area should include agreed-on parameters for dealing with problems that all humans face in moving toward a truly global society, with its many cultural cleavages. That emerging society is itself seeking a new identity. Drawing on the bequest of the human rights regime developed after World War II, it says that *human identity* has a moral core that cannot tolerate discrimination based on "race, color, sex, language, religion, political or other opinion, national or social origin, property, birth, or other status," in the language of the Universal Declaration of Human Rights.[16] With a focus on this "species identity," much of the psychic and social damage from adverse discrimination and oppositional identities would gradually pass away.

Social Compact

Such outcomes bring up the nature of the social compact that human societies must accommodate if they are to survive. Modern societies are grounded on the successive refinement of an implicit or explicit understanding that human beings join together to form organized social organisms and assure the mutual protection and common well-being of each individual.[17] This social compact has, at times, required governments not only to provide police and military protection but also to protect civil and political rights, such as freedoms of conscience, the press, and the right to vote as well as to supply social services and support the physical infrastructure. Part of the Cold War hinged on the nature of the "social contract," on the rivalry in which liberal democracy deemphasized the social and economic in preference for the civil and political while the socialist system did the opposite. The U.S. Constitution itself speaks of the government's obligation to promote the "general welfare," but this has been interpreted to mean that the subordinate units of government (the states) should deal with such matters rather than the federal government.

In contrast to the United States, Europe has embraced a significant body of social rights—in health care, education, and housing, for example—but it has come under considerable pressures recently to restrict immigrants' access to those rights.[18] Some European Union citizens in Eastern Europe feel a deep sense of deprivation. With communications technology, including access to social media, people compare what they think they are socially entitled to with what they, in fact, have access to. They are less willing to wait for benefits associated with social rights to trickle down. The edifice of political systems is under stress, with a growing willingness to sacrifice the political to ensure the survival of the economic system.

The Universal Declaration of Human Rights, unlike the liberal democratic or Marxist socioeconomic orders, is the product of thinking that understands the social compact as a fundamental commitment *combining* civil and political rights with social, economic, and cultural rights in an integrated whole. Rights would be defined in terms of both *freedom from* (from varying kinds of abuse—including arbitrary arrest, detention, or exile—or torture and other forms of cruel and degrading treatment) and *freedom to* (to free speech, press, religion, fair trials, and asylum; to associate and participate in elections; to education, medical care, food, housing, work, fair wages, social security, and the fruits of scientific progress; and to participate in the cultural life of the community). Indeed, what are called "third generation" rights, inspired by the Universal Declaration of Human Rights, would include solidarity rights for individuals and groups: the right to self-determination and to a safe and sustainable environment, development, and peace.

This comprehensive outlook anticipates what U.S. Representative Alexandria Ocasio-Cortez has called the Green New Deal.[19]

A true leader will know that it is impossible to speak of freedom if the demands of a hungry belly are not met—to speak honestly of human dignity without ensuring housing or respect for life, which wars of mass destruction wantonly degrade. One cannot genuinely speak of the democratic entitlement to participate in free elections without education or honorably speak of the rights to development and share in scientific progress while destroying the environment from which development and scientific progress come. The right to work requires self-respect, improvements in material well-being, and the greater range of choices from which freedom springs.

The categories of rights cannot, with integrity, be separated. The question is whether the current dominant economic system and its ideology can accommodate this social contract. In its current form, it cannot, but modified in certain areas, it might be able to do so. A true leader, whether an individual or a nation, must be willing to take on the dominant economic culture and outlook when the social contract requires it. After all, the social contract is the reason for the organization of society. Therefore, there can be no morally defensible reason for society if the aims of that contract cannot be realized.

Historically, the free-market economy has willingly sacrificed everything on the altar of profits and growth, which it sees as belonging to shareholders. The thinking is that shareholders take risks and must be rewarded, whether those returns are negative or positive. It is also based on the idea that all people are "economic animals" motivated by material things and equipped with rational ingenuity that together impel forces of growth and profits. Also, because no government can anticipate or effectively regulate the complex routes and breakthroughs to growth and profits, the thinking goes, competition as the mechanism of regulation will redound to the social good.

However, liberal democracy, twinned with the free-market economy, cannot accommodate the social compact. This system has not done so for over two hundred years, and there is no reason to suppose it will in the future if left unreformed. Indeed, the system continues to produce the reverse of the social compact, externalizing costs (transferring certain costs to society, such as environmental pollution or cancers caused by tobacco) and engineering the strangulation of society itself. Two dramatic demonstrations of this are the Great Depression of 1929–1939 and the Great Recession of 2007–2009, the former inducing Franklin Roosevelt to call attention to "economic Royalists" seeking to control the economy and reduce individuals to a condition of material inequality and sociopolitical powerlessness. Karl Polanyi, in *The Great Transformation,* a 1944 work that carefully examined the free market, contended that the unregulated market would destroy society. In more specific terms, he predicted the defiling of neighborhoods and landscapes, the pollution of rivers, the destruction of agriculture, and the impairment of military safety.[20]

The existing order, absent reforms, will not serve today's needs because the norm of equality at the heart of democracy is at odds with the inequality that capitalism invariably sponsors, a contradiction that the scholarly work of Thomas Piketty captures so well.[21] In the United States and other societies where capitalism has succeeded in containing government regulation, the emerging global society accumulates untold riches, but those riches go to increase socioeconomic inequality and the resulting social problems.[22] Recent reports that deaths outnumber births among U.S. whites is only one of several indicators of the social problems the nation faces, with the lack of education, health care, and sense of worth among the leading causes of the demographic challenge.[23]

The free-market model, as is, cannot accommodate the social compact because it does not allow for ideological or conceptual competition (even though it considers competition one of its core values). In the United States, it limits competition, first of all, by undermining or short-circuiting debate. In political life, as recently observed by economist Paul Krugman (and long ago by Franklin Roosevelt), "[e]veryone who wants to make life in a market economy less nasty, brutish, and short gets denounced as socialist."[24] Today Americans most often associate the terms *socialist* and *socialism* not with the people or social systems of Sweden, Denmark, Norway, or Germany but with the former Soviet Union, Venezuela, or Cuba. The Chinese experiment, with what it calls market socialism, must therefore be fought in every possible way.

The free-market economy, as is, cannot serve because many of its claims and assumptions are wrong. Human beings are not economic animals but social beings, to the extent that they seek economic outcomes to satisfy social needs or aspirations. The market about which the ideology speaks is not a neutral entity, as seen in battles to control banks or grant capital ascendency over labor. The individualism it espouses flies in the face of the social cooperation required to produce. Moreover, the revered attribute of competition is often breached in fundamental ways, offering ample opportunities for monopolistic practices. Also, capitalism's hierarchical nature of leadership is out of sorts with the digital age, and the use of individual and group human attributes as raw material for the future economy threatens to enslave, not liberate. Ironically, the free-market focus on individuals and individualism actually deemphasizes the role of power in economic life, leading to misallocated blame when thing go wrong, as they often do. Individuals need communities for rootedness and renewal, just as the community needs the individual for creative breakthroughs.

All that said, the system could work if modified to promote genuine competition, incentives for risk taking, and shared prosperity, with profits shared across a range of stakeholders—workers, communities, and the government in addition to business owners. Moreover, an explicit emphasis on social cooperation must be nurtured. Businesses benefit from an educated population and from parents' work in rearing children as well as from roads, airports, ports, railways, sponsored research, the police, the courts, legislation, and regulation.[25]

A further enabling change would be to accept social rights as coequal with civil and political rights, along with recognition for the dignity of labor. In this case, both Pres. Theodore Roosevelt and President Lincoln, whom Roosevelt admired and frequently quoted, afforded labor equal importance with capital (e.g., money, technology, plants, factories), with an emphasis on labor's contributions to emotional fulfillment, the drive that work done well can engender. Lincoln stated, "Labor is prior to and independent of capital. Capital is only the fruit of labor, and it could never have existed if labor had not first existed."[26] He was for equal compensation for equal work but not against the idea of becoming rich or the idea of wealth. The socialized respect for labor would help workers organize and enjoy the power to check, in a form of competition, capital and vice versa so that legal structures, such as tax laws, would not routinely transfer wealth to the richest or those who control capital.[27]

Such changes will not come about easily. They will anger those who assume that debates about the market economy have been largely settled. This is not true, of course. Future discussions may not be settled in favor of capitalism "as is." Suggesting otherwise is the direction of much contemporary thinking—Roman Catholicism's social teachings, neo-Confucianism's community emphasis, Islam's focus on the well-being of *ummah*, the orientation of social democracy in Europe (the seeming rising ascendency of the Right on certain issues, notwithstanding), and the inclinations of peoples in Africa and South America toward a different economic order.

Leadership is needed, a quality exhibited by Franklin Roosevelt, who was unafraid to attack "the privileged princes" who, "wrapped in the use of their robes of legal sanction," wielded their power to thwart the popular will and impose an industrial dictatorship.[28] He went on to say the following:

> For too many of us, the political equality we had won was meaningless in the face of economic inequality. A small group had concentrated in their own hands an almost complete control over other people's property, other people's money, other people's labor—other people's lives. For too many of us, life was no longer free, liberty no longer real; men no longer follow the pursuit of happiness.[29]

Apart from capturing the psychological terrain of 1936, a terrain that closely mirrors our present condition, Roosevelt's metaphors induced comparisons with the search for independence in 1776. He sought a new spiritual independence with a new conception of self. Nothing less would allow for the type of American leadership that is needed now.

Earth's Ecology

Turning to humanity's place in the ecology of the earth and the universe, no single nation or subgroup of nations can deal with the threat that climate change poses to life on this planet and the life of the planet itself, a threat principally caused by human activities. A leader of this cause must be able to elicit responses coextensive with the problem faced and those who must be enlisted in helping solve it.

The economist Jeffrey D. Sachs would begin plotting "sustainable development" by noting that the world's output for 2018, measured by international prices, was about $134 trillion or $17,000 for each person on the planet.[30] Sachs is well-intentioned, but he starts in the wrong place. We as humans must first establish our place in nature and determine how that place may help save the planet as well as our enhanced place in it. While all living things communicate with one another, not all are conscious of how those communications interact. Only human beings seem potentially able to comprehend that interaction, and their capacity to do so has evolved over human history and with the evolution of the planet itself. With insightfulness, humans have "visited" the earth before our presence on it to discover how those beginnings and their development shaped the present and will help shape our individual and collective future. It also seems clear that humanity and the rest of the earth cohere, as demonstrated by way of new modes of thinking and experimenting—modes by which nature discloses more and more to our consciousness, including how we understand ourselves. It is from this consciousness and understanding about ourselves and the rest of nature that humanity, as nature's lead steward, can help effect a mutually advantageous, evolving future.

Just as we are learning to think historically and mathematically, we must think environmentally, bearing in mind nature's near self-sufficiency, variety, spontaneity, and self-organizing attributes, along with its interconnectedness. Then we will understand why the universe is a single though differentiated entity, why the earth is a single though differentiated community, why the human family is a single though differentiated society, and that what is differentiating can also be unifying. Only by dealing with the general and the particular, the single and the differentiated, in all their complexities, and in recognizing the interdependence of all things can we properly deal with the environment and climate change.

The decision at the 2015 Paris Conference to place sustainable development and the Sustainable Development Goals at the center of global economic development is praiseworthy, as is the apparent ratification of that decision by the 2019 Conference of Parties (CoP) in Katowice, Poland. What remains to be seen is whether the Katowice Agreement on rules for putting the 2015 Paris Agreement into practice can be implemented successfully—including rules on how governments must measure, report, and verify claimed results from emission-reducing policies. The year 2020 will also reveal much; at that time, countries must detail their progress on meeting their carbon emissions commitments and produce shared plans for new targets for 2030 and beyond. In Katowice, however, the United States joined with Russia, Saudi Arabia, and Kuwait in seeking to water down the IPCC's 2018 report on threats posed by climate change without drastic changes to limit global warming to one and a half degrees centigrade. The European Union, joined by many other industrial countries and with overwhelming support from the Global South, pledged a commitment to the one-and-a-half-degree limit.

There is cause for hope. Although carbon emissions, after years of stabilization, show signs of increasing, clean energy is emerging faster than predicted and at declining costs. Also, U.S. technology has capabilities that can benefit the nation and the world. What are needed are inspirational leaders to tell the story of the earth, including the interdependence of all things and how the major changes that have to take place as well as the costs, material and otherwise, must be borne collectively—including changes in industrial plants, buildings, transportation, and farming, in how we organize ourselves, in consumption, and in attitudes, among other things.

Bearing the burdens collectively will require reallocating material resources. For example, nations will have to rethink the current use of funds to buy weapons of mass violence, estimated at $14 trillion in 2018. Should nations invest in research directed at reversing the threat of climate change or weapons systems for the militarization of space?[31] After all, the building, maintenance, and use of those weapons run contrary to the interdependence of things, the integrity of the environment, and the dignity of human beings. The structures that have allowed the world's two-thousand-plus billionaires to hold $9.1 trillion in wealth will have to be modified, and trillions in "hidden wealth" will have to be unhidden, along with a cleansing of political life from the poison of money, which helps fuel the maldistribution of societal material resources. A modest portion of this money could help the world deal with climate change and address the UN's Millennium Development Goals within a program of sustainable development, including addressing social ills deriving from shortcomings in education, health care, and housing.[32]

Place in Earth's Ecology

U.S. leadership would make a major difference in the two other areas: education in the face of rapid technological change and the global quest for common security.

The education challenge speaks to developments such as artificial intelligence, the loss of privacy, gene editing, the gathering and sharing of huge databases on individuals and groups, and the potential outcomes of viewing humans as mere raw material for use in the consumption markets. According to the Universal Declaration of Human Rights, education "shall be directed to the full development of the human personality and to the strengthening of respect for human rights . . . It shall promote understanding, tolerance, and friendship among all nations, racial, or religious groups and shall further the activities of the UN for the maintenance of peace."[33] Part of these roles for education should be to enable *everyone* to enjoy the "right freely to participate in the cultural life of the community, to enjoy the arts, and to share in scientific achievements and its benefits."[34]

Today every country seeks to excel in the information and communications revolution called artificial intelligence. In the United States, concerns have arisen respecting the application of artificial intelligence to using data and decision-making algorithms to foment social and racial unrest, its role in fatal crashes from the operation of drones and other autonomous vehicles, robots taking jobs from "natural individuals," economic competition from other nation-states, and potential threats from new forms of intelligence, the operations of which are unknown.[35] Concerns have been raised about the regulation of these technologies, fearing that their use by self-interested businesses (claiming to use them for societies' benefit) could lead to results paralleling those of the tobacco industry and its connections to cancer and the fossil fuel industry's culpability in climate change.[36] Accusations of the misuse of artificial intelligence to manipulate people, especially voters, have been aired but mostly against Russia rather than in principle, even though the most democratic nations have indulged in the same practices.

While all these concerns are undeniable, they say nothing about how technologies with global reach will contribute to the type of education to which human beings are, by right, entitled. Neither is much said about the overarching context of nature, the complexities of great demographic changes and the transborder movement of peoples, and the material and cultural inequalities that undergird social and psychological anxieties, let alone the education needed to begin any collective and individual responses to these many fundamental questions.

Shoshana Zuboff, in *The Age of Surveillance Capitalism*, captures the context and character of the challenge of artificial intelligence. That challenge is nothing less than the danger of a new economic order that claims the entirety of human constitution and experiences as raw material to be tracked, parsed, mined, modified, and used as data and hence to create knowledge, wealth, and power. The challenge is the mining of the mind and individual conduct, under an invisible system of digital surveillance, to predict patterns of and effect changes in individual and collective behavior.[37] Those collections of data will enable banks, insurance companies, hospitals, retail institutions, restaurants, and moviemakers, catering to broadly awakened narcissisms long ago recognized by advertisers and consumer-led economics, to prey with predictive certainty on a new quality of demand: "consumption my way, what I want, when I want it, where I want it."[38] Information shared with commercial interests can also be shared with political interests, including governments. Facebook's much-publicized sharing of data with Cambridge Analytica to influence the 2016 elections is but one example.

The artificial intelligence–led information and communications revolution could help develop the human personality and the self-determination and autonomy of individuals and communities, nurture the human dignity on which self-determination is grounded, and expand the capacity to cultivate broader cultural understanding, tolerance, and friendship among peoples and nations, along with a deeper appreciation for interdependence among countries and with the rest of nature. Instead, that revolution is currently geared to diminishing human liberty, quashing self-determination, and, in many respects, doing to *human* nature what the Industrial Revolution and its associated activities did to non-human nature and how they, in so doing, shaped a socioeconomic and political legacy that haunts the survival of life on earth.

The "human grandeur" about which Marilynne Robinson reminds us and that undergirds the human rights movement, including the idea of a continuing unfolding of the human personality, is being left further and further behind.[39] Our historical self-absorption is being reinforced and extended, and our remaining capacity to sustain the habit of duty to larger communities and self-government, expressive of that duty, is being further eroded.[40]

The Age of Surveillance Capitalism contributes toward understanding the scope of today's challenge. In this regard, the European Union's General Data Protection Regulation is a commendable example of what governments can do to constrain the shape of the artificial intelligence revolution. However, current constraints are insufficient. What is needed is a commitment to change how people learn, in terms of both the tenor and the methodology of education's curricular content.

The first requirement is for a curriculum that fearlessly examines contemporary culture and exposes its focus on attachments to or the struggle for self-satisfaction and the search for privileges without any corresponding focus on duties. This concerns what Ortega y Gasset calls the "mass culture" that societies, including so-called elites, imbibe and embody.[41]

Second, whatever the character of individual experience, it is but part of a flow through time, an episode, however profound, that does not, by itself or even together with other episodes, define a person. Each person can rise above current circumstances, including whatever the information and communications revolution holds in store.

Third, individuals are not as comfortable with freedom as they might suppose. Freedom calls on each person to think and judge, wander at the edges and debate the strangers there, and face and live with ambiguities. Here, the danger persists that people would willingly give over the burden of freedom and the difficulties of judging to those who offer certainty—this is part of what artificial intelligence promises—and material satisfaction, again confirming Dostoevsky's warning in "The Grand Inquisitor."[42]

Finally, part of what equips people for the future is the ability to recognize patterns. This gives them a measure of control over their lives and an orientation to things, including the nonhuman environment and the universe itself. Therefore, the education of the future must enable students to deal with ambiguities that reside in the multiplicity of experiences each person encounters, including thinking environmentally.[43] This kind of education can best be assured through what are traditionally called the liberal arts but renewed to be less abstract and more transdisciplinary and transcultural, with classics from all continents, enabling learning by doing before moving to higher levels of abstraction and encouraging the study of languages and literatures as, in part, forms of discovering, coding, and signaling.

The education of the future should insist on pattern recognition as among the best forms of learning and teaching, with practice in *judging* an overarching requirement. Such skills help people become less vulnerable to the mere presence of opinion and popular taste and the news bias of the moment. Government will be spared the soft legitimacy that springs from public opinion and, where merited, enjoy a deeper support.[44]

Common Security

Leadership is needed to induce collaboration and deal with the will to power. Its absence will not only aggravate the asymmetry of power represented by new technologies but also encourage futile national comparisons. Who is ahead? Who is catching up? Who is a greater threat and to whom?

In no area is the struggle between the will to national power and the need for global leadership more difficult than in the realm of coercive power, expressed in the form of what is called the military–industrial complex, including its relationship with the law. We must also wrestle with what we worship, as instructed by Aeschylus in *Prometheus Bound*. The classic god was the all-powerful, thunder-dispensing, torture-inflicting, and law-evading Zeus; today it is national security—the bomb-dropping, would-be all-destroying, law-bypassing, sometimes law-breaking, self-justifying doctrine of the modern nation-state system. Over the years, that doctrine has gained greater and greater hold on America's consciousness as dangers supposed, exaggerated, and actual have made it appear valid. The country was born of a military conflict; the Civil War, the greatest threat to the nation's survival to date, is understood to have been concluded by military action; its most important strategic, territorial gains resulted from wars with Mexico and Spain, along with drawn-out conflicts with Native Americans; and World War II, followed by the conflicts engendered by the Cold War, are taken as further validation.

Abstract teaching, complementing lived experience, has also had its way with the general public and prospective leaders through military academic institutions and the more general body of academic culture. An example is the speech that Oliver Wendell Holmes Jr. delivered to the Harvard graduating class on Memorial Day in 1895—a speech that influenced generations and is said to have resulted in his nomination to the Supreme Court, where he served from 1902 to 1932. Holmes bemoaned the commercial culture that was supplanting war in commanding the attention of people, the cosmopolitanism of unions, socialists, societies such as that for the "prevention of cruelty to animals"; and the "whole literature of sympathy [that had] sprung into being [pointing] out in story and in verse how hard it is to be wounded in the battle of life and how terrible and how unjust it is that anyone should fail."[45]

Holmes believed that "the struggle for life is the order of the world, at which it is vain to repine," that now, "at least and perhaps as long as man dwells upon the globe, his destiny is battle, and he has to take his chances in war," and that if "our business is to fight, the book of the army is a war-song."[46] The question for Holmes was to decide what kind of world we want: that of the soldier or one of the gentleman who parasitically builds a name on the "soldier's choice of honor rather than life?" His answer goes further into faith and knowledge:

> I do not know what is true. I do not know the meaning of the universe. But in the midst of doubt, in the collapse of creeds, there is one thing I do not doubt, that no man who lives in the same world with most of us can doubt, and that is that the faith is true and adorable which leads a soldier to throw away his life in observance to a blindly accepted duty, in a cause which he little understands, in a plan of campaign of which he has little notion, under which he does not see the use.[47]

Holmes wanted to give his audience of future political leaders and soldiers a raw sense of battle where, in Philip Ziegler's portrayal, men are "made mad" from groveling fear, shrieking fear, unspeakable fear.[48] Holmes did so in a series of "ifs":

> [If you] have heard and seen shrieking fragments go tearing through your company and have known that the next . . . shot carries your fate, if you have advanced in line and have seen ahead of you the spot where you must pass, where the rifle bullets are striking, if you have ridden at night . . . where, for twenty-four hours, the soldiers were fighting on two sides . . . and, in the morning, the dead and dying lay piles in a row six deep . . . if you have had a blind fierce gallop against the enemy, with your blood up and a pace that left no time for fear . . . you know that there is such a thing as the faith I spoke of. You know your weakness and are modest, but you know that man has in him that [which] is unspeakable somewhat, which makes him capable of miracle, able to [lift] himself by the might of his own soul, unaided, able to face annihilation for blind belief.[49]

He urged his listeners to "follow the gleam"—a quest for something honorable, holy, untarnished, as he quoted from Tennyson's poem "Merlin and the Gleam."

The details here are important. Holmes focuses not so much on war but on the culture of war and warfare before and within the nation-state system. That culture offers the very opposite of what global leadership requires—the struggle for life; the terror and triumph that are part of that struggle; the unspeakable thing that comes from the might of the soul; the suspicion of sympathy, unions, socialism, and cosmopolitanism; the blind belief in and acceptance of duty; the threat of physical annihilation; the constant in the pursuit of honor, defined as commitment to the idea of the warrior, even in the face of changing creeds; and the miracle that can be wrought when one, with blood up and at a pace that allows no time to fear, gallops blindly and fiercely ahead, indeed because there is no time to reflect.

This culture of war is exactly what Simone Weil inveighed against in her examination of *The Iliad*. In the eyes of policy makers, citizens, and even those doing the actual fighting, most wars are purportedly fought to pursue some just claims, but where there is "no room for reflection," for even fear, "there is none either for justice or prudence."[50] The very values needed for global leadership are those that the culture of war, as captured by Holmes, cannot allow.

Theodore Roosevelt, a person concerned with justice but more focused on honor, thought mostly in terms of the honor of the nation and the role of the culture of war within it—a culture that, at all times, should prepare both soldiers and the nation psychologically for war. Two years after Holmes delivered his Harvard address, Theodore Roosevelt, who much admired the Harvard speech, delivered his own at the Naval College in Newport, Rhode Island. The soon-to-be president observed that consistent with that culture, "a country has to be prepared for war" as "the most effectual means to promote peace." In the nurturing of the most valuable qualities of "soldierly virtues" resides the honor and greatness of America—virtues for which, in "a nation, as in an individual, no refinement, no culture, no wealth, no material prosperity can atone."[51]

As Brooks Adams argued at the beginning of the twentieth century, "political innovation," unless it seeks to conserve much of what exists, always affects people for "whom a change in what they have been trained to respect is tantamount to sacrilege." To Adams, for liberals and conservatives alike, "[t]he temper of the mind is conservativism. It resists instinctively and not intelligently, and it is the conservatism which largely causes those violent explosions of pent-up energy which we term revolution."[52] This takes us back to Aeschylus and *Prometheus Bound,* in which the change sought and gained was to conserve. It is not easy to insist that people share a consciousness of security beyond the nation-state, beyond the narrow confines of the god of national interest, defined by soldiers (and societies) prepared to die to kill other people without reflection, without any impulse to justice or prudence, in blind obedience, trained to use weapons that would destroy life on earth or large portions of it. People have learned to worship national security and its way of being part of what gives meaning to life.

Changing that belief will be regarded as sacrilege in many quarters, including businesses, their employees, their customers, and citizens in general, and the challenge is especially great in the United States. Like dominant powers since the time of Assyria, the capacity to conquer, dominate, subjugate, and exploit other peoples has been associated with greatness—part of what Theodore Roosevelt included in his Naval College speech in reference to great races. No state has been considered great unless it subdued others.[53] The United States—following "the gleam," as admonished by Holmes—has sought to build and sustain its military presence and dominance in every domain: land, sea, air, space, and cyberspace.

It is true, as posited by Jeffrey Sachs, that exceptionalism, realism, and internationalism have taken turns, especially since World War II, as guiding principles for U.S. foreign policy.[54] However, advocates of all three have sought U.S. preeminence, with the internationalists allowing more dialogue ("soft power," with coercive power in the background) than the realists would tolerate, preferring a prompt application of military and economic power to gain objectives, and the exceptionalists, who would put the military at the forefront. In fact, in many ways, all three groups, as identified by Sachs, are exceptionalists, with different preferences concerning the timing of coercion. All hold that the capacity to coerce must be overwhelming, reinforced by technological excellence in the information and communications revolution, outer-space and deep-sea explorations, the neuroscience frontier, and so on.

The push to excel technologically, when successful, often becomes a zero-sum game. The winner takes all prestige and power, but a catch-up dynamic drives other countries, such as China, Russia, India, and the confederation called the European Union, led by Germany. South Korea and Israel as well as an increasingly confident Brazil, a reorienting Japan, and others have varying ambitions to catch up, if only in certain technology sectors. Accusations that China steals intellectual property, something that the United Kingdom and other European nations accused the United States of doing during the nineteenth century, subtly reinforce the idea of U.S. exceptionalism. They also reinforce the psychological terrain that supports the idea domestically that "others"—Jews, blacks, Hispanics, Indians, etc.—are taking something from long-suffering Americans. The accusations feed the frequent implication that nonwhites are incapable of original thinking, that they are mere memorizers and imitators, even though whites have benefited so much from ideas originating in the nonwhite world.[55]

Burnishing the exceptionalist brand also conceals the fact that in trade, for example, the efforts of other nations to catch up have also benefited the United States. During the first two decades of Beijing's experiments with the market, cheap Chinese imports eased social tensions in the United States at a time when U.S. wages stagnated. Why is there an outcry about China's cheating rather than about the United States' unwillingness to work with people of *all* countries to build a community with what Sachs calls a "shared future for mankind"?[56]

The reason, in part, is China's experiment with what it calls the "socialist market" system. That experiment, if successful, will dilute America's claim of an exceptional place in human history. It would subvert efforts to portray "American principles" as universally valid.[57] Without doubt, much of the current and likely future rivalry between Beijing and Washington will be as much economic as military, with a fight for the world's consumers, including those in China, and for control of the technologies that will shape world economic development for decades to come.[58] From the standpoint of the exceptionalists, whose views would have to change if the "will to global leadership" is to prevail, an "America First" can dominate the world; a "China First" (or any other emerging rival) cannot challenge that domination.

A final challenge here derives from the title "lone superpower" as not simply a title or a fact of status but as a value; it has become a sort of moral category, like liberty or justice, beyond question. The United States takes any action by a country or a combination of countries or regions to challenge America's right to the title as a form of impiety deserving punishment. The U.S. stance echoes that taken by the United Kingdom during the height of the British Empire, as captured by the historian A. P. Thornton: a sort of faith that the empire would *lead* the world "in the arts and civilization," bring "light to dark places," teach the "true political method," and "nourish and protect" the tradition of liberalism. As well, the United Kingdom would serve as trustee for the weak and less fortunate and teach humility to the arrogant. As such, it represented itself and its objectives as embodying "the highest aims of human society. 'It was to command and deserve a status and prestige shared by no other.'"[59]

The United States—in its claim to exceptionalism, indispensability, or superior status—follows the United Kingdom in seeking a position that can be "shared by no other," with a self-interested national security defined by coercion and domination, fully aware than this could lead to an abyss, destroying the earth and slaughtering our blood sisters and brothers.[60] The United States, as the lone superpower and representative of the liberal tradition, would be the protector of the weak—Eastern Europe and the Baltic countries against Russia, Kuwait against Iraq, Georgia against Russia, Taiwan against China, and Latin American countries against Cuba. It would contain the strong (Russia) and teach humility to the arrogant (Saddam Hussein, Muammar Gaddafi, Slobodan Milosevic) who would presume to question or disrespect the U.S. standing.[61]

No country has willingly made the adjustments required to concede the status and associated privileges of the lone superpower. To the average person, the loss of prestige becomes a matter of mental health, as Strachey related on what happened in Britain. Individual Britishers came to "feel a sense of personal loss—almost an amputation—when some colony . . . became independent."[62] This helps in understanding the pressures that a leader and government will bear and the temptations to reclaim any seeming loss of status. The lowering of the American flag, as was the case with the Union Jack, will bring a sense of humiliation, yet it is a necessary path if the United States is to pursue true global leadership. The United Kingdom used a pretended global interest to pursue its will to power, and the United States followed suit; the United Kingdom found an adjustment of sorts through the British Commonwealth of Nations led from London and later, as the commonwealth's ties became less and less substantive, by joining the European Union. The United States can find an adjustment far more substantive in actually leading a global community of common interests. The returns will justify the pain, and even long-neglected national challenges can be addressed with fewer risks to national integrity.

In 1987, Gorbachev observed that for the first time in its history, humankind has become "capable of resolving many problems that were hindering progress over centuries."[63] Given existing and newly created resources and technologies, he argued, no impediments remained to feeding a population of many billions . . . providing it with education, affording it with housing, and keeping it healthy. Further, he opined, conceding differences and potentialities among peoples, "there has taken place a prospect for ensuring befitting conditions of life for the inhabitants of the Earth."[64]

"Alas," Gorbachev complained, "many influential forces continue adhering to outdated conceptions concerning ways to ensuring national security . . . The world is in an absurd situation whereby persistent efforts are being made to convince it that the road to an abyss is the most correct one."[65]

The Prometheus (special enlightenment) of the human rights regime sought to avoid this abyss and hoped that the United States would see through the "influential forces" that continue "to adhere to the outdated conceptions" of national security.

The emerging global, societal interests are broadly articulated in the human rights regime, the emerging environmental regime encompassing sustainability goals, and the broader concerns of international law, including those areas dealing, even if imperfectly, with the transborder movement of peoples, reforms of the global financial system, the elimination of the war system, and the creation of a constitution for protecting the world's oceans, regulating outer space, and reforming the UN.

That community of societal interests is not represented by the nationalists, whose exclusivist preference has shaped the nation-state system defining the U.S.-led global order. It is not the Marxists, who have sought to build an international community based on solidarity among proletarians or industrial workers—a solidarity that, like that of the nationalists, diminishes, excludes, and sometimes extinguishes other identities. Neither is it that of co-religionists, in general, who largely focus on sameness among communicants only, or of civilizationists, who would divide the world into large cultural aggregates.

Each of these groups has one attribute that the human rights regime, guided by the Universal Declaration of Human Rights, would seek to overcome—a community imagined and constituted in terms of how one's own group of persons differs from others. Singaporeans, for example, think of themselves in terms of how they ostensibly differ from non-Singaporeans and Lutherans in terms of how they differ from non-Lutherans. The Universal Declaration of Human Rights begins by claiming that all humans share a common identity, that this common identity and our moral obligations exist before other identities, such as Japanese, proletarians, women, Muslims, poor, and Westerners.

In short, the community to which the human rights regime calls us is composed of humanity as a whole. This would-be community, so painfully carved out of the experiences of World War II and the insights of leaders who chose to represent all of humanity while drafting the Universal Declaration of Human Rights, embraces each individual and subgroup of individuals. All are part of the human family, and the declaration asks all to discover a largely unknown wider self and loyalty that, in turn, links to partial identities tied to home, village, city, nation, and other sociocultural entities.

In accepting this community and its associated identities, humanity cannot, in the words of Gorbachev, allow (as Holmes and others would have it) the "uncontrollable fury of nuclear weapons . . . [to] be held in the hands of any mere mortal ever again, for any reason," including so-called national security.[66]

Domestically and internationally, human beings have generally been guilty of failing, of an evil, in Niebuhr's words, "for evil is *always* [emphasis added] the assertion of some self-interest without regard for the whole, whether the whole be conceived as the immediate community or the total community of mankind or the total community of the world."[67] Were Washington to choose that path, it will be following "the gleam" that Oliver Wendell Holmes bequeathed to it, progressively losing legitimacy at home and abroad, and inviting further steps toward militarism. President Trump's references to fake news and his surrounding of the presidency with military personnel, with little questioning from Congress or the political class in general, follow logically from the policies of President Reagan, hurried on by the Bush–Cheney team, and from the historical uses to which the United States has put the doctrine of national security.[68]

The United States can help purge that potential, partial evil by refocusing on the global community as a whole, and Holmes could have cited a different vision from Tennyson but also from "Locksley Hall." If the United States elects to pursue true global leadership, it raises the possibility of a world where "the war-drum throbb'd no longer, and the battle flags were furl'd/In the Parliament of man, the Federation of the World."

7

A FINAL CHANCE: COMMON SECURITY

What common attributes operate across the topics of this book? How are those attributes so enmeshed in relationships among the topics that they cannot be addressed properly outside their enmeshment? What path might the United States, with other countries, take going forward to use that enmeshment to forge a common purpose, including dealing with the environment?

The feature that joins them is the concept of common security: military security (with or without disarmament), economic security, racial and social class security, cultural security, and leadership security—the type of leadership that might ensure security. The path forward revolves around this concept, and it includes merging certain ends contemplated by the U.S. Constitution and the UN Charter as well as bringing into being some modest modifications to the UN Charter that would reduce military spending and facilitate arms reduction, focus more tightly on social issues, identify funds to pursue UN responsibilities, and lead to the declaration of an environmental emergency. A failure to adopt common security will haunt the country and the world in the years to come and in many ways.

Security Defined

The generally accepted meaning of security in modern culture is a military one. Here, we will deal with security in a broader sense. As used here, security refers to the presence of economic and sociopolitical conditions, within and among societies, that enable individuals and groups to feel that their individual and collective well-being is not threatened. This security can also be defined as the relative (there is no absolute) absence of fear that one's well-being is threatened or likely to be threatened.

Defined as such, security is the overarching concern of Americans as well as human beings in general within national and among international societies. The founders of the United States had intimations of this and gave it textual expressions; the creators of the UN thought likewise, with similar literal evidence. In the U.S. Constitution, the preamble superimposes security in its purpose to "promote the general welfare." James Madison, recognizing the insufficiency of national institutions alone to ensure the general welfare, wisely moved from the review of individuals and local assemblies to national bodies. He then urged the inclusion of the "judgement of nations" in the U.S. Constitution:

> An attention to the judgement of other nations is important to every government for two reasons: one is that independently of the merits of any particular plan or measure, it is desirable . . . that it should appear to other nations as the offspring of a wise and honorable policy; the second is that in doubtful cases, particularly where the national councils may be warped by strong passion or momentary interest, the presumed or known opinion of the impartial world may be the best guide that can be followed. What has not America lost by her want of character with foreign nations; and how many errors and follies would she not have avoided if the justice and propriety of her measures had, in every instance, been previously tried by the light in which they would probably appear to the unbiased part of [hu] mankind?[1]

The UN Charter begins with the ingredients for the general welfare of national and global societies:

We the peoples of the UN determined

- to save succeeding generations from the scourge of war, which twice in our lifetime has brought untold sorrow to mankind,
- to reaffirm faith in fundamental human rights, in the dignity and worth of the human person, in the equal rights of men and women and of nations large and small,
- to establish conditions under which justice and respect for the obligations arising from treaties and other sources of international law can be maintained, and
- to promote social progress and better standards of life in larger freedom . . .

In short, security, the general welfare (national and global), can best be assured if the opinion of humankind is sought and used to help shape policy.

Initial Demonstration

Focusing first on "military" security, the choice of coercion over disarmament is enmeshed in every phase of a wider understanding of security. Thus, little if any security has been based on the broader, nonconventional definition of military security. While the military's principal occupation is fighting (that is, how most people measure it in their minds), many other aspects of the armed forces are important. For example, the armed forces are linked in civilian life to families who feel stress—the children, wives, husbands, fathers, mothers, grandparents, uncles, and aunts, among others, left behind. It has its own fully functioning communities, composed of physicians, drivers, cooks, police, religious leaders, teachers, gas stations, post offices, and theaters, with provisions for housing, childcare, health care, etc. for the 1.3 million men and women on active duty and 850,000 in the reserves.[2]

In other words, the military is largely a social institution, and most of its operations, outside of training and fighting, replicate civilian life, including socially and demographically. Class, racial, religious, and other differences can easily destroy loyalty to the "community"—often taken to mean unquestioning reliance and dependence on fellow members of the armed forces—and form the basis for security or insecurity in every branch of the armed forces, as for society.[3] Racial and ethnic minorities make up more than 40 percent of the U.S. military, up from 25 percent in 1990.[4] The issue of who serves from poor families and who serves from more affluent ones also bears on considerations of commitment, loyalty, and the sense of community.[5]

Conceptions of security also bear on economics and economic models, confronting neoliberalism with the extent to which government involvement in everything through the armed forces contradicts its insistence on limited government.[6] This pervasive involvement, of course, has to do with Washington's increasing dependence on coercive force as policy as the United States loses its moral clout as well as the fact that today's "wars"—cyberwarfare and war by non-state actors—are more diffused than traditional wars and extend to wider areas of societies.

The military is enmeshed in various areas of the economy as well, including its share of the federal budget, the pay of veterans, and the consumption of energy. The military gets a 54 percent share of the discretionary budget of the United States.[7] Among other things, this severely restricts spending on all other programs, be they education and other social programs, including those associated with diplomacy, and often link to building community and common security. It follows that common security has but limited prospect each year.

Annual funding commitments to the military mask the long-term commitments the society makes when it links security closely (sometimes seemingly exclusively) to the military. Veterans benefits offer a glimpse. The United States is still paying for surviving children from the War of 1898, the last Confederate widow died in 2008, and in 2016, it was reported that Irene Triplett was still alive and collecting a veteran's pension from the Civil War.[8] Clearly, long-term financial commitments like these affect the broader society. Support for veterans of wars in Afghanistan, Iraq, and Vietnam, added to those of Korea and two world wars, will be daunting, especially now that mental health has begun receiving its rightful attention.[9] These commitments, justly earned, at least marginalize and, in some instances, exclude new social, infrastructural, and cultural programs. No nation-state has ever augmented its security for long by piling up obligations to veterans. Similarly troubling is the intergenerational neglect entailed in increased obligations.

Although the private sector accounts for the overwhelming share of energy use in the United States, energy absorbs a significant proportion of the Pentagon budget. The Defense Department is "the largest institutional consumer of fossil fuel in the world," according to CBS News, based on a Brown University study.[10] The consumption, 70 percent of which is for moving troops and weapons and supporting the overall work of the U.S. Air Force, makes the department one of the nation's largest emitters of greenhouse gases. Damage to the environment from these emissions undermines security, yet the public debate about environmental degradation usually says little about the military.[11]

Looking more broadly at economic models and the U.S. economy leads to a similar concern for security. Mercantilism's focus on government control of the economy had its birth in concerns for the state's security. The dominant thinking has been that wealth (in the form of gold and other precious metals) was the most important guarantor of power and that this power could be used to protect and defend the state. Today the talk is less of gold and other precious metals than in terms of a favorable balance of trade and payments. Regardless, mercantilist policies and practices, ancient and modern, have sought to earn a country more than they purchase in exchanges with other countries. Exports should exceed imports.

Because this practice came to be regarded as national selfishness that limited trade and invited wars, liberalism gradually modified and largely replaced it. In particular, the neoliberal wing has argued that national and international security can best be gained through free trade. Free trade would commit countries to mutual security because its network of entanglements would bring interdependence. Domestically, people would see the benefits of free trade, and their outlook would become more international and cosmopolitan. As such, they would become less likely to relapse into national sentiments and their associated prejudices, inviting wars, wholesale displacements of people, and increasing numbers of refugees and asylum seekers.

The neoliberal reasoning, to the extent that it is valid, is grounded on three elements: a quasi-central bank to ensure adequate financing for trade and investment; a currency usable by all participants; and rules for pursuing trade and investment safely. Without the effective operation of these elements, common security and faith in it rapidly disintegrate.

Because the U.S. dollar served as a global currency, its central bank acted as the world's central bank, and U.S.-advanced rules and practices dominated the GATT after World War II and its successor, the WTO. These Washington institutions would have to act neutrally and consistently, at home and abroad, if people within the United States and the larger global system were to enjoy security as defined here. In practice, however, the GATT and WTO skewed matters in favor of U.S. business interests.[12] Internationally, the tilted agenda came under the banner of a "nationalism" that rejected 1970s proposals for a more neutral currency issued by the IMF.[13] Two related topics are especially important here: the 2019 tariffs that President Trump unilaterally imposed on China and continuing reliance on the dollar as the world's key currency.

The United States imposed the tariffs used to contain China's perceived challenge to the U.S. identity as the world's lone superpower outside the rules of the WTO and thus in violation of international trade law as well as the principle of "neutral third party" decision making in settling international disputes—something countries have fought for since the Hague Conference of 1898.[14] It also violates Madison's urging, in his considerations of security, that the United States should consult the opinion of other countries before adopting policies. Moreover, while the tariffs target China, they affect every region and, in so doing, undermine the security of workers, consumers, investors, and businesses in general. For instance, China earns fewer dollars when it sells fewer goods and services to the United States. In turn, China purchases less from Europe, Africa, and Latin America, so those regions earn fewer dollars and spend less on U.S. goods and services. For countries whose economies depend largely depend on exports—Germany and Ethiopia, for example—the effects on autoworkers, farmers, small businesses, and the poor have been significant whether one looks at education, health care, housing, or even food. As China retaliated to the tariffs, soybean, fish, and meat sales in the United States declined. Some farmers faced difficulties paying for their loans.[15]

The environment was implicated as well when Brazilian farmers and would-be farmers sought to increase their soybean sales to China after it shifted purchases away from the United States. The Brazilians joined others in setting fire to Amazon forests, sometimes called the earth's lungs because they provide over 20 percent of the planet's oxygen. This threatened the security and well-being not only of Brazil but also of the earth at large.[16] Just as important from the perspective of common security, the chagrin expressed by Europe and the Global

North about the burning has provoked reactions among some Brazilians, including Pres. Jair Bolsonaro. This raises the possibility of heightening suspicions that the Global North, the leader in fossil fuel emissions for over a century, now wants the Global South to bear most of the burden in protecting the world against climate change.[17] Thus, the tariffs have undermined extended negotiations centered on the environment, from the 1972 Stockholm Declaration in 1972 to the 1992 Rio Conference and since, to address this wound in North–South relations.

With respect to the dollar, every country is aware of its critical role in the financial security of the nation's and the world's economy. The increasing use of the dollar to further the perceived national interest of the United States has threatened the security of other countries, the international system, and private companies, including some U.S.-based multinationals.[18] For this reason, the governor of the Bank of England has called for "a new virtual currency."[19] Were that call implemented, the United States would be in a far worse position than it was in the 1970s. Among other things, it would be affected by interest rates worldwide. In particular, it would have to pay a range of interest rates on a national debt that will continue to grow to maintain enormous armed forces (with even more elaborate expressions, including cyberwarriors, killer robots, and DNA-linked weapons).[20]

Alternatively, under the current dollar-dominant world financial system, the U.S. *interest* on the debt for post-9/11 wars has been estimated at $8 trillion by 2050. At the very least, the cost to finance the debt would increase. If the dollar were to lose its status as the dominant international currency, the debt would likely increase even further absent a change in how the nation finances its wars.[21] Whether or not the dollar remains internationally dominant, U.S. society would not survive as we know it if Washington continues to maintain its large armed forces. Security, as defined here, would be but an idle dream.

Further Demonstration

A determined oligarchy has pitted racial identity against social class to ensure its self-claimed sense of security, thereby creating and ensuring insecurity for its victims. No wave of migration has escaped this "pitting against." When Lincoln said that "a house divided against itself cannot stand," he was quoting the Bible: "Every kingdom divided against itself is brought to desolation; and every city or house divided against itself shall not stand."[22] The actual or even potential desolation resulting from race and class cleavages affects employment, purchasing power, the economy, the armed forces, the organization and distribution of knowledge, the manner of presenting and receiving political and popular culture, and the physical and social environment in which people live as well as the nonhuman environment.

An even broader fault line is implicated here, one for which race and class are but two promontories within a sea of invidious discrimination, inequality,

125

and felt powerlessness. This rather extendable sea is captured by the concept of "relative deprivation," which is the actual or presumed existence of demonstrable disparities between value expectations and one's life conditions, including goods, services, and other self-defining values. In other words, there is a deeply felt contradiction, most often accompanied by moral outrage, between what one believes one is entitled to and that to which one may reasonably aspire.[23]

With the communications revolution, social discrepancies—based on religion, gender, sexual orientation, disability, indigenous status, old age, geography, language, single parenthood, U.S.-born children of foreign-born parents, and those who have fallen or harbor fears of falling in status—began to coalesce with the more pronounced and broadly recognized categories of race and class in the form of growing anxieties. For many Americans, a so-called strong economy does not allay those anxieties or the sense of relative deprivation; on the contrary, a strong economy accentuates those feelings. So too does a political culture that speaks of progress, the self-making individual, and liberty when people feel more and more imprisoned by life's condition.[24] Certainly, their sense of self-esteem is diminished.

Thus, relative deprivation constitutes the major fault line undermining the traditional view of security—simultaneously crying out for a broader idea of security, one that social and economic *rights* (not just programs) could significantly address, that a proper merging of the subject areas covered here would reveal, and that Russia exploited in the 2016 elections. It is also, in part, what former secretary of defense James Mattis warned about—"What concerns me most as a military man is not our external adversaries. It is our internal divisiveness. . . . We are dividing into hostile tribes cheering against each other, fueled by emotion and a mutual disdain that jeopardizes our future, instead of rediscovering our common ground and finding solutions."[25]

The creation of "internal divisiveness" is something oligarchies always foster. That process is the essence of masking class through a manipulation of race. However, such manipulation implicates the ruling oligarchy more openly this time, and part of its manifestation will be the unwillingness of those who see themselves as relatively deprived to listen to traditional excuses and explanations. This refusal to listen will precipitate fear among oligarchs of the end of their exalted position as leader; it will also trigger ill-considered responses that have characterized all oligarchies that fear extinction.

Political and popular culture partake of the same enmeshments as the military, the environment, and the economy—except more so in that they deal with the basic sociocultural identities of individual and national selves. Political and popular culture bear weightily on the nature, success, or failure of everything else: what we know about climate change and solutions to it, the understanding of and responses to the economy, actual or felt inclusion or exclusion in or from the "national community," the scientific and technological advantages we seek and enjoy, the type of leadership developed, and the capabilities of armed forces. In case of the last, for example, military and military-related work employs over half of our scientists and engineers, and the funds budgeted per civilian for education pale in comparison with that budgeted per person for the military.[26] There is but limited security in such a restricted deployment of talent.

Even more important here is to look at the expectations of civil society and the military after 9/11. Rosa Brooks has observed,

> [T]he average member of the military is now better paid than civilian federal workers with comparable education and experience, and members of the military and their females can also lay claim to some of America's most generous social programs. The military offers free health care to service members and their dependents, discount groceries, tax-free shopping, subsidized childcare, tuition assistance that can be transferred to spouses and children, and a host of other services.[27]

The members of this nationally revered institution learn to shape an "other-oriented" self to ensure the success of its purpose. This orientation is reinforced by social programs and the expectation of them. Civilian life, on the other hand, centers on the individual self (which can be transformed into an aggregated national self), with the emphasis on the individual and the private. Complementing all this, the consumer bypasses the producer in importance and replaces the individual in the corporate and commercial culture. The average self-making individual must accept the idea that education is a private good, increasingly out of financial reach. The consequence? Little or no security.

That average person is asked to pay for programs she or he cannot have—programs with their other-oriented or community-focused culture and associated with the military, regarded as the most effective and respected national institution.[28] Far more important is that the military's social programs symbolize an increasing separation of the armed forces from civilian life, a condition pregnant with insecurity. It results from the work of academic economists, led by Milton Friedman of the University of Chicago, the leading neoliberal of his day.[29] Arguing that the draft is contrary to liberty, they advocated introducing market forces into the army: replace conscription with a volunteer army that would be well enough compensated to meet the armed forces' recruiting needs.[30] To those like President Nixon, whose tenure is linked to the end of the draft, this course of action was intended to lessen opposition to the Vietnam War, like hiding body bags from public gaze, and thereby provide more national security. In fact, as then senator Hubert Humphrey of Minnesota suggested, the cost of all-volunteer armed forces would be prohibitive, and it would enlist those who had the fewest choices in life.[31]

The most important loss in terms of common security is a principle on which the republic was established—to promote the general welfare, every person has an obligation to serve the country and not as a paid venture but as a moral commitment, a common duty of all in the community. Money does not purchase security, as the conduct of mercenary groups during the Gulf War disclosed.[32]

Despite the costs to support the military, its domestic and global reach continue expanding.[33] The academy, the media and other corporations, corporation-financed research institutes, and Wall Street collude to shape a national political culture largely defined by the passive reception of prepackaged information.[34] That culture advances the psychological and social separation of the civilian population from the military, except as an institution to which deference is owed. It raises the growing possibility that many wars will become "background noise," continuing from one decade to another.

Multiple Insecurities or Common Security?

As these demonstrations suggest, all the issues that this book touches on are enmeshed and must be addressed together. Dealing with them separately, as the traditional definition of security would urge, has led to multiple insecurities. In other words, common security is the only answer to the apparently separate and multiple insecurities that the United States now faces.

The idea of common security is implicit in a human rights regime, one that includes the United States working closely with an international system built upon a range of global constitutional arrangements, one that could lead to Tennyson's dream of a "federation of the world." In this view, the merger of common security and human rights could join the "larger freedom" of the UN Charter with the "general welfare" of the U.S. Constitution, along with following Madison's advice concerning listening to the "judgement of nations" or, updating the phrasing, the opinion of humankind.

Providing for the General Welfare and Larger Freedom

To provide for the general welfare, domestically and internationally, common security would require resources for dealing with mounting social problems (symbolized in the growth of relative deprivation) and the environment, understood in its broadest sense but centered on climate change. Other challenges, such as ideology and the place of morality in society's development, would also have to be addressed.

Increasing the UN's enforcement authority could partially provide the needed resources with changes to its Military Staff Committee, created in 1945 to advise the Security Council on military matters.[35] That change would involve amending the UN Charter, under Article 108, to enlarge the committee from the five permanent members of the Security Council to all its members, simultaneously enlarging the Security Council from fifteen members to perhaps thirty. Decisions to apply military force or other forms of coercion should draw on the advice of a broader representation of the human community. One committee member would be the equivalent of the chair of the U.S. joint chiefs of staff.

Along with those changes should be the creation of a "Joint Committee on Disarmament," composed of members from the Security Council and the General Assembly, unless today's UN Disarmament Commission can effectively take on the tasks suggested here. Created in 1952, the commission works with the Military Staff Committee to suggest ways to implement Article 43 of the UN Charter, which calls for states to make "available to the Security Council, on its call, armed forces, assistance, facilities, including rights of passage necessary for the purpose of maintaining international peace and security." This article authorizes the council to impose on wrongdoing countries "complete or partial interruption of economic relations and of rail, sea, air, postal, telegraphic, radio, and other means of communication."[36] The Security Council also has the authority to "take action by air, sea, and land forces" to make possible the type of common military security sought by each nation-state and the world at large, with the understanding that an attack on any member state would constitute an attack on every UN member.[37] A major role of the Joint Disarmament Committee or the UN Disarmament Commission would be to establish a schedule for global disarmament, ensuring progressive reductions in national armaments as the UN increases the armed forces under its control, financed by a tax on all transnational transactions.[38]

As all UN members contribute to common military security, as is required under the charter, they will contribute to their own security under collective defense. Like an insurance policy, this will reduce the cost to individual states. Each state would be able to invest its saving in social and cultural programs to promote social progress, raise living standards, and expand freedoms. People will come to understand that far from the zero-sum game now defining their lives, the freedom of others enlarges that which they themselves actually or potentially enjoy.

Regardless of how this larger freedom is defined, common security's global collaboration (including North–South collaboration) offers opportunities for the greater material well-being of all.[39] It suggests that the Speech and Debate Clause of the U.S. Constitution as well as the First Amendment mean more than we have come to think of them.[40] Together, they are grounded in the understanding of "larger freedom"—that the knowledge and insights gained from freely shared, uncensored information and unconstrained debate should accrue not so much to individuals for the sake of the individual but to the people at large, the community, the individual writ large. Together, as an informed society, they should direct the government on the path they judge best.

Larger freedom also bears on common security in connection with the "public trust" theory of education, which relates, in turn, to a more equitable sharing of power and wealth. This theory—embraced by U.S. schools, including colleges, until the beginning of the twentieth century—holds that educational institutions, both public and private, should operate as public trusts. In other words, they should see themselves as cultural and social resources to be protected and maintained for public use and the common good. In short, these institutions, while ministering to the education and development of individuals, should do so in a way that their physical and intellectual resources serve the national (and now international) community.

With respect to the equitable sharing of wealth and power, the collective military defense would contribute to common security in three general areas (with spillover effects in others): the relations between labor and capital, the financial arrangements among nation-states, and the direction of economic approaches to societal and human development.

Regarding capital and labor, the realm of workers (producers) would be accorded a standing of importance equal to that of the realm of capital (owners). The idea that labor occupies a place at least as important as capital has been part of this country's intellectual tradition but without gaining much expression in policy. A full recognition in policy would offer a more favorable societal view of labor organizing and collective bargaining, and labor would join in the shared management of companies to ensure a greater balance of power. This shift in relations would have an effect on the capital-poor but labor-and-natural-resource-rich Global South, which seeks greater respect in its bargaining with the capital-rich Global North. Coupled with this shift could be another: that individuals and societies pursue wealth to achieve social ends rather than for its own sake, as neoliberalism has advocated for fifty years. That recognition would make it easier for the United States to accept economic, social, and cultural rights, along with the common security they offer.

Regarding how common military security would enable a better financial arrangement among nations, consider the U.S. insistence on keeping the dollar as the key global currency. The current course of action has helped the United States maintain a military presence almost everywhere on earth, but that has proven inadequate even for transnational businesses, and allies and other nations resent its sponsorship of inequality among them.[41] Meanwhile, the U.S. national debt has accumulated, rising from 30 percent of U.S. gross domestic product in 1980 to 65 percent in 1990 and 100 percent today.[42] With a common military defense, the United States could gracefully give up the dollar's role as key currency, making way for a true global currency, given appropriate reform of the IMF.[43] The opening up of ideological space for different modes of social and human development could also follow, with the result that nation-states and even "cultural areas" ("civilizations") would become less resentful of the United States and the neoliberal economic order it has led.

The newly opened ideological space could admit the following: that economic prosperity is possible outside liberal democracy; that countries such as Japan, Singapore, Taiwan, South Korea, and Vietnam—not to mention China and, to an extent, Turkey, India, and Brazil—have successfully experimented with non-liberal models of development; that Islam, Confucianism, and Hinduism have modes of organizing and patterns of insights that can add to human development; and that many Western European countries (and, to an extent, Canada) offer important approaches to national and human development. We may even be able to admit that while liberalism as an economic system has been associated with political democracy, its primary objective has never been to establish or advance democracy.[44]

Declaring an Emergency

The single most important result of committing to common military security could be the individual and collective freedom to address climate change, a challenge that requires the declaration of an emergency. The nature of what humanity produces and the socioeconomic and political organization to produce it must undergo massive change, giving capitalism a new purpose and direction.

As a country, the United States has responded to emergencies before, even without a formal declaration. It created the Manhattan Project (1939–1946) to produce atomic weapons before Germany did in World War II and the Apollo Program (1969–1972) to respond, in part, to fears of the Soviet Union's technological accomplishments, including in exploring outer space. In other words, the United States can successfully organize to pursue large-scale planning.

That said, an excellent precedent for declaring a state of emergency to address climate change would be the creation of the War Production Board (WPB) after the 1941 attack on Pearl Harbor. Established in January 1942 and lasting through the end of World War II, the WPB directed the conversion of peacetime industries to the demands of the war, reallocated scarce resources, established priorities for production and distribution, and encouraged, often through financial incentives, coordinated investments.[45] Just as Ford Motor, for example, converted its automobile factories to the wartime production of aircraft engines and military vehicles, the new emergency would require conversion from an economy based on fossil fuels to one that fully embraces alternative energy. The scientific and technical talents now consumed by the military would largely convert to civilian use.[46] The focus and staff of many research universities, research institutes, and technical labs, among others, would center more on the environment, broadly understood, including the physical infrastructure of countries and the wider social environment. As well, the curricular structure of schools at all levels would come to reflect a new narrative, with nature itself as the original curriculum.

Declaring an emergency is necessary now because of the lost opportunity since the 1992 Rio Summit and because, despite progress by some countries, there is an urgent need for the collective leadership that the Security Council could provide if the United States chose to lead the initiative. We also know of the 2015 Paris Accord and its targets for fighting global warming, which require oil and gas production to fall by 20 percent by 2030 and by about 55 percent by 2050.[47]

However, the major oil companies have invested at "least $50 billion in fossil fuel projects" since 2018 while devoting "just 1 percent of their capital investment to low-carbon energy sources."[48] Their investment patterns disclose not only a lack of support for the fight against global warming but also that we cannot trust the private sector, whose greed for profits has made societies more and more dependent on the principal sources of global warming. While urging trust in the market, the oil giants have made societies less secure under even a narrow definition of security: reflect on how drone strikes in 2019 disrupted the global oil supply.[49] Well aware of their influence at the centers of decision making, these same corporations now seek to persuade the public that the needed changes will come from major oil and gas companies. "[T]he trillions of dollars of investment," declared Royal Dutch Shell CEO Ben van Beurden, "is only going to come from companies with resources and scale."[50]

Those required costs and scale are part of the rationale for declaring an emergency to complement and, to a degree, justify the focus on common military security. The task in meeting the challenge of global warming is war of another kind, requiring worldwide sacrifice, along with a willingness to impose sanctions on countries or businesses that would subvert efforts to save the planet and provide human security. The terms of the Montreal Protocol are an excellent model, especially if their enforcement is closely coordinated with the WTO and the Group of 77.[51]

An emergency is also needed when, in the midst of the 2019 UN Climate Summit, U.S. president Donald Trump, reflecting on years of self-interested influence by oil companies and neglecting Madison's counsel on canvassing the judgment of nations, never once mentioned the environment in addressing the General Assembly.[52] That silence is especially troubling given the worldwide call by young people for action to ensure that they have a future and the chilling words of sixteen-year-old Greta Thunberg just a day before President Trump's speech:

This is all wrong. I shouldn't be up here. I should be back in school on the other side of the ocean . . . You have stolen my dreams and my childhood with your empty words. And yet I'm one of the lucky ones. People are suffering. People are dying. Entire ecosystems are collapsing. We are in the beginning of a mass extinction, and all you can talk about is money and fairy tales of eternal economic growth. How dare you![53]

How dare the nations of the world not declare an emergency!

This leads to added dividends resulting from such a declaration: the proposed emphasis on environmental matters could help foster the reform of capitalism itself. This economic system has some potential to transform the material lives of individuals and societies but not as long as it remains grounded on two false premises that allow little room for morality: that human beings are economic animals and that they are fundamentally selfish.[54] These premises have sown great havoc and insecurity for society and individuals.

The idea that anyone or anything (be it an individual, business, or nation) is an economic animal, selfishly seeking material things for personal or individual ends, serves as grounds for competition, an essential feature of capitalism. In that competition, issues of morality have no bearing (unless they further selfish ends, which would mean no morality at all).[55] However, human beings are actually social animals, and they survive only as part of a group. They have competed, often for the zest and passion it invites, but they have also created rules governing that competition—rules of inclusion, belonging, loyalty, mutual respect, and reciprocal obligation.

The pursuit of material things has always been strong, but it has been to serve the social ends and moral purposes that generate esteem, belonging, care, and the sense of fairness. One cannot purchase these attributes (unless they are fake and thus sacrifice integrity and truthfulness).[56] Even more compelling is the realization that social collaboration has produced multiple times the returns of individual efforts. Protecting the environment requires worldwide social collaboration and the belonging, care, esteem, and security that collaboration can produce. The absence of these values causes relative deprivation.

An ethic based on greed is unconcerned with what happens to the other and encourages the exploitation of every perceived opportunity to increase one's material circumstances, even if civilization, the ecosystem, and the earth suffer. In the past decade or so, through what Shoshana Zuboff has termed "surveillance capitalism," that ethic has cynically used the human thirst for social connection to reap undreamt-of profits.[57] The transformation of capitalism to recognize human beings as social could help give this economic model a moral purpose for dealing with the environment.[58] Within a common security system, one no longer linked to national insecurity, worldwide collaboration in the regulation of technology and data use might follow, and the tendency of governments to spy on their citizens could be gradually contained.

Solidarity? There Is No Plan B

This focus on common security says that despite its past, the United States still has a chance, domestically and internationally, for intellectual and moral overhaul and solidarity internally and globally. When it comes to declaring an environmental emergency, demonstrating children remind us with signs saying, "There Is No Plan B." If the United States does not embrace common security, the country will be prey to five torments that will corrode and bleed society: greatness based on military power, the inheritances of colonialism and slavery, the weakness of the law, the exposure of neoliberalism, and the loss of human dignity.

Military Greatness

If the United States continues seeking greatness based on military power, it will lose an opportunity for the moral renewal and solidarity that would come from common security. Left with its military power and largely military-related technology, it may retain, for a brief while, its standing in a very insecure world. Asserting "national interest," the United States may continue pursuing global dominance and thus continue a pattern of endless war as it misinterprets any unfavorable change in dominance as a loss. Such losses are inevitable unless existing global power relations remain unchanged—an impossibility, especially in the light of demographic and socioeconomic changes.[59] Increasingly, the military will be involved in nonmilitary activities while funding declines for other organs of government. The title "commander in chief" will become the most important attribute of the presidency in a country defined by militarism.

Indeed, the United States might even return to the century-old "Vancouver to Vladivostok" ambition that sought not so much to spread democracy as to dominate Eastern Europe and Russia, control of which many once believed would ensure global dominance.[60] China, pursuing its "One Belt One Road" initiative, appears to be looking at the same area, from a different direction, to increase its own global influence. Conflicts will ensue.[61]

Three Inheritances

The United States has two inheritances from the United Kingdom (and imperial Europe) and one from the institution of domestic slavery. Without the moral force of common security, both are likely to haunt the United States, resulting in a socially toxic mix when the three inheritances are linked.

During the nineteenth century and the early part of the twentieth century, the United Kingdom's ruling oligarchy almost perfected a psychology that portrayed it as "natural" that the highest fulfillment for India and other colonies should reside in the feeding and otherwise nurturing of Britain so that it could become "great and do great things for [hu]mankind," in the words of the Indian poet, musician, and writer Rabindranath Tagore.[62] The British believed that downtrodden colonial subjects would, through their identification with greatness, substitute the empire's great accomplishments for their own lowliness. The corporate oligarchy of that which rules the United States likewise sees it as natural that workers in general should find their fulfilment in the accumulation of wealth by a few who, along with the upper crust in the armed forces, are seen as leaders doing great things, recreating and sustaining "the greatest country in the world," while the workers who are without health care and a morally acceptable wage—faced with gentrification, reduced longevity, an increasingly gigged economy, and student debt—are expected to find satisfaction in the nation's greatness.

This is the context out of which the anger of the Tea Party was born, out of which in desperation President Trump was elected, appealing to the "forgotten American." People feel cheated. The state of being of feeling cheated (and there are racial and other factors in this feeling) is part of the context for the ongoing demand for reparation to the offspring of American slaves, who were denied the benefits of the promised forty acres and a mule to compensate for the heritage of slavery. Although not exactly the same, workers who have felt cheated (especially those whose experience of "whiteness" is understood such that they had been promised at least a marginally better status than nonwhites) are looking for a "reparation of sorts," and there will be bitter internal conflicts without it. What of Native Americans and others experiencing relative deprivation?

Linked to this push by black Americans for reparation and workers (especially some white workers for a "reparation of sorts") is the idea of the United States as heir to British global power—an inheritance that Conrad, in *Nostromo*, predicted.

> We in this country know just about enough to keep indoors when it rains. We can sit and watch. Of course, some day we shall step in. We are bound to. But there's no hurry. Time itself has got to wait on the greatest country in the whole of God's universe. We shall be giving the word for everything: industry, trade, law, journalism, art, politics, and religion, from Cape Horne clear over Smith's Sound and beyond too . . . And then we shall have the leisure to take in hand the outlying islands and the continents of the earth. We shall run the world's business

whether the world likes it or not. The world can't help it—and
neither can we, I guess.[63]

The speaker is a San Francisco financier who is backing the British owner of
a Latin American mine. He does not want either himself or the United States to be
involved in local troubles; he wants, instead, "to keep indoors" and bide his time.
In due course, everything would be at Washington's command. That time came
when the United States proclaimed the New World Order and all that it stood for
after the demise of the Soviet Union, although few fully comprehended what that
pronouncement meant. It meant, among other things, that the United States had
become the full successor to the European empires that had formerly exploited
the non-European areas of the world. As such, it would be required to help offer
reparations for the trauma of plunder.

The little recognized conjunction among the repression of workers, the
empire, and slavery contains ingredients for trouble that a commitment to
common security can deal with. Without common security, many who continue
seeing the United States in terms of a majority-white, ancestrally Northwest
European, English-speaking, and Christian nation are prepared to fight to keep
it that way.[64] For them, a new vocabulary has emerged to deal with demographic
transformations, and among its most important concepts, originating in France
and spreading throughout Europe and the United States, is the idea of "the great
replacement."[65] Thus, demonstrators during the 2017 Charlottesville riot declared
that "Jews will not replace us." The same message was subtly contained in
President Trump's 2019 speech to the UN General Assembly when he emphasized
the central value of national identity and urged countries to defend their "history,
culture, and heritage." He encouraged the "free world" nations to embrace their
"national foundations" and to never "attempt to erase them or replace them."[66]

As successor to European empires, however, the United States would be
required to offer reparations for the trauma and plunder, including the plunder
of nature, symbolized by the mine in Conrad's novel. Many people, in a number
of countries in the Global South, see what the writer Seketu Mehta terms
"immigration as reparation."[67] This means, among other things, that they see the
opening of the national doors of former imperial states to would-be migrants from
former exploited areas of the globe as partial reparation. It is a form of justice. The
internal push for reparation is being joined by and external one.

The Weakness of the Law

The downtrodden in general and minorities for at least the past seventy years
have viewed U.S. laws as a means to relieve exclusion and relative deprivation.
For the corporate oligarchy, the law has undergirded the claim that the United

States is a work in progress, moving toward a more perfect union. However, under the pressure of feared replacement, "walls within walls" restrain both visions in a pattern begun in 1846 in the case of *U.S. v. Rogers* and, most recently reaffirmed, in the 2018 case of *Trump v. Hawaii*. That pattern will likely become more menacing for the country in the years to come.[68]

In *U.S. v. Rogers*, the Supreme Court recognized plenary powers residing in the presidency to separate Native Americans, that "unfortunate race," from the rest of the United States and to treat them differently, including the unlimited power to take their lands and other resources.[69] Pres. Franklin Roosevelt used that plenary power in establishing concentration camps, officially called "relocation centers," to wall off Japanese Americans during World War II.[70] Plenary power enabled President Trump to impose a Muslim travel ban, bypass First Amendment prohibitions, and enforce the separation of Hispanic children from their parents, placing those children in detention camps.[71] The doctrine of plenary powers undermines the checks and balances designed to counterbalance centers of influence in the government. It has walled off the executive branch, concentrating unaccountable power within it to deal with racial issues. That power will have many effects, in many other areas, including what the nation asks the military to do if the United States does not embrace common security.

Neoliberalism Exposed

Unreformed capitalism, especially as expressed in neoliberalism, has its large-scale operational origins (some will say its theoretical origins as well) in the United States. Expanded to the rest of the world with the exception of a few nations, this model boasts of its unprecedented creation of wealth, revolutions in technology (including artificial intelligence, seen as initiating the next transformation of economic and social life), and a commitment to progress, economic growth, liberty, and peace. Little is said about the wars the model has incited, its production of social inequality, its refusal or inability to deal with issues of the environment, and its universal practice of externalizing costs, a practice that returns to us in many forms, including contaminated rivers and oceans, greenhouse gases, and unprecedented weather events that destroy farms, overrun military bases, and devastate communities.[72]

Nor is much said about capitalism's willingness, through the greed it nurtures, to use or countenance artificial intelligence's use of the most intimate properties of individuals everywhere to profit from the control of their consciousness.[73] Because of possible competition, U.S. corporate and political leaders express concerns about China's gaining dominance in this field and how it might use that dominance against its people, but there is no concern with what "creating and managing experiences" (a favorite artificial intelligence expression) means for human beings, including individual privacy, and just as little concern about corporate–government collusion to silence anyone who challenges the type of society that the nation's leaders are creating. Among the worst silences is the glaring absence of attention to standards of fairness and reciprocity. People's intimate properties (their thoughts and emotions, for example) can be appropriated for private use, for the accumulation of unheard-of levels of material wealth, with little or no returns to the property owners who furnish the resources for the wealth.

That type of capitalism is founded on the commitment to the idea that greatness, economic growth, progress, and civilization depend on limiting the life chances of the overwhelming majority of humans and, most fundamentally, on denying their human rights, especially economic, social, and cultural rights. This denial represents nothing less than a profound moral offense against and reproach to any spiritually alive sensibility. It is part of what will continue to haunt the United States as the world awakens to it.

Human Dignity

The modern human rights movement revolves around a central principle that emerged out of World War II: the sanctity of human dignity. Fundamental to the principle is the moral equality of every person, an equality that must be acknowledged and nurtured in certain dimensions of power and authority, usually under the broad umbrella of self-determination. Politically, the principle envisions communities in which actors—individuals or human social collectivities, such as nations—share in power and authority. The very idea of democracy assumes that sharing.

The U.S. ruling oligarchy insists that Washington's self-interest demands that it have no equals. Even within the nation's borders, equality and human dignity continue to be denied to many individuals and groups. More broadly, a person, a subnational group, or a country that cannot accept equals of necessity frowns on the idea of self-determination and must seek to limit what others do or can dream of doing. Such an oligarchy cannot be trusted to advance a community interest that, by definition, would limit perceived self-interest. To remind us of a quote in Chapter 6 from Reinhold Niebuhr, evil is "always the assertion of some self-interest without regard for the whole, whether the whole be conceived as immediate community or the total community of [hu]mankind or the total order of the world."[74]

Limiting what others may do or become is a sin; seeking to assert perceived self-interest against that of the national, international, or the earth community is a sin as well, particularly so when done deliberately under the pretense of the national or global interest. The pretense is also morally damaging to the asserters and their victims because it invites widespread hypocrisy. Thus, the

United States accuses other countries of subsidizing businesses, a practice that directly contradicts liberalism, but insists on doing the same thing for U.S. farmers and the fossil fuel industry, among others. The United States acts unilaterally, contrary to accepted legal norms, but claims to be the exemplar of a law-governed nation. It pursued mercantilism for 60 percent of its constitutional history but cannot support a few decades of that economic model for others. It views nuclear weapons as a threat to peace and opposes their possession by Iran and Iraq but refuses to support the abolition of those weapons. It accuses China of violating the rights of Muslim minorities but denies rights not only to Muslims but also to Native Americans and many others.

Every substitution of the partial interest for the community's security has beneficiaries. It may be the fossil fuel industry colluding with political leaders to thwart global attention to climate change. It may be the military–industrial complex as it resists arms limitation and disarmament. It may be the pharmaceutical and biotech industries that inveigh against models of health care for all. It may be members of a political class that gerrymander electoral constituencies. It may be the broader aggregation that undermines the noble cause of education, the surest route to social and cultural equality.

Fundamental fairness and equal respect for all require that human beings mutually enhance one another's life chances. To dominate, domestically or internationally, means limiting life chances and to diminish an individual or group. Russia has felt that diminishment since the demise of the Soviet Union, as does the U.S. South from defeat in the Civil War, as do many poor whites today; so too do the Kurds, the Palestinians, and the Kashmiri as well as many Muslims, most minorities, Native Americans, women—as do all who have been compelled, under force, to do something of which the self has disapproved. Robert Frost, in his poem "The Oven Bird," posed the question of "what to make of a diminished thing." Just as important is the question of what a diminished thing "makes" of itself and others, including those seen as the source of its diminishment.

The human rights regime would put the interest of the species first—not the interest of the citizen, the coreligionist, the rich, the poor, or any ethnic or racial grouping. It follows that the common interest, common security, should come first. Today's liberal model of economic development cannot accommodate that common interest, and nor can liberal democracy if unmodified. The political class, notwithstanding the talk of some presidential candidates about structural changes, has not comprehended that fact. Much of the rest of the world appears to have. Let us look for common security. There is no Plan B.

Epilogue

As I read the final proofs of the book, the U.S. House of Representatives voted to impeach President Donald Trump. The central charge against him was that of his "inciting violence" and insurrection against the government of the United States for the purpose of overturning the results of the November 2020 presidential election that were unfavorable to him. That insurgency, which took place on January 6, 2021, resulted in death and destruction, generated great fear among members of Congress, many of whom were humiliatingly in hiding, and occasioned images of physical assaults on the US Capitol that few citizens or people abroad ever imagined they would see.

Those who voted for the impeachment shared much of Representative Liz Cheney's charged—that there "has never been a greater betrayal by a president of the United States to his office and to his oath to the Constitution"; some thought broader developments throughout the four years of the Trump's administration, not simply what had taken place in the preceding few weeks, were responsible for the insurrection. The contention of this book, especially in chapters three, four, and six, and seven, is that the problems associated with the Trump administration have been long buried in the country's social, political, and moral culture. They will remain with us, may even destroy us, unless fundamental changes are sought and implemented.

Bibliography

A

Adams, Brooks. *The Law of Civilization and Decay.* New York: The MacMillan Company, 1896.
———. *The New Empire.* New York: MacMillan, 1902.
Albright, Madeleine. "Harvard University Commencement Address, Cambridge Massachusetts, June 5, 1997."
Alcoff, Linda M. *The Future of Whiteness.* Cambridge: Polity Press, 2016.
Aoun, Joseph E. "Boston Can Be Hub for Artificial Intelligence," in *Boston Globe,* January 7, 2019.
Appelbaum, Binyamin. *The Economists' Hour: False Prophets, Free Markets, and the Future of Society.* New York: Little, Brown and Company, 2019.
Appiah, Kwame Anthony. *The Lies That Bind: Rethinking Identity: Creed, Country, Class, Culture.* New York: Liveright Publishing, 2018.
Arendt, Hannah. *Eichmann in Jerusalem.* New York: Penguin Books, 1977.
Arkin, William A. *Top Secret: The Rise of the New American Security State.* Boston: Back Bay Books, 2012.
Auth, Janice. *To Beijing and Beyond.* Pittsburgh: University of Pittsburgh Press, 1998.

B

Bacevich, Andrew. *The New American Militarism.* New York: Oxford University Press, 2013.
Barker, Ernest. *Greek Political Theory: Plato and His Predecessors.* London: Methuen & Co. Ltd., 1964.
Basic Writings of Mo Tzu, Hsun Tzu, and Han Fei Tzu. New York: Columbia University Press, 1964.

Basso, Keith. *Wisdom Sits in Places: Landscape and Language Among Western Apache.* Albuquerque: University of New Mexico Press, 1996.

Berger, Bethany R. "'Power Over This Unfortunate Race': Race, Politics, and Indian Law in *United States v. Rogers,*" in *William and Mary Review,* vol. 45, no. 5, 2004, pp. 1957–2020.

Berry, Thomas. *The Great Work: Our Way into the Future.* New York: Bell Tower, 1999.

Bremmer, Ian. *Us vs. Them: The Future of Globalism.* New York: Portfolio Penguin, 2018.

Breyer, Stephen. *The Court and the World: American Law and the New Global Realities.* New York: Vintage, 2016.

Brooks, Rosa. *How Everything Became War and the Military Became Everything.* New York: Simon & Schuster, 2016.

C

Camus, Albert. *The Rebel: An Essay on Man in Revolt.* New York: Alfred A. Knopf Inc., 1956.

Cannadine, David. *Margaret Thatcher: A Life Legacy.* Oxford: Oxford University Press, 2017.

Carsen, Rachel. *Silent Spring.* Boston: Houghton Mifflin, 1962.

Chivers, C. J. *The Fighters: Americans in Combat in Afghanistan and Iraq.* New York: Simon & Schuster, 2018.

Chow, Daniel C. K. "Why China Established the Asian Development Bank." *Vanderbilt Journal of International Law,* vol. 49, 2016, pp. 1255–1298.

Collier, Paul. *The Future of Capitalism.* New York: Harpers Collins, 2018.

Conrad, Joseph. "The Heart of Darkness," in *A Conrad Argosy,* with an introduction by William McFee and woodcuts by Hans A. Mueller. New York: Doubleday, Doan & Company Inc., 1942, pp.

———. *Nostromo.* New York: Penguin Classics, 2007.

Coolidge, Calvin. First Annual Message to Congress, December 6, 1923.

———. Armistice Day Address, Kansas City, Missouri, November 11, 1926.

Cooper, Kent. *Barriers Down.* New York: J. J. Little and Ives Company, 1942.

Cribb, Julian. *The Coming Famine: The Global Food Crisis and What We Can Do About It.* Berkeley: University of California Press, 2010.

Curr, Robert T. "A Causal Model of Civil Strife: A Comprehensive Analysis Using New Indices," in *American Political Science Review,* vol. 62, December 1968, pp. 1104–1124.

Curr, Robert T., and Barbara Harff. *Ethnic Conflict in World Politics.* Boulder: Westview Press, 1994.

Cushman, Robert E., and Robert F. Cushman, eds. *Cases in Constitutional Law.* New York: Appleton-Century-Croft, 1968.

D

Dalton, George, ed. *Primitive, Archaic, and Modern Economies: Essays of Karl Polanyi.* Boston: Beacon Press, 1971.

Dawkins, Richard. *The Selfish Gene.* New York: Oxford University Press, 1989.

Deneen, Patrick. *Why Liberalism Failed.* New Haven: Yale University Press, 2018.

Dostoevsky, Fyodor. *The Brothers Karamazov.* New York: Farrar, Straus and Giroux, 2002.

Dred Scott v. Stanford 19 How 393 (1857).

E

Ehrlich, Paul R. *The Population Bomb.* New York: Ballentine Books, 1968.

Ellul, Jacques. *Propaganda: The Formation of Men's Attitudes.* New York: Vintage Books, 1973.

Ewan, Stuart. *Captains of Consciousness: Advertising and the Social Roots of Consumer Culture.* New York: McGraw Hill Book Company, 1976.

F

Falk, Richard. "Challenging Nuclearism: The Test Ban Treaty Assessed." *The Asian Pacific Journal*, vol. XV, July 15, 2017, pp. 1–

Faulkner, William. *Light in August.* New York: Vintage International, 1985.

Fisher, Max, and Audrey Carlsen. "How the Rise of China Is Challenging Longtime American Dominance in Asia." *New York Times,* March 16, 2018.

Frederickson, George. *Black Image in the White Mind.* New York: Harper & Row Publishers, 1971.

Freeman, James, and Vern McKinley. *Borrowed Time.* New York: Harper Business, 2018.

Friedman, Milton. *Capitalism and Freedom.* Chicago: University of Chicago Press, 1962.

Friedman, Milton, and Rose Friedman. *Free to Choose.* New York: Harcourt, 1980.

Friedman, Thomas L. "A Green New Deal Revisited!" *New York Times*, January 9, 2019.

Fromm, Erich. *The Anatomy of Human Destructiveness.* Chicago: Holt, Rinehart and Winston, 1973.

Fukuyama, Francis. *The End of History and the Last Man.* New York: Free Press, 1992.

———. *Identity: The Demand for Dignity and the Politics of Resentment.* New York: Farrar, Straus and Giroux, 2018.

G

Gibney, Frank. *The Fragile Superpower.* New York: Penguin, 1986.

Giridharadas, Anand. *Winners Take All.* New York: Alfred A. Knopf, 2018.

Goel, Vindu. "New Law in India Is a Problem for US Companies." *New York Times,* October 6, 2018.

Gorbachev, Michael. "The Reality and Guarantees of a Secure World." *Transnational Perspectives,* vol. VIII, no. 3, 1987, pp.

———. *The Search for a New Beginning: Developing a New Civilization.* San Francisco: Harper Collins, 1995.

Gore, Albert A. *The Future: Six Drivers of Social Change.* New York: Random House, 2013.

Greider, William. *Secrets of the Temple: How the Federal Reserve Runs the Country.* New York: Simon & Schuster, 1987.

———. *Who Will Tell the People: The Betrayal of American Democracy.* New York: Simon & Schuster, 1993.

Grim, John, and Mary Evelyn Tucker. *Ecology and Religion.* Washington, D.C.: Island Press, 2014.

Grozier, Michael, Samuel P. Huntington, and Joji Watanuke. *The Crisis of Democracy: Report on the Governability of Democracies to the Trilateral Commission.* New York: New York University Press, 1975.

Guinier, Lani. *The Tyranny of the Meritocracy.* Boston: Beacon Press, 2015.

Gurtov, Melvin. *The United States Against the Third World: Antinationalism and Intervention.* New York: Praeger, 1974.

H

Hall, David, and Robin de la Molte. *Dogmatic Development: Privatization and Conditionalities in Six Countries.* London: University of Greenwich, Public Services International Unit, 2004.

Hamilton, Alexander. *Final Version of the Report on the Subject of Manufactures, December 5, 1791.* Online at https://founders.archives.gov/documents/Hamilton/01-10-02-0001-0007

———. "The Reports of Alexander Hamilton," in George T. Crane and Abla Amawi (eds.), *The Theoretical Evolution of International Political Economy: A Reader.* New York: Oxford University Press, 1991, pp. 37–47.

Hansberry, Lorraine. *A Raisin in the Sun.* New York: Vintage Books, 1994.

Harrington, Brooke. *Capital without Borders: Wealth Managers and the One Percent.* Cambridge: Harvard University Press, 2016.

Hathaway, Donna A., and Scott J. Shapiro. *The Internationalists: How a Radical Plan to Outlaw War Remade the World.* New York: Simon & Schuster, 2017.

Hayek, F. A. *The Road to Serfdom: Text and Documents.* Bruce Caldwell, ed. Chicago: University of Chicago Press, 2007.

Hedges, Chris. *Death of the Liberal Class.* New York: Nation Books, 2010.

Herman, Arthur. *Freedom's Forge: How American Business Produced Victory in World War II.* New York: Random House, 2012.

Hochschild, Arlie. "Male Trouble," in *New York Review of Books,* October 11, 2018, pp. 13–15.

Holmes, Oliver Wendell Jr. "The Soldier's Faith," address delivered at Harvard University, Memorial Day, May 30, 1895.

Honey, Michael K. *To the Promised Land.* New York: W. W. Norton, 2018.

Huntington, Samuel P. "The Clash of Civilizations?" *Foreign Affairs,* vol. 72, no. 3, 1993, pp.

———. *Who Are We? The Challenge of American National Identity.* New York: Simon & Schuster, 2005.

I

Ikeda, Daisaku. "Mahayana Buddhism and the Twenty-First Century Civilization," a speech delivered at Harvard University, September 24, 1993.

Ingraham, Christopher. "The Richest 1 Percent Now Owns More of the Country's Wealth than at Any Time Its Past 50 Years." *Washington Post*, December 6, 2017.

Intergovernmental Panel on Climate Change. "Summary for Policy Makers," in *Global Warming of 1.5°C,* IPCC, 2018. Online at https://archive.ipcc.ch/pdf/special-reports/sr15_spm_final.pfd (accessed July 30, 2019).

International Legal Materials.

Irwin, Neil. "In Trade Pacts, Signs Emerge of a Strategy." *New York Times,* October 7, 2018.

J

Jansson, Bruce S. *The Reluctant Welfare State: Past, Present, and Future.* Belmont: Wadsworth/Thompson Learning, 2001.

Johnson, Chambers. *MITI and the Japanese Miracle.* Redwood: Stanford University Press, 1982.

Johnson, Dennis, and Valerie, Marians. *What Do We Do Now?* London: Melville House, 2017.

K

Kagan, Robert. *Of Paradise and Power: America and Europe in the New World.* New York: Alfred A. Knopf, 2003.

Kakutani, Michiko. *The Death of Truth.* New York: Tim Duggan Books, 2018.

Karasz, Palko, and Stanley Reed. "Saudi Oil Supply Is Put in Danger by Drone Strikes." *New York Times,* September 24, 2019.

Kennan, George E. Address in accepting the Albert Einstein Peace Prize, May 19, 1981.

Kennedy, Paul. *The Rise and Fall of the Great Powers.* New York: Vintage Books, 1987.

Kerrison, Catherine. *Jefferson's Daughters: Three Sisters, White and Black in Young America.* New York: Ballantine Books, 2018.

Kerry, John, and Julie Packard. "The Urgent Need to Save Our Oceans." *Boston Globe,* October 30, 2018.

Kissinger, Henry. *On China.* New York: Penguin, 2011.

Kohn, Hans. *Prophets and Peoples.* London: Collier-Macmillan, 1964.

Korematsu v. United States 323 U.S. 214 (1944).

Koren, Marina. "What Does Trump Mean by 'Space Force'?" *Science,* March 13, 2018.

Kramer, Andrew E. "Trump's Treaty Pullout Isn't the Work of a 'Great Mind,' Gorbachev Says." *New York Times,* October 22, 2018.

Krestedemas, Philip. *The Immigration Crucible.* New York: Columbia University Press, 2012.

Krugman, Paul. "Something Not Rotten in Denmark." *New York Times,* August 17, 2018.

Kutner, Robert. *Can Democracy Survive Global Capitalism?* New York: W. W. Norton & Company, 2018.

L

Langley, Winston. "Why Did the U.S. Withdraw from UNESCO?" *The Scandinavian Journal of Development Alternatives*, vol. VIII, 1989, pp.

———. "Teaching, Learning, and Judging," in Esther Kingston-Mann, ed., *Achieving Against the Odds: How Academics Became Teachers of Diverse Students.* Philadelphia: Temple University Press, 2001, pp. 160–179.

———. "What Have We Learned from the Wars of the Twentieth Century?" in Padraig O'Malley, Paul Atwood, and Patricia Patterson, eds., *Sticks &*

Stones: Living with Uncertain Wars. Amherst: University of Massachusetts Press, 2006, pp. 19–32.

Lash, Peter. *The Revolt of the Elites and the Betrayal of American Democracy.* New York: W. W. Norton, 1966.

Lauren, Paul G. "First Principles of Racial Equality: History and Politics and Diplomacy of Human Rights Provisions in the United Nations." *Human Rights Quarterly,* vol. 5, no. 1, Winter, 1983, pp. 1–28.

Lifton, Robert Jay. *The Climate Swerve: Reflections on Mind, Hope, and Survival.* New York: The New Press, 2017.

Lila, Mark. *The Once and Future Liberal.* New York: Harper Collins, 2017.

Lincoln, Abraham. First Annual Message to Congress, December 3, 1861.

Londono, Ernesto. "China's Long, Quiet Push into Latin America." *New York Times,* July 29, 2018.

Loth, Renee. "The Climate Can't Wait for A 'Green Deal.'" *Boston Globe,* January 10, 2019.

M

Mackinder, H. J. "The Geographical Pivot of History." *The Geographical Journal,* vol. XXIII, no. 4, April 1904, pp. 298–321.

Mahan, Alfred Thayer. *The Influence of Sea Power upon History, 1660–1783.* Boston: Little, Brown and Company, 1898.

Maritain, Jacques. *On the Use of History: Three Essays.* New York: Athenaeum, 1969.

Marshall, George. "The 'Marshal Plan' Speech at Harvard University," June 5, 1947. Annual Meeting of the Harvard Alumni Association on Commencement Day, June 5, 1947.

Marshall, T. H. *Class, Citizenship, and Social Development.* New York: Doubleday & Company Inc., 1964.

Matlock, Jack F. *Reagan and Gorbachev: How the Cold War Ended.* New York: Random House, 2005.

McDermott, John F. *Economics in Real Time.* Ann Arbor: University of Michigan Press, 2007.

McKibben, Bill. "2050: How Earth Survived." *Time* (Special Issue), September 23, 2019.

McNamara, Robert. *The Essence of Security.* New York: Harper, 1968.

Meadows, Donella H., Jorgen Randers, and Dennis L. Meadows. *Limits to Growth: Club of Rome's Project on the Predicament of Mankind.* New York: Universe Books, 1972.

Mehta, Seketu. *This Land Is Our Land: An Immigrant's Manifesto.* New York: Farrar, Straus and Giroux, 2019.

Morita, Akio. *Made in Japan.* New York: Penguin Books, 1985.

N

National Academy of Sciences. *Changing Climate.* Washington, D.C.: National Academy Press, 1983.

Negrin, Ellott. "The California Gold Rush: How USC Helped Point the Way." *Union of Concerned Scientists,* vol. XVIII, 2018.

Niebuhr, Reinhold. *The Irony of American History.* Chicago: University of Chicago Press, 1952.

———. *Moral Man and Immoral Society.* New York: Scribner, 1932.

———. *The Children of Light and the Children of Darkness.* New York: Scribner's Sons, 1960.

Norris, Bruce. *Clybourne Park.* New York: Farrar, Straus and Giroux, 2011.

Nye, Joseph. *Born to Lead: The Changing Nature of American Power.* New York: Basic Books, 1990.

O

Obradovich, Nick, et al. "Beware of Corporate 'Machine-Washing' of AI." *Boston Globe,* January 7, 2019.

Omni, Michael, and Howard Winant. *Racial Formation in the United States: From the 1960s to the 1980s.* New York: Routledge, 1994.

O'Neil, Joseph. "Real Americans." *New York Review of Books,* vol. LVI, no. 13, August 2019, pp. 14–15.

Ortega y Gasset, Jose. *History as a System.* New York: W. W. Norton, 1961.

———. *The Revolt of the Masses.* New York: W. W. Norton, 1932.

P

Painter, Neil Irwin. *The History of White People.* New York: W. W. Norton & Company, 2010.

Patterson, James T. *America's Struggle Against Poverty, 1900–1944.* Cambridge: Harvard University Press, 1995.

Payutto, P. A. *Buddhist Economics.* Bangkok: Buddhadhamma Foundation, 1998.

Pfaff, William. *The Wrath of Nations: Civilization and the Furies of Nationalism.* New York: Simon & Schuster, 1993.

Pierre-Louis, Kendra. "Oceans Warming Much Faster Than Thought, Study Finds." *New York Times,* November 1, 2018.

Piketty, Thomas. *Capital in the Twenty-First Century.* Cambridge: Harvard University Press, 2014.

Plasencia, Adolfo. *Is the Universe a Hologram?* Cambridge: MIT Press, 2017.

Plumber, Brad, and Lisa Friedman. "Climate Change and the Mid-term Elections: Five Takeaways." *New York Times,* November 8, 2018.

Polanyi, Karl. *The Great Transformation.* New York: Octagon Books, 1975.

Popper, Karl. *The Open Society and Its Enemies.* Princeton: Princeton University Press, 2013.

Priest, Dana. *The Mission.* New York: Norton & Company, 2004.

R

Reagan, Ronald. "Address to the Nation on Defense and National Security," March 23, 1983.

Redmond, S. A, et al. "A Brief Introduction to the Military Workplace Culture." *Work*, vol. 50, 2015, pp. 9–20.

Reese, Byron. *The Fourth Age.* New York: ATRIA Books, 2018.

Reich, Robert. *Saving Capitalism for the Many.* New York: Vintage Books, 2016.

Report of the Independent Commission on International Development. *North–South: A Program for Survival.* Cambridge: MIT Press, 1980.

Report of the International Commission for the Study of Communication Problems. *Many Voices One World.* Paris: UNESCO, 1980.

Report of the World Commission on Environment and Development. *Our Common Future.* Oxford: Oxford University Press, 1987.

Resplandy, L., et al., eds. "Quantification of Ocean Heat Uptake from Changes in Atmospheric O2 and CO2 Composition." *Nature,* vol. 563, 2018.

Rhodes, Richard. *Arsenals of Folly: The Making of Nuclear Weapons Race.* New York: Random House, 2007.

Rich, Nathaniel. "Losing the Earth: The Decade We Almost Stopped Climate Change." *New York Times Magazine*, August 1, 2018.

Riley, Glenda. "Frederick Jackson Turner Overlooked the Ladies." *Journal of Early Republic*, vol. 14, no. 2, 1993, pp. 216–230.

Robbins, James S. *Erasing America: Losing Our Future by Destroying Our Past.* Washington, D.C.: Regnery Publishing, 2018.

Robinson, Marilynne. *What Are We Doing Here? Essays.* New York: Farrar, Straus and Giroux, 2018.

Roosevelt, Franklin D. Message to Congress, May 16, 1933.

———. "A Rendezvous with Destiny," speech before the 1936 Democratic Convention, in Philadelphia, December 27, 1936.

Roosevelt, Theodore. Annual Message to Congress, 1904.

———. Speech at Osawatomie, Kansas, August 31, 1910.

———. *The Works of Theodore Roosevelt*, vol. XII. New York: Charles Scribner's Sons, 1926.

Rosen, Stephen P. "Military Effectiveness: Why Society Matters." *International Security*, vol. 19, no. 4, Spring, 1996, pp. 5–31.

Rosenbloom, Joseph. *Redemption*. Boston: Beacon Press, 2018.

Rothstein, Richard. *The Color of Law: The Forgotten History of How Our Government Segregated America*. London: Liveright Publishing Corporation, 2017.

Rowland, Christopher. "Pentagon Sees Outer Space as New Frontier." *Boston Globe,* August 19, 2018.

Roy, Ramashray. "Modern Economics and the Good Life: A Critique." *Alternatives*, vol. XVII, 1994, pp.

Russell, Bertrand. *Unpopular Essays*. New York: Simon & Schuster, 1950.

S

Sachs, Jeffrey D. *A New Foreign Policy: Beyond American Exceptionalism*. New York: Columbia University Press, 2018.

Sakamoto, Yoshikazu. "The Global Context of Democratization." *Alternatives*, vol. XVI, 1991, pp. 119–128.

Sakharov, Andrei D. *My Country and the World*. New York: Alfred A. Knopf, 1975.

Sandal, Michael J. *What Money Can't Buy: The Moral Limits of Markets*. New York: Farrar, Straus and Giroux, 2013.

Scott, James C. *Hidden Transcripts*. New Haven: Yale University Press, 1992.

Serwer, Andy, et al., eds. *American Enterprise: A History of Business in America*. Washington, D.C.: Smithsonian Books, 2015.

Shan, Weijian. "The Fights for China's Consumers." *New York Times*, January 8, 2019.

Shultz, George. *Turmoil and Triumph*. New York: Charles Scribner's Sons, 1993.

Smith, Adam. *The Wealth of Nations*. New York: Modern Library, 937.

———. *The Theory of Moral Sentiments*. Oxford: The Clarendon Press, 1976.

Smith, Woodruff D. *Consumption and the Meaning of Respectability*. New York: Routledge, 2002.

———. *The Public University and the Public Sphere*. New York: Palgrave MacMillan, 2011.

Sokol, Jason. *The Heavens Might Crack*. New York: Basic Books, 2018.

Solzhenitsyn, Alexander I. *The Moral Danger*. New York: Harper & Row Publishers, 1981.

Song, Bing. "Confucianism, Gapponshugi, and the Spirit of Capitalism." Paper presented at a conference on Confucianism, Boston University, April 17, 2018.

Spykman, Nicolas J. *American Strategy in World Politics.* New York: Harcourt, Brace and Company, 1942.

———. *The Geography of Peace.* New York: Harcourt, Brace and Company, 1944.

Stearns, Peter N., ed. *Peacebuilding Through Dialogue.* Fairfax: George Mason University Press, 2018.

Strachey, John. *The End of Empire.* New York: Random House, 1960.

Suzuki-Morris, Tessa. *A History of Japanese Economic Thought.* London: Routledge, 1989.

T

Tagore, Rabindranath. *Rabindranath Tagore: An Anthology.* Krishna Dutta and Andrew Robinson, eds. New York: St. Martin's Press, 1997.

Tate, Merze. *The Disarmament Illusion: The Movement for a Limitation of Arms to 1907.* New York: Macmillan, 1942.

———. *The United States and Armaments.* Cambridge: Harvard University Press, 1948.

Taubman, William. *Gorbachev: His Life and Times.* New York: W. W. Norton & Company, 2017.

Tavernese, Sabrina. "In Most States, White Deaths Outnumber Births." *Boston Globe,* June 21, 2018.

Tegmark, Max. *Life 3.0: Being Human in the Age of Artificial Intelligence.* New York: Alfred A. Knopf, 2017.

Teunissen, Jan Joost. "The International Monetary Crunch: Crisis or Scandal?" *Alternatives,* vol. XII, 1987, pp. 359–395.

Thatcher, Margaret. "Unfinished Business, New Challenges." Speech delivered to the Heritage Foundation, September 23, 1991.

The Bhagavad Gita, compiled and adopted by Yogi Ramacharaka. Chicago: The Yogi Publications Society, 1930.

Thomas, Evan. *The War Lovers.* Boston: Little, Brown and Company, 2010.

Thornton, A. P. *The Imperial Idea and Its Enemies.* New York: St. Martins, 1959.

Thunberg, Greta. "Full Transcript of Greta Thunberg's Speech at the UN Climate Action Summit, September 23, 2019." *NPR News,* September 23, 2019.

Toynbee, Arnold. *A Study of History,* abridged version by D. C. Somerville. New York: Simon & Schuster, 1993.

Tucker, Mary Evelyn. *Worldly Wonder: Religions Enter Their Ecological Phase.* Chicago: Open Court, 2003.

Tucker, Mary Evelyn, and John Grim, eds. "Religion and Ecology: Can the Climate Change?" *Daedalus,* vol. 130, no. 4, 2001.

Tyson, Neil deGrasse. *The Unspoken Alliance between Astrophysics and the Military.* New York: W. W. Norton & Company, 2018.

U

Unger, Craig. *The Fall of the House of Bush.* New York: Scribner, 2007.
United States Statutes at Large, vol. 42, part 2.
U.S. Department of the Army. *Department of the Army Fiscal Year (FY) 2019 Budget Estimates Vol. I, Operation and Maintenance, Army: Justification Estimates,* February 2018.

V

Vance, Cyrus. "Human Rights and Foreign Policy." *Georgia International Law Journal,* vol. VII, 1977, pp. 223–229.
Vitalis, Robert. *White World Order, Black Power Politics: The Birth of American International Relations.* Ithaca: Cornell University Press, 2015.
Vogel, Ezra. *Japan as Number One: Lessons for America.* New York: Harper Torchbooks, 1985.

W

Ward, Peter. *The Flooded Earth.* New York: Basic Books, 2010.
Washington, George. *George Washington Papers, Series 2, Letterbooks — 1799: Letterbook 24, April 3, 1793–March 3, 1797.* M/Mixed Material. Online at https://www.loc.gov/item/mgw2.024/
Washington, James M., ed. *A Testament of Hope: The Essential Writings and Speeches of Martin Luther King Jr.* New York: Harper Collins, 1986.
Wawro, Geoffrey. "How 'Half-Americans' Won World War I." *New York Times,* September 13, 2018.
Weil, Simone. *The Iliad or The Poem of Force.* Wallinford: Pendle Hill, 1976.
Weston, Burns H., Richard A. Falk, and Anthony A. Damato, eds. *Basic Documents in International Law and World Order.* St. Paul: West Publishing, 1990.
Williams, Appleton William. *Empire as a Way of Life.* New York: Oxford University Press, 1980.
Williams, Joan C. *White Working Class: Overcoming Class Cluelessness in America.* Boston: Harvard Business Review Press, 2017.
Wilson, William Julius. *The Declining Influence of Race.* Chicago: University of Chicago Press, 1980.
Wolferen van, Karel. *The Enigma of Japanese Power.* New York: Vintage, 1990.
Wuebbles, D. J., et al., eds. "2017: Executive Summary," in *Climate Science*

Special Report: Fourth National Climate Assessment Volume I. Washington, D.C.: US Global Change Research Program, 2017.

Z

Ziegler, Philip. *Soldiers: Fighting Men's Lives, 1901–2001.* New York: Penguin Books, 2003.

Zuboff, Shoshana. *The Age of Surveillance Capitalism: The Fight for a Human Future at the New Frontier of Power.* New York: Public Affairs, 2019.

Zucman, Gabriel. *The Hidden Wealth of Nations: The Scourge of Tax Havens.* Chicago: University of Chicago Press, 2015.

Endnotes

Introduction

1　See, for example, Frank Bruni, "What Kind of Democrat Can Best Trump?" *New York Times* (November 4, 2018), p. SR3.

Chapter 1

1　As quoted in Merze Tate, *The Disarmament Illusion: The Movement for a Limitation of Arms to 1907* (New York: Macmillan Company, 1942), p. 168. The language—from the August 27, 1898, published statement of Tsar Nicholas—embraces the aim of both conferences, although the reluctance of nations resulted in a marked de-emphasis on dealing with arms limitation in 1907. Tate's book remains a fundamental reference of early movements for arms limitation.

2　See President McKinley's second annual message to Congress, December 3, 1898.

3　Tate, *Disarmament Illusion*, p. 292.

4　Ibid.

5　Tate, *The United States and Armaments* (Cambridge: Harvard University Press, 1948), p. 15.

6　Tate, *Disarmament Illusion*, p. 306.

7　Ibid., p. 308.

8　See Theodore Roosevelt's annual message to congress for 1904; House Records HR 58A-K2; records of the U.S. House of Representatives; Record Group 233; Center for Legislative Archives; National Archives.

9　Roosevelt, annual message to Congress for 1904.

10　Ibid.

11　Ibid.

12 Tate, *Disarmament Illusion*, p. 300.

13 Ibid., pp. 344–345.

14 From time to time, philosophers and jurists would get together to discuss issues of war and peace.

15 Tate, *Disarmament Illusion*, p. 245.

16 Tate, *United States and Armaments*, p. 50.

17 See Evan Thomas, *The War Lovers* (Boston: Little, Brown and Company, 2010), pp. 57–59; see also Glenda Riley, "Frederick Jackson Turner Overlooked the Ladies," *Journal of Early Republic,* vol. 14, no. 2 (1993), pp. 216–230.

18 Roosevelt, annual message to Congress for 1904.

19 Thomas, *War Lovers,* p. 259. Roosevelt met Frederick Jackson Turner at the 1893 meeting of the American Historical Association, at which Turner presented the "frontier thesis."

20 Roosevelt, annual message to Congress for 1904.

21 Alfred Thayer Mahan, *The Influence of Sea Power upon History, 1660–1783* (Boston: Little, Brown and Company, 1898). Reading carefully, one sees how spending would increase indefinitely, as House Speaker Read had noted, to support the army and navy. It should also be observed that Roosevelt created the first plans for concurrent wars in the Caribbean/Atlantic and the Pacific.

22 Thomas, *War Lovers*, pp. 364–365

23 See Pres. Calvin Coolidge's first annual message to Congress, December 6, 1923.

24 Dona A. Hathaway and Scott J. Shapiro, *The Internationalists: How a Radical Plan to Outlaw War Remade the World* (New York: Simon & Schuster, 2017), pp. 111–112.

25 See Pres. Calvin Coolidge's Armistice Day address in Kansas City, Missouri, November 11, 1926.

26 See Norman H. Davis's (chair of the U.S. delegation) address to the General Disarmament Conference, Geneva, May 22, 1933.

27 Davis, General Disarmament Conference, Geneva. Germany's position was consistent with Part IV of the Treaty of Versailles.

28 See Franklin D. Roosevelt's message to Congress, May 16, 1933.

29 Then as now, even the definition of offensive weapons constituted a problem.

30 See the contention of Hugh Gibson, U.S. representative to the disarmament talks, in Tate, *U.S. and Armaments*, p. 95.

31 The pact was also known as the Kellogg–Briand Pact, named after U.S. Secretary of State Frank B. Kellogg and his French counterpart, Aristide Briand.

32 *United States Statutes at Large*, vol. 42, part 2, p. 2343.

33 Hathaway and Shapiro, *Internationalists*, pp. 158–182.

34 This came to be known as the Stimson Doctrine, named after Secretary of State Henry Stimson. It states that the United States would not recognize international territorial changes brought about through force.

35 See the sentiment expressed in George F. Kennan's address in accepting the Albert Einstein Peace Prize, May 19, 1981.

36 See Kennan's 1981 address. The United States also had "counter-force" and "counter-value" strategies, depending, respectively, on whether one first attacks military targets or industrial areas and cities.

37 George Shultz, *Turmoil and Triumph* (New York: Charles Scribner's Sons, 1993), p. 6.

38 Ibid., p. 6.

39 For a fairly balanced overview, see William Taubman, *Gorbachev: His Life and Times* (New York: W. W. Norton & Company, 2017).

40 Ronald Reagan, "Address to the Nation on Defense and National Security," March 23, 1983.

41 Ibid.

42 In this proposal, Gorbachev repeated some of what he had offered in a January 15 letter to Reagan but to which he had received an inadequate response.

43 See "Reykjavik Summit: The Legacy and Lessons for the Future" from the James Martin Center for Non-Proliferation Studies at the Institute of International Relations, Monterey, California, 2017.

44 A January 14, 1986, letter from Gorbachev to Reagan contained some of what was later proposed at Reykjavik in October. Using the letter for which he had been prepared instead of the unexpected, far bolder, and more comprehensive "new" proposals at Reykjavik was an important initial tactic.

45 Secretary of Defense Casper Weinberger gave Deputy Secretary Richard P. Perle the arms control portfolio and allowed him to exercise too weighty an influence on the direction of discussions despite Perle's opposition to the Gorbachev plan.

46 See Article 1 of the Treaty on the Prohibition of Nuclear Weapons at A/CONF 229/2017/8 (July 7, 2017).

47 See Richard Falk, "Challenging Nuclearism: The Test Ban Treaty Assessed," *The Asia Pacific Journal*, vol. XV (July 15, 2017), p. 1.

48 See Marina Koren, "What Does Trump Mean by 'Space Force'?" in *Science* (March 13, 2018), p. 1. See also the Treaty on Principles Governing the Activities of States in the Exploration and Use of Outer Space, Including the Moon and Other Celestial Bodies, 610 UNTS 205/18 UST 2410.

49 See Kennan's 1981 address.

50 Christopher Rowland, "Pentagon Sees Space as Next Frontier," *Boston Globe* (August 19, 2018), p. 1.

51 As quoted in Richard Rhodes, *Arsenals of Folly: The Making of the Nuclear Weapons Race* (New York: Random House, 2007), p. 223.

52 See, for example, David Cannadine, *Margaret Thatcher: A Life Legacy* (Oxford: Oxford University Press, 2017).

53 See Jack F. Matlock Jr., *Reagan and Gorbachev: How the Cold War Ended* (New York: Random House, 2005), pp. 259–264.

54 See, for example, Shultz, *Turmoil and Triumph*, p. 773.

55 Neil deGrasse Tyson, *Accessory to War: The Unspoken Alliance between Astrophysics and the Military* (New York: W. W. Norton & Company, 2018), p. 253.

56 See Rowland, "Pentagon Sees Space."

57 See, for example, Francis Fukuyama, *The End of History and the Last Man* (New York: The Free Press, 1992).

58 See Andrew Bacevich, *The New American Militarism* (New York: Oxford University Press, 2013), and Rosa Brooks, *How Everything Became War and the Military Became Everything* (New York: Simon & Schuster Paperbacks, 2016).

59 See Andrew E. Kramer, "Trump's Treaty Pullout Isn't the Work of a 'Great Mind,' Gorbachev Says," *New York Times* (October 22, 2018), p. A4, and Cass Sunstein, Geoffrey R. Stone, Michael J. Morell, Peter Swire, and Richard A. Clarke, *NSA Report: Liberty and Security in a Changing World* (Princeton: Princeton University Press, 2016).

Chapter 2

1 George Washington. *George Washington Papers, Series 2, Letterbooks — 1799: Letterbook 24, April 3, 1793–March 3, 1797.* 1793. M/Mixed Material. Online at https://www.loc.gov/item/mgw2.024/

2 See Alexander Hamilton, "Federalist No. 30."

3 Alexander Hamilton, Final Version of the Report on the Subject of Manufactures, December 5, 1791. Online at https://founders.archives.gov/documents/Hamilton/01-10-02-0001-0007

4 From "The Reports of Alexander Hamilton," in George T. Crane and Abla Amawi (eds.), *The Theoretical Evolution of International Political Economy: A Reader* (New York: Oxford University Press, 1991), pp. 37–47.

5 "Reports of Alexander Hamilton," pp. 37–47.

6 Ibid., p. 41.

7 The United States currently pursues this course of action against China.

8 "Reports of Alexander Hamilton," pp. 37–47.

9 See Friedrich Lit, "Political and Cosmopolitical Economy," in Crane and Awami, *Theoretical Evolution*, pp. 48–54.

10 See Point 3 of Wilson's Fourteen Points; see also Article 23 of the League of Nations Covenant.

11 Some felt that the United States should have forgiven the loans because they were incurred under a joint effort to defeat a common enemy.

12 For a look at weaknesses such as the absence of social protection for people, see Bruce S. Jansson, *The Reluctant Welfare State: Past, Present and Future* (Belmont, CA: Wadsworth/Thompson Learning, 2001), and James T. Patterson, *America's Struggle Against Poverty, 1900–1944* (Cambridge: Harvard University Press, 1995).

13 George Dalton (ed.), *Primitive, Archaic, and Modern Economies: Essays of Karl Polanyi* (Boston: Beacon Press, 1971), pp. 7–46.

14 Karl Polanyi, *The Great Transformation* (New York: Octagon Books, 1975), pp. 85–143.

15 Ibid.

16 See the speech by Pres. Theodore Roosevelt at Osawatomie, Kansas, August 31, 1910.

17 See the purposes and principles of the UN Charter in Burns H. Weston, Richard A. Falk, and Anthony A. Damato (eds.), *Basic Documents in International Law and World Order, 2ⁿᵈ edition* (St. Paul: West Publishing, 1990), p. 16.

18 Ibid., p. 24.

19 The United States made the dollar convertible into gold at a fixed rate of $35 per ounce. For a fair summary of post-1945 issues, see Robert Kutner, *Can Democracy Survive Global Capitalism?* (New York: W. W. Norton & Company, 2018).

20 See George Marshall, "The 'Marshall Plan' Speech at Harvard University," June 5, 1947, at the annual meeting of the Harvard Alumni Association on Commencement Day, June 5, 1947.

21 Ibid.

22 Ibid.

23 Jan Joost Teunissen, "The International Monetary Crunch: Crisis or Scandal?" *Alternatives*, vol. XII (1987), pp. 359–395.

24 Melvin Gurtov, *The United States Against the Third World: Antinationalism and Intervention* (New York: Praeger Publishers, 1974).

25 The Middle East and West Asia are synonymous terms in many respects but reflect different viewpoints.

26 Bretton Woods institutions refer to the IMF and the World Bank, both of which were created in 1944 at Bretton Woods, New Hampshire. Other institutions, linked to both, have since been created, such as the "soft loan window," the International Development Association.

27 Weston, Falk, and Damato, *Basic Documents*, pp. 550–575.

28 Ibid., p. 550.

29 This is very similar to the impact on U.S. trade partners when President Trump threatened in 2018 to withdraw from the World Trade Organization.

30 Teunissen, "The International Monetary Crunch," p. 390.

31 Reagan and Thatcher were preparing assaults on social programs within their own countries as well.

32 Winston Langley, "Why Did the U.S. Withdraw from UNESCO?" *The Scandinavian Journal of Development Alternatives*, vol. VIII (March 1989), p. 30.

33 See Report of the International Commission for the Study of Communication Problems, *Many Voices One World* (Paris: UNESCO, 1980).

34 See Herbert I. Schiller, "Strengths and Weaknesses of the New International Information Empire," in Philip Lee (ed.), *Communication for All* (New York: Orbis Books, 1985), pp. 27–32.

35 See David Hall and Robin de la Molte, *Dogmatic Development: Privatisation and Conditionalities in Six Countries* (London: Public Services International Unit, University of Greenwich, 2004).

36 Obama's tax cut, which extended his predecessor's, should be analyzed differently. His was not designed to starve the government.

37 See the speech by Margaret Thatcher to the Heritage Foundation, "Unfinished Business, New Challenges," delivered on September 23, 1991. Thatcher was perhaps the most eloquent spokesperson on privatization as public policy. President Reagan's Commission on Privatization made the recommendations indicated in 1988, but there was not enough time during his last term to implement them.

38 The United States did not go as far with privatization as the United Kingdom under Margaret Thatcher. Her government privatized water and electricity, British Airways, aerospace, petroleum, telecom, oil and gas, steel, and certain airports.

39 See Frank Gibney, *The Fragile Superpower* (New York: Penguin, 1986); Akio Morita, *Made in Japan* (New York: Penguin, 1985); Tessa Morris-Suzuki, *A History of Japanese Economic Thought* (London: Routledge, 1989); Ezra Vogel, *Japan as Number One: Lessons for America* (New York: Harper Torchbooks, 1985); Karel van Wolferen, *The Enigma of Japanese Power* (New York: Vintage, 1990); and Chambers Johnson, *MITI and the Japanese Miracle* (Redwood, CA: Stanford University Press, 1982). See also Bing Song, "Confucianism, Gapponshugi, and the Spirit of Capitalism," paper presented at Boston University, April 17, 2018, at a conference on Confucianism.

40 No one argued that Washington could spend less.

41 See Shultz, *Turmoil and Triumph*, pp. 180–181.

42 Ibid.

43 See James Fallows, "Containment of Japan," *Atlantic Monthly* (May 1989).

44 The proposed Trans-Pacific Partnership included Australia, Brunei, Canada, Chile, Japan, Malaysia, Mexico, New Zealand, Peru, Singapore, and the United States. It was signed on February 4, 2016.

45 The Trump administration has also renegotiated the North American Free Trade Agreement bilaterally, first with Mexico and then with Canada.

46 Francis Fukuyama, *The End of History and the Last Man* (New York: The Free Press, 1992).

47 Gorbachev, unlike Chinese leaders, advanced political reforms too rapidly, with no economic improvements, such as consumer goods, to show for those reforms. As well, China had been a member of the World Bank and the IMF since 1945; in 1980, the People's Republic of China took over that membership from the Republic of China (Taiwan).

48 See Madeleine Albright, "Harvard University Commencement Address, Cambridge Massachusetts, June 5, 1997." Online at http://secretary.state. gov/www/statements/970605.html

49 Ibid. Although Africa was rarely positively mentioned in U.S. policy circles, Albright included almost all regions of the globe in her speech.

50 See "Interview Secretary of State Madeleine Albright with Matt Lauer," Columbus, Ohio, February 19, 1998.

51 For a compelling treatment of the subject, see Craig Unger, *The Fall of the House of Bush* (New York: Scribner, 2007).

52 Ibid., pp. 4–12.

53 Ian Bremmer, *Us vs. Them: The Failure of Globalism* (New York: Portfolio Penguin, 2018), and Brooke Harrington, *Capital without Borders: Wealth Managers and the One Percent* (Cambridge: Harvard University Press, 2016).

54 Joan C. Williams, *White Working Class: Overcoming Class Cluelessness in America* (Boston: Harvard Business Review Press, 2017).

55 Robert C. Reich, *Saving Capitalism for the Many, Not the Few* (New York: Vintage Books, 2016).

56 Christopher Ingraham, "The Richest 1 Percent Now Owns More of the Country's Wealth than at Any Time in Its Past 50 Years," *Washington Post* (December 6, 2017).

57 There have been some challenges to the union, especially because of problems in Brazil, but the group is working to solve them.

58 See, for example, Vindu Goel, "New Law in India Is a Problem for US Companies," *New York Times* (October 6, 2018), p. 1.

59 Henry Kissinger, *On China* (New York: Penguin Press, 2011), pp. 415–428.

60 See Daniel C. K. Chow, "Why China Established the Asian Development Bank," in *Vanderbilt Journal of International Law,* vol. 49 (2021), pp.

1255–1298.

61 Kissinger, *On China*, p. 455. See also "Special Advertisement produced by Xinhua News Agency" and carried by *New York Times* (June 8, 2017), p. A9.

62 See Ernesto Londono, "China's Long, Quiet Push into Latin America," *New York Times* (July 29, 2018), p. A1; Max Fisher and Audrey Carlsen, "How the Rise of China Is Challenging Longtime American Dominance in Asia," *New York Times* (March 16, 2018), p. A1.

63 Glenn Thrush, "China's Weight Fuels Reversal by Trump on Foreign Aid," *New York Times* (May 15, 2018), p. B1.

64 See Neil Irwin, "In Trade Pacts, Signs Emerge of a Strategy," *New York Times* (October 7, 2018), p. Y15.

65 Ibid.

66 See F. A. Hayek, *The Road to Serfdom: Text and Documents,* Bruce Caldwell (ed.) (Chicago: University of Chicago Press, 2007). This work, on which so much of neoliberalism rests, could have been more fully debated. For the same reflection, see also James Freeman and Vern McKinley, *Borrowed Time* (New York: Harper Business, 2018).

Chapter 3

1 Gender differences, which are less of a focus here, speak to how societies culturally construct females and males, with the former almost invariably suffering less-than-equal treatment.

2 George Dalton (ed.), *Primitive, Archaic, and Modern Economies: Essays of Karl Polanyi* (Boston: Beacon Press, 1971), pp. 3–58.

3 T. H. Marshall, *Class, Citizenship, and Social Development* (New York: Doubleday & Company Inc., 1964).

4 Ibid., p. 78.

5 Ernest Barker, *Greek Political Theory: Plato and His Predecessors* (London: Methuen & Co. Ltd., 1964), p. 7.

6 See Alexander Hamilton, "Federalist No. 10."

7 See Article 1, Section 2, Clause 3 of the U.S. Constitution.

8 See Alexander Hamilton, "Report on Manufactures," in Crane and Awami, *The Theoretical Evolution,* pp. 37–47.

9 William Faulkner, *Light in August* (New York: Vintage International, 1985), p. 253. This is the voice of Ms. Burton, the "Yankee," as she was called.

10 This is not unlike the shadow of "invasion" by immigrants that occupied the mind of Brenton Harrison Tarrant, the 2019 mass murderer of Muslims in New Zealand.

11 See *Dred Scott v. Sanford* 19 How 393 (1857), in Robert E. Cushman and Robert F. Cushman (eds.), *Cases in Constitutional Law* (New York:

Appleton-Century-Croft, 1968), pp. 1130–1131.

12 Ibid.

13 Ibid, p. 1132.

14 Ibid.

15 Ibid., p. 1133.

16 This reference to a Massachusetts court decision points to the inaccurate belief that these separations were primarily in the South.

17 Cushman and Cushman, *Cases in Constitutional Law*, p. 1032.

18 See *United States v. Wong Kim Ark* 169 U.S 649, in Cushman and Cushman, *Cases in Constitutional Law*, p. 1139.

19 Cushman and Cushman, *Cases in Constitutional Law*, p. 1030.

20 One can imagine the complaints then when observing the views of today's opponents of citizenship for the children of Central American and Mexican immigrants.

21 See 261 U.S. 204.

22 This is what President Trump was saying when he indicated that he wanted Norwegians as immigrants, not people from Africa.

23 See, for some interesting forms of genetic thinking, Catherine Kerrison, *Jefferson's Daughters: Three Sisters, White and Black in Young America* (New York: Ballantine Books, 2018).

24 See Philip Krestsedemas, *The Immigration Crucible* (New York: Columbia University Press, 2012), p. 105. Historically, the use of facial angles, the size and orientation of the skull, and claims of beauty or the lack of it were used in the United States.

25 Nell Irvin Painter, *The History of White People* (New York: W. W. Norton & Company, 2010), p. 133.

26 Ibid., pp. 201–227.

27 Ibid., pp. 256–360.

28 Ibid. This book is filled with reservations from leaders—be they anthropologists, such as Josiah Nott (1804–1873); presidents, such as Jefferson, who feared the possibility that the United States might become a mongrel nation; legislators such as Henry Cabot Lodge, who was anxious about racial suicide; and public intellectuals such as Emerson, who was among the earliest advocates of the myth concerning Anglo-Saxon greatness, which the United States must preserve.

29 Linda Martin Alcoff, *The Future of Whiteness* (Cambridge: Polity Press, 2016), p. 9.

30 See Bruce Norris, *Clybourne Park* (New York: Farrar, Straus and Giroux, 2011).

31 See Joseph Conrad, "The Heart of Darkness," in *A Conrad Argosy*, with an introduction by William McFee and woodcuts by Hans A. Mueller (New

York: Doubleday, Doan & Company, Inc., 1942), p. 30.

32 Noel Ignatiev, *How the Irish became White* (New York: Routledge, 1995).

33 Ibid. Ignatiev covers this quite well, although power could receive a bit more emphasis.

34 See Alcoff, *The Future of Whiteness*, pp. 11–12.

35 Painter, *History of White People.*

36 Richard Rothstein, *The Color of Law: The Forgotten History of How Our Government Segregated America* (London: Liveright Publishing Corporation, 2017), pp. 60–61. This was part of a campaign to encourage people to bypass renting in favor of home ownership.

37 Ibid. See Rothstein's chapter on "racial zoning." Banks included savings and loans and credit unions.

38 Ibid., p. 156.

39 Ibid., p. 167.

40 See Geoffrey Wawro, "How 'Half-Americans' Won World War I," *New York Times* (September 13, 2018), p. A27.

41 See Paul Gordon Lauren, "First Principles of Racial Equality: History and the Politics and Diplomacy of Human Rights Provisions in the United Nations," in *Human Rights Quarterly,* vol. 5, no. 1 (Winter 1983), pp. 1–26.

42 See the preamble as well as Article 55 of the UN Charter.

43 Recall the treatment of U.S. citizens of Japanese ancestry during the war.

44 As cited in George Frederickson, *Black Image in the White Mind* (New York: Harper & Row Publishers, 1971), pp. 310–311. See also Brooks Adams, *The Law of Civilization and Decay* (New York: The MacMillan Company, 1986), and Theodore Roosevelt, *The Works of Theodore Roosevelt Vol. XIII* (New York: Charles Scribner's Sons, 1926), pp. 322–323, 331.

45 See Lauren, "First Principles," pp. 18–21.

46 See text of Senator Humphrey, July 14, 1948, at the Democratic National Convention in Philadelphia; online at http://speechoday.blogspot.com/2009/05/landmark-civil-rights-speech-by-hubert.html. See also James Taub, "The Party of Hubert Humphrey," in *The Atlantic* (April 7, 2018).

47 Robert McNamara, *The Essence of Security* (New York: Harper, 1968).

48 See Rothstein, *Color of Law,* pp. 177–179.

49 For a review of the civil rights movement and some aspects of the Great Society programs, including the effects of the efforts of some civil rights leaders to forge a collective push on behalf of *all* poor people, see Michael K. Honey, *To the Promised Land* (New York: Norton, 2018); Joseph Rosenbloom, *Redemption* (Boston: Beacon Press, 2018); Jason Sokol, *The Heavens Might Crack* (New York: Basic Books, 2018); and James M. Washington (ed.), *A Testament of Hope: The Essential Writings and Speeches of Martin Luther King Jr.* (New York: Harper Collins, 1986).

50 Robert Vitalis, *White World Order, Black Power Politics: The Birth of American International Relations* (Ithaca: Cornell University Press, 2015), pp. 126–127.

51 Ibid.

52 Ibid, p. 128.

53 Ibid, p. 110; see also Lauren, "First Principles," pp. 14–15.

54 Quoted in Lauren, "First Principles," pp. 133–134.

55 Ibid., pp. 111.

56 See Article 26.

57 It must be noted in this context that the welfare policies of the New Deal and the Great Society were programs that could be repealed. They did not confer civil or political rights, such as the rights to speak, to vote, and to trial by jury.

58 See Secretary of State Cyrus Vance's Law Day address at the University of Georgia, April 30, 1977, "Human Rights and Foreign Policy," carried in *Georgia International Law Journal,* vol. VII (1977), pp. 223–229.

59 See *International Legal Materials,* vol. XIV (1975), p. 1292.

60 The brief interval of Barack Obama and his national health-care plan did not derail neoliberalism's sway.

61 Speaker of the House Nancy Pelosi at her new conference of November 7, 2018.

62 See Christopher Ingraham, "The Richest 1 Percent Now Owns More of the Country's Wealth than at Any Time in the Past 50 Years," in *Washington Post* (December 16, 2017); see also Venkat Venkatatasubramanian, "How Much Income Inequality Is Fair: Nash Bargaining Solution and Connection to Entropy," presented at the University of Massachusetts Boston, October 10, 2018.

63 See Joseph O'Neill, "Real Americans," *New York Review of Books,* vol. LVI, no. 13 (August 15, 2019), pp. 14–15.

64 The U.S. Census Bureau classifies Arabs as white for "affirmative action" purposes.

65 Alcoff, *The Future of Whiteness*, p. 29.

66 Michael Omi and Howard Winant, *Racial Formation in the United States: From the 1960s to the 1980s* (New York: Routledge, 1994).

67 Alcoff, *The Future of Whiteness*, p. 95.

68 See Ian Bremmer, *Us vs. Them* (New York: Penguin, 2018).

69 Samuel P. Huntington, "The Clash of Civilizations?" *Foreign Affairs,* vol. 72, no. 3 (Summer 1993). His later *Who Are We? The Challenge of American National Identity* (New York: Simon & Schuster, 2005) is also relevant. Omi and Winant's *Racial Formation* deals with disproportionate distributions of resources that help fed identities.

70 Huntington, "The Clash of Civilizations?" p. 24.

71 Ibid., p. 25.

72 Ibid., p. 40. In this vein, see Joseph Nye, *Born to Lead: The Changing Nature of American Power* (New York: Basic Books, 1990).

73 *The Guardian* (October 27, 2018), p. 3. Note the need to reestablish, to put back.

74 See William Julius Wilson, *The Declining Influence of Race* (Chicago: The University of Chicago Press, 1980).

75 See Lauren, "First Principles," p. 133.

76 See reports of alleged influence of Trump's campaign and the racial attacks, *Boston Globe,* October 28, 2018. See also Ivan Krastevi, "Steve Bannon's New Best Friend," *New York Times* (August 20, 2018), p. A19, and Emma Green's "Why Charlottesville Marchers Were Obsessed with Jews," *The Atlantic* (August 15, 2017).

77 See the text of "Fair Harvard" before its 2017 changes; see also Stanley Hoffman, "Discord and Community: The North Atlantic Community as a Partial International System," *International Organization,* vol. XVII (1963), p. 523.

78 See Neil Swidey, "How the Democrats Would Be Better Off Today If Bill Clinton Had Never Been President," in *Boston Globe Magazine* (July 15, 2018), pp. 14–21.

79 See David Leonard, "We're Measuring the Economy All Wrong," *New York Times* (September 16, 2018), p. SR1.

80 See Richard A. Friedman, "The Neuroscience of Hate Speech," *New York Times* (November 1, 2018), p. A25.

81 Just as President Eisenhower was unprepared for the Global South's drive for independence movement, so too are Americana unprepared for the broad demographic changes they face.

Chapter 4

1 Hans Kohn, *Prophets and Peoples* (London: Collier-Macmillan, 1964). See also Winston Langley, "Liberation Theology and the Politics of Transformation," *Transnational Perspectives,* vol. XV (1989), pp. 23–29.

2 Passerin d'Entreves, *The Notion of the State* (Oxford: The Clarendon Press, 1967), p. 180.

3 Arnold Toynbee, *A Study of History*, abridged version by D. C. Somerville, vol. I (London: Oxford University Press, 1947), p. 299.

4 William Pfaff, *The Wrath of Nations: Civilization and Furies of Nationalism* (New York: Simon & Schuster, 1993), p. 161.

5 Andy Serwer, David Allison, Peter Liebhold, Nancy Davis, and Kathleen G. Franz (eds.), *American Enterprise: A History of Business in America*

(Washington, D.C.: Smithsonian Books, 2015), p. 55.

6   Seeing who is represented at the bottom of social structures provides a certain type of knowledge: bus drivers, nurse's aides, delivery people, gardeners, hotel maids, childcare workers, nannies, domestic workers, construction workers, dishwashers, short-order cooks, doormen, luggage handlers, prison guards, poultry workers, fruit pickers, farmworkers, cafeteria workers, shoe shiners, and traffic cops, among others. See Alcoff, *The Future of Whiteness*, p. 27.

7   Pfaff, *Wrath of Nations*, p. 176.

8   See William McKinley's speech to Congress, December 5, 1898.

9   Pfaff, *Wrath of Nations*, p. 179.

10   Ibid., p. 165.

11   See Reinhold Niebuhr, *The Irony of American History* (Chicago: University of Chicago Press, 1952), pp. 24–25.

12   Pfaff, *Wrath of Nations,* p. 185. See also Niebuhr, *Irony of American History*, p. 24.

13   Yoshikazu Sakamoto, "The Global Context of Democratization," *Alternatives,* vol. XVI (Spring 1991), pp. 119–128.

14   There was always concern about the social inequalities linked to capitalism, especially in the face of the equality boasted by communism.

15   Ramashray Roy, "Modern Economics and the Good Life: A Critique," *Alternatives,* vol. XVII (Summer 1992), p. 374.

16   Adam Smith, *The Wealth of Nations* (New York: Modern Library, 1937); *The Theory of Moral Sentiments* (Oxford: The Clarendon Press, 1976), reprinted by Liberty Fund Inc., Indianapolis, IN, 1979. In the latter book, Smith's view of human nature is far less selfish, more communally oriented. Also observe that the root meaning of economics does not separate the social from the economic.

17   Is today's competition among Apple, Google, Facebook, and Twitter to engage the young, including children, any different?

18   See the proposed NIEO in Chapters 2 and 3, *North-South: A Program for Survival, Report of the Independent Commission on International Development Issues* (Cambridge, MA: MIT Press, 1980), and Janice Auth, *To Beijing and Beyond* (Pittsburgh: University of Pittsburgh Press, 1998). The conferences took place in Mexico City in 1975, Copenhagen in 1980, Nairobi in 1885, and Beijing in 1995.

19   See Jose Ortega y Gasset, *History as a System* (New York: W. W. Norton, 1961), pp. 150–151.

20   Japan and South Korea have moved into this way of thinking. To an extent, China appears to be moving in this direction as well. Israel and Germany have cultures that complement it.

21 Marilynne Robinson, "The Sacred Human," in *What Are We Doing Here? Essays* (New York: Farrar, Straus and Giroux, 2018), pp. 51–68. This view is rarely stated explicitly except by critical thinkers such as Robinson.

22 See Kent Cooper, *Barriers Down* (New York: J. J. Little and Ives Company, 1942).

23 This is unlike the situation when the Global South, in the 1970s, called for a new information and communication order.

24 Cooper, *Barriers Down*, pp. 18–19.

25 Stuart Ewen, *Captains of Consciousness: Advertising and the Social Roots of Consumer Culture* (New York: McGraw Hill Book Company, 1976).

26 Woodruff D. Smith, *Consumption and the Meaning of Respectability* (New York: Routledge, 2002).

27 Ewen, *Captains of Consciousness*, p. 85.

28 Ibid., p. 90.

29 Ibid., p. 91.

30 For an academic view of the concept of embeddedness, see Wayne Baker and Robert Faulkner, "Social Capital, Double Embeddedness, and Mechanisms of Stability and Change," *American Behavioral Scientist,* vol. 52 (July 2009), pp. 531–555.

31 See Jeremy Stahl, "Incompetence or Coverup," *Future Tense*, October 27, 2017.

32 See Woodruff D. Smith, *The Public University and the Public Sphere* (New York: Palgrave MacMillan, 2011); Margaret O'Mara, "The End of Privacy Began in the 1960s," *New York Times* (December 6, 2018), p. A31; and David Lleonhardt, "The Monopolization of America," *New York Times* (November 26, 2018), p. A23.

33 See Richard L. Trumka, "Does 'American Enterprise' Exist in the Global Era?" in Serwer, *American Enterprise*, pp. 200–201. President Trump has seen an opening here, but he has exploited it wrongly.

34 See, for example, *The Living Thoughts of Thomas Jefferson Presented by John Dewey* (New York: Premier Books, 1957), pp. 137–139.

35 See, for example, Craig Unger, *The Fall of the House of Bush* (New York: Scribner, 2007).

36 See, for example, Reinhold Niebuhr, *Moral Man and Immoral Society* (New York: Scribner, 1932); *The Children of Light and the Children of Darkness* (New York: Scribner's Sons, 1960); and *The Irony of American History* (Chicago: University of Chicago, 2008; originally published in 1952).

37 In the United States, the term *patriotism* is more commonly used than *nationalism*.

38 See Niebuhr, *Moral Man*, pp. 88–107.

39 See Niebuhr, *Irony*, p. 7.

40 Michel Grozier, Samuel P. Huntington, and Joji Watanuke, *The Crisis of Democracy: Report on the Governability of Democracies to the Trilateral Commission* (New York: New York University Press, 1975). Private citizens from Western Europe, Japan, and North America formed the Trilateral Commission in 1973 to promote cooperation on common problems affecting the three regions.

41 Ibid., p. 76.

42 Alexander I. Solzhenitsyn, *The Moral Danger* (New York: Harper & Row Publishers, 1981), pp. 60–66.

43 Andrei D. Sakharov, *My Country and the World* (New York: Alfred A. Knopf, 1975), pp. 51–53.

44 See Article 13 of the Universal Declaration of Human Rights.

45 Read Niebuhr's *Children of Light*, Section 5, with *The Irony of American History*.

46 Michael J. Sandel, *What Money Can't Buy: The Moral Limits of Markets* (New York: Farrar, Straus and Giroux, 2013).

47 See Stephen Breyer, *The Court and the World: American Law and the New Global Realities* (New York: Vintage, 2016).

48 In addition to Breyer, *Court and the World*, see Adam Liptak, "Justice Breyer Sees Value in a Global View of Law," *New York Times* (September 12, 2018), p. A20.

49 See, for example, Robinson, *What Are We Doing Here? Essays*; Chris Hedges, *Death of the Liberal Class* (New York: Nation Books, 2010); Peter Lasch, *The Revolt of the Elites and the Betrayal of American Democracy* (New York: W. W. Norton, 1996); Patrick Deneen, *Why Liberalism Failed* (New Haven: Yale University Press, 2018); Mark Lilla, *The Once and Future Liberal* (New York: Harper Collins, 2017); Robert Kuttner, *Can Democracy Survive Global Capitalism?* (New York: W. W. Norton, 2018); Dennis Johnson and Valerie Marians, *What Do We Do Now?* (London: Melville House, 2017); Francis Fukuyama, *Identity* (New York: Farrar, Straus and Giroux, 2018); and Lani Guinier, *The Tyranny of the Meritocracy* (Boston: Beacon Press, 2015).

50 See John F. McDermott, *Economics in Real Time* (Ann Arbor: The University of Michigan Press, 2007); Thomas Piketty, *Capital in the Twenty-First Century* (Cambridge: Harvard University Press, 2014); Anand Giridharadas, *Winners Take All* (New York: Alfred A. Knopf, 2018); and Robert Reich, *Supercapitalism* (New York: Alfred A. Knopf, 2007).

51 Bertrand Russell, *Unpopular Essays* (New York: Simon & Schuster, 1950), p. 16.

52 A still-valuable classic is Jacques Ellul, *Propaganda: The Formation of Men's Attitudes* (New York: Vintage Books, 1973). A viewer of "The Art of Influence: Propaganda Postcards from the Era of World Wars" at the Boston

Museum of Fine Arts (December 18, 2018–January 21, 2019) cannot but affirm Ellul's insights.

53 Karl Popper, *The Open Society and Its Enemies with a New Introduction by Alan Ryan and an Essay by E. H. Gombrich* (Princeton: Princeton University Press, 2013).

54 See Albert Camus, *The Rebel: An Essay on Man in Revolt* (New York: Alfred A. Knopf Inc., 1956).

55 V. S. Naipaul, "Our Universal Civilization," *City Journal* (Summer, 1991).

56 Karl Polanyi, *The Great Transformation: The Political and Economic Origins of Our Time* (Boston: Beacon Press, 1957).

57 See Niebuhr, *Children.*

58 Jacques Maritain, *On the Use of Philosophy: Three Essays* New York: Athenaeum, 1969), p. 11.

59 James C. Scott, *Hidden Transcripts* (New Haven: Yale University Press, 1992).

60 Hannah Arendt, *Eichmann in Jerusalem* (New York: Penguin Books, 1977).

61 Lorraine Hansberry, *A Raisin in the Sun* (New York: Vintage Books, 1994).

62 This inbred family of ideas has succeeded in socializing risks and failure while privatizing wealth and success on the promise of assured success through something called the "free market." Also, it has successfully resisted possible relief from this unfair system; thirty years of delay in dealing with climate change is but one example.

Chapter 5

1 See Rachel Carsen, *Silent Spring* (Boston: Houghton Mifflin, 1962); Paul R. Ehrlich, *The Population Bomb* (New York: Ballentine Books, 1968); and Donella H. Meadows, Dennis L. Meadows, Jorgen Randers, and William W. Beherns III, *The Limits to Growth: Club of Rome's Project on the Predicament of Mankind* (New York: Universe Books, 1972).

2 See the text of the Convention on International Trade in Endangered Species of Wild Fauna and Flora in *International Legal Materials*, vol. XII (1973), p. 1085.

3 See the text of the declaration in *International Legal Materials*, vol. XI (1972), p. 1416.

4 See Principles 22 and 24 of the declaration, *International Legal Materials.*

5 Ibid.

6 See Article 30 of the charter in *International Legal Materials,* vol. XIV (1975), p. 251.

7 See "The Challenge of Climate Change" in Adolfo Plasencia, *Is the Universe a Hologram? Scientists Answer the Most Provocative Questions* (Cambridge:

MIT Press, 2017), pp. 55–64.

8   See texts of the World Charter for Nature in *International Legal Materials*, vol.
    XXII (1983), p. 455; Vienna Convention in *International Legal Materials*, vol.
    XXVI (1987), p. 1529; Montreal Protocol in *International Legal Materials*,
    vol. XXVI (1987), p. 1550; and World Commission on Environment and
    Development, *Our Common Future* (Oxford: Oxford University Press, 1987).

9   See National Academy of Sciences, *Changing Climate* (Washington, D.C.:
    National Academy Press, 1983). For those interested in the energy policy
    debate, see "S.2667 — 100th Congress, National Energy Act of 1988" (www.
    gov/Track.us), 1988. It was never enacted.

10 See the preface to NAS, *Changing Climate*, p. xiii.

11 Ibid., p. 1.

12 Ibid.

13 Ibid.

14 Ibid.

15 See the preamble of the World Charter for Nature.

16 See the Vienna Convention.

17 See the Montreal Protocol.

18 See Article 10 of the Montreal Protocol. While countries other than those
    of the Global South obtained technical assistance, those associated with the
    label were the overwhelming beneficiaries. See also *North–South: A Program
    for Survival, The Report of the Independent Commission on International
    Development Issues under the Chairmanship of Willy Brandt* (Cambridge:
    MIT Press, 1980).

19 See G. Victor Buxton, "Covenant with the Future," in *Our Planet,* vol. IX,
    no. 7 (1987), p. 7.

20 Buxton's "Covenant" offers a compelling presentation of this.

21 For proposals on financing, see WCED, *Our Common Future*, pp. 340–342.

22 Ibid., p. 325

23 See Nathaniel Rich, "Losing the Earth: The Decade We Almost Stopped
    Climate Change," *New York Times Magazine* (August 1, 2018). The issue was
    devoted to a comprehensive review of U.S. conduct from 1979 to 1989. The
    Reagan administration claimed that the evidence for global warming was
    inconclusive.

24 See "S.2667 — 100th Congress: National Energy Policy Act of 1988" (www.
    gov/Track.us).

25 See the National Energy Policy Act of 1988.

26 The Group of 7 is an informal bloc of industrialized countries: Canada,
    France, Germany, Italy, Japan, the United Kingdom, and the United States.

27 See GA/Res/44/207 (December 22, 1989).

28 See Point 10 of the resolution.

29 See the Rio Declaration on Environment and Development, *International Legal Materials*, vol. XXI (1992), p. 874.

30 See the Convention on Biologic Diversity, *International Legal Materials*, vol. XXXI (1992), p. 818.

31 Ibid., Article 1.

32 Six greenhouse gases are identified—carbon dioxide, methane, nitrous oxide, hydrofluorocarbons, perfluorocarbons, and hexa-fluorocarbons.

33 See Christiana Figueres, "The Power of Policy: Reinforcing the Paris Trajectory," *Global Policy*, vol. VII (September 2016), p. 1.

34 See the narrative by Rich, *Losing the Earth*.

35 See George H. W. Bush, "News Conference in Rio de Janeiro, June 13, 1992."

36 See Klaus Topper's editorial in *Our Planet*, vol. X (1999), p. 3. The references to damage that was done or being done were current when written about two decades ago. See also Julian Cribb, *The Coming Famine: The Global Food Crisis and What We Can Do About It* (Berkeley, CA: University of California Press, 2010); Peter Ward, *The Flooded Earth* (New York: Basic Books, 2010); and Al Gore, *The Future: Six Drivers of Social Change* (New York: Random House, 2013).

37 See Figueres, "The Power of Policy," p. 449.

38 The Millennium Development Goals include the eradication of extreme poverty and hunger; achieving universal primary education; realizing gender equality and empowerment for women; reducing child mortality; improving maternal health; combatting AIDS, malaria, and other diseases; ensuring environmental sustainability; and fighting poverty and climate change.

39 The alliance is made up of California, Colorado, Connecticut, Delaware, Hawaii, Maryland, Massachusetts, Minnesota, New Jersey, New York, North Carolina, Oregon, Vermont, Virginia, Washington, and Puerto Rico.

40 See Brad Plumber and Lisa Friedman, "Climate Change and the Mid-term Elections: Five Takeaways," *New York Times* (November 8, 2018), p. F11.

41 Ibid. See also *Ecological Civilization: Proceedings of the International Conference on Ecological Civilization and Environmental Reporting*, sponsored by the Communications University of China and Yale School of Forestry and the Environment, held at the Yale Center, Beijing, June 16, 2015, Part 42.

42 Brad Plumber, "Clean Energy Is Surging, Just Not Fast Enough to Fix Global Warming," *New York Times* (November 13, 2018), p. A7.

43 Elliott Negrin, "The California Green Rush: How USC Helped Point the Way," in *Union of Concerned Scientists,* vol. XVIII (Fall 2018), pp. 8–11, 20.

44 Intergovernmental Panel on Climate Change, "Summary for Policy Makers," in *Global Warming of 1.5°C* (IPCC, 2018). Online at https://archive.ipcc.ch/pdf/special-reports/sr15/sr15_spm_final.pdf, accessed July 30, 2019.

45 D. J. Wuebbles, D. W. Fahey, K. A. Hibbard, B. DeAngelo, S. Doherty, K. Hayhoe, R. Horton, J. P. Kossin, P. C. Taylor, A. M. Waple, and C. P. Weaver (eds.), "2017: Executive Summary," in *Climate Science Special Report: Fourth National Climate Assessment, Volume I* (Washington, D.C.: U.S. Global Change Research Program, 2017), pp. 12–34. Online at https://science2017.globalchange.gov/chapter/executive-summary, accessed July 30, 2019.

46 See Topper's editorial in *Our Planet*, p. 3. His references to damage were current when written about two decades ago. See also Julian Cribb, *The Coming Famine: The Global Food Crisis and What We Can Do About It* (Berkeley, CA: University of California Press, 2010); Peter Ward, *The Flooded Earth* (New York: Basic Books, 2010); and Al Gore, *The Future: Six Drivers of Social Change* (New York: Random House, 2013).

47 Kendra Pierre-Louis, "Oceans Warming Much Faster Than Thought, Study Finds," *New York Times* (November 1, 2018), p. A10; John Kerry and Julie Packard, "The Urgent Need to Save Our Oceans," *Boston Globe* (October 30, 2018), p. A8; and L. Resplandy, R. F. Keeling, Y. Eddebbar, M. K. Brooks, R. Wang, L. Bopp, M. C. Long, J. P. Dunne, W. Koeve, and A. Oschlies, "Quantification of Ocean Heat Uptake from Changes in Atmospheric O_2 and CO_2 Composition," *Nature,* vol. 563 (2018), pp. 105–108.

48 Some people have thought that human existence is absurd, mysterious, or, to take a word from postmodernism, meaningless, but examining this kind of thinking reveals that the claimed absurd, the mysterious, and the meaningless imply, in their own way, the very opposite of what they espouse.

49 Thomas Berry, *Evening Thoughts* (San Francisco: Sierra Club Books, 2006), pp. 17–20.

50 For example, see the letter from Chief Seattle to President Pierce in 1852. *Genesis* is seen as authorizing an insensitive manipulation of nature for human benefit, but Chief Seattle does not share this view. See also Munjed M. Murad, "Islamic Philosophy and the Environment," at Religion, Ecology, and Our Planetary Future, a conference held at Harvard Divinity School on October 14–16, 2016.

51 Charles Hirschfeld (ed.), *Classics of Western Thought: The Modern World* (New York: Harcourt, Brace & World, 1968), p. 2.

52 P. A. Payutto, *Buddhist Economics* (Bangkok: Buddhadhamma Foundation, 1998).

53 WCED, *Our Common Future*, p. 5.

54 See Laurel Kearns, "Conspiring Together," a paper presented at Religion, Ecology, and Our Planetary Future, a conference held at Harvard Divinity School on October 14–16, 2016.

55 See Hirschfeld, *Classics of Western Thought*.

56 Ibid. This is also part of the thinking of Thomas Berry, *The Great Work: Our Way into the Future* (New York: Bell Tower, 1999); Robert Jay Lifton, *The Climate Swerve: Reflections on Mind, Hope, and Survival* (New York: The New Press, 2017); and Keith Basso, *Wisdom Sits in Places: Landscape and Language Among the Western Apache* (Albuquerque: University of New Mexico Press, 1996).

57 For example, the poor, to survive, must often resort to practices destructive of sustainability, such as burning coal.

Chapter 6

1   The text of NSC-68 (April 14, 1950) called for the containment of the Soviet Union.

2   Erich Fromm, *The Anatomy of Human Destructiveness* (Chicago: Holt, Rinehart and Winston, 1973), p. 235.

3   Robert Kagan, *Of Paradise and Power: America and Europe in the New World Order* (New York: Alfred A. Knopf, 2003), pp. 85–87.

4   Paul Kennedy, "The American Prospect," *New York Review of Books,* vol. 4 (1993), p. 42.

5   Ibid.

6   Christopher Rowland, "Pentagon See Space as Next Frontier," *Boston Globe,* August 19, 2018, p. 1.

7   In this context, gender includes the problems of white males who, faced with declining power and influence, are unable to adjust socially or psychologically. The political consequences are becoming evident. See, for example, Arlie Hochschild, "Male Trouble," *New York Review of Books* (October 11, 2018), pp. 13–15.

8   See "America at War," *Smithsonian*, vol. 49 (January–February 2019), p. 29. This article estimates that the United States has been at war in 93.5 percent of the calendar years between 1775 and 2018.

9   Dana Priest, *The Mission* (New York: Norton & Company, 2004), p. 27.

10 Kagan, *Of Paradise and Power*, p. 76.

11 Price Waterhouse Cooper, "Project Blue." Online at www.pwc.com/gx/en/industries/financial-services/projectblue/about-project-blue.html, accessed August 1, 2019.

12 See Ana Swanson, "Six Maps That Will Make You Rethink the World," *Washington Post,* April 29, 2016. Online at www.washingtonpost.com/news/wonk/wp/2016/04/29/six-maps-that-will-make-you-rethink-the-world/?utm_term=.feff33bc44bc (subscription required), accessed August 1, 2019.

13 Migration from Syria into Europe or from Honduras and Guatemala into the United States is but a recent example of transborder migration caused by

climate change.

14 Francis Fukuyama, *Identity: The Demand for Dignity and the Politics of Resentment* (Farrar, Straus and Giroux, 2018); Kwame Anthony Appiah, *The Lies That Bind: Rethinking Identity: Creed, Country, Class, Culture* (New York: Liveright Publishing, 2018).

15 In general, children can adjust more easily than parents can.

16 See Article 2 of the Universal Declaration of Human Rights.

17 Because of the timing of its political ascendency, the West has strong claims to being the most influential at the explicit or theoretical level, with the works of Hobbes, Locke, Rousseau, and Hume, among others, dominating. Works such as *Basic Writings of Mo Tzu, Hsun Tzu, and Han Fei Tzu*, translated by Burton Watson (New York: Columbia University Press, 1964), reveal equally impressive explicit approaches. Muslim societies can point to the Koran as requiring it, Confucianism has always championed it, and traditional African and other societies made it central to their reason for being.

18 Europe's embrace of these rights was less extensive than in the Marxist system led by the Soviet Union.

19 Renee Loth, "The Climate Can't Wait for A 'Green New Deal,'" *Boston Globe* (January 10, 2019), p. A10; Thomas L. Friedman, "A Green New Deal Revisited!" *New York Times* (January 9, 2019), p. A23.

20 Polanyi, *The Great Transformation*, pp. 3–4, 73, 131.

21 Piketty, *Capital in the Twenty-First Century.*

22 Brooke Harrington, *Capital Without Borders: Wealth Managers and the One Percent* (Cambridge: Harvard University Press, 2016); see also Gordon S. Wood, *Friends Divided: John Adams and Thomas Jefferson* (New York: Penguin, 2018), and Theodore Roosevelt's "The New Nationalism" speech on August 31, 1910, in Osawatomie, Kansas.

23 Sabrina Tavernise, "In Most States, White Deaths Outnumber Births," *Boston Globe* (June 21, 2018), p. A2.

24 Paul Krugman, "Something Not Rotten in Denmark," *New York Times* (August 17, 2018), p. A25.

25 See an interesting article on this issue by Bret Stevens, "What Have the Elites Ever Done for Fox?" in the *New York Times* (January 5, 2019), p. A19.

26 See Lincoln's first annual message to Congress, December 3, 1861; see also Roosevelt, "The New Nationalism."

27 See Piketty, *Capital in the Twenty-First Century;* see also a citation in the *Boston Globe*, "Study Finds Corporate Policies Help Transfer Wealth to the Richest" (January 2, 2019), p. B6.

28 See "A Rendezvous with Destiny," FDR's speech before the 1936 Democratic National Convention in Philadelphia, December 27, 1936.

29 Ibid.

30 Jeffrey D. Sachs, *A New Foreign Policy: Beyond American Exceptionalism* (New York: Columbia University Press, 2018), p. 207.

31 Ibid., p. 208.

32 Ibid., pp. 208–209; Gabriel Zucman, *The Hidden Wealth of Nations: The Scourge of Tax Havens* (Chicago: University of Chicago Press, 2015); and Harrington, *Capital Without Borders.*

33 See the Universal Declaration of Human Rights, Article 26(2).

34 Ibid., Article 27(1).

35 See Nick Obradovich, William Powers, Manuel Cebrian, and Iyad Rahwan, "Beware of Corporate 'Machine-Washing' of AI," *Boston Globe* (January 7, 2019), p. A8; and Joseph E. Aoun, "Boston Can Be Hub for Artificial Intelligence," *Boston Globe* (January 7, 2019), p. A9. The first article is from a research group at MIT's Media Lab; the second is from the president of Northeastern University, which is focusing heavily on AI.

36 Obradovich et al., "Beware of Corporate 'Machine-Washing' of AI."

37 Shoshana Zuboff, *The Age of Surveillance Capitalism: The Fight for a Human Future at the New Frontier of Power* (New York: Public Affairs, 2019).

38 Ibid., p. 28. For a variation on this body of reflection, see Max Tegmark, *Life 3.0: Being Human in the Age of Artificial Intelligence* (New York: Alfred A. Knopf, 2017).

39 See Marilynne Robinson, "What Are We Doing Here?" in *What Are We Doing Here? Essays* (New York: Farrar, Straus and Giroux, 2018), pp. 32–33.

40 Michiko Kakutani, *The Death of Truth* (New York: Tim Duggan Books, 2018), pp. 64–65.

41 Jose Ortega y Gasset, *The Revolt of the Masses* (New York: W. W. Norton, 1932).

42 See "The Grand Inquisitor" in *The Brothers Karamazov.*

43 For all its problems, the United States leads in certain areas of education but could benefit from experiences in many countries, including Cuba, South Korea, Vietnam, and Germany, among others.

44 Winston E. Langley, "Teaching, Learning, and Judging," in Esther Kingston-Mann, *Achieving Against the Odds: How Academics Became Teachers of Diverse Students* (Philadelphia: Temple University Press, 2001), pp. 160–179.

45 Oliver Wendell Holmes Jr., "The Soldier's Faith," address delivered at Harvard University, Memorial Day, May 30, 1895.

46 Ibid.

47 Ibid.

48 Philip Ziegler, *Soldiers: Fighting Men's Lives, 1901–2001* (New York: Penguin Books, 2003).

49 Holmes, "The Soldier's Faith."

50 Simone Weil, *The Iliad or the Poem of Force* (Wallinford, PA: Pendle Hill,

1976); see also how contemporary she is in C. J. Chivers, *The Fighters: Americans in Combat in Afghanistan and Iraq* (New York: Simon & Schuster, 2018).

51 Theodore Roosevelt, "Naval War College Address," June 2, 1897. In the same speech, Roosevelt noted that all the master races have been fighting races.

52 Brooks Adams, *The New Empire* (New York: MacMillan, 1902), p. xiii.

53 John Strachey, *The End of Empire* (New York: Random House, 1960), p. 210.

54 Sachs, *A New Foreign Policy,* pp. 9–20.

55 To cite a recent example, China, not the United States, has led the world in patent applications since 2011. See the *Boston Globe* (December 4, 2019), p. 3.

56 Sachs, *A New Foreign Policy,* p. 121.

57 See Henry Kissinger, *On China* (New York: Penguin Books, 2011), pp. 447–486. This shows important differences in China's and the United States' views.

58 Weijian Shan, "The Fight for China's Consumers," *New York Times* (January 8, 2019), p. A23. This is an aspect of the fight symbolized by the quarrel about the reach of China's telecom giant Huawei.

59 A. P. Thornton, *The Imperial Idea and Its Enemies* (New York: St. Martins, 1959), pp. ix–x.

60 *The Bhagavad Gita*, complied and adapted by Yogi Ramacharaka (Chicago: The Yogi Publications Society, 1930), pp. 23–24.

61 Much of this humiliated Russia, something that the country will not soon forget.

62 Strachey, *The End of Empire*, p. 204.

63 Michael Gorbachev, "The Reality and Guarantees of a Secure World," *Transnational Perspectives,* vol. XIII, no. 3 (1987), p. 6.

64 Ibid., pp. 6–7.

65 Ibid.

66 Michael Gorbachev, *The Search for A New Beginning: Developing a New Civilization* (San Francisco: Harper Collins, 1995), p. 5.

67 Reinhold Niebuhr, *The Children of Light and the Children of Darkness* (New York: Charles Scribner's Sons, 1944), p. 9.

68 See Andrew J. Bacevich, *The New American Militarism* (New York: Oxford University Press, 2013), and Dana Priest and William A. Arkin, *Top Secret: The Rise of the New American Security State* (Boston: Back Bay Books, 2012). I share Bacevich's position on how militarist thinking has recently shaped U.S. foreign policy and the critical developments, including religious and political coalitions, that supported it during the latter part of the twentieth century and the first decade of the twenty-first. However, this mode of thinking began in the 1890s, gained traction after World War II, and accelerated under Reagan and Bush. The final stages are now emerging.

Chapter 7

1   See Alexander Hamilton, Federalist No. 63. The second most remarkable portion of the U.S. Declaration of Independence is that dealing with "a decent respect for the opinions of mankind."

2   S. A. Redmond, S. L. Wilcox, S. Campbell, A. Kim, K. Finney, Barr, and A. M. Hassan, "A Brief Introduction to the Military Workplace Culture," *Work,* vol. 50 (2015), pp. 9–20; K. K. Rebecca Lai, Troy Griggs, Max Fisher, and Audrey Carlsen, "Is America's Military Big Enough?" *New York Times* (March 22, 2017), p. A1.

3   Stephen Peter Rosen, "Military Effectiveness: Why Society Matters," *International Security,* vol. 19, no. 4 (Spring 1996), pp. 5–31. In *The Essence of Security,* the former U.S. secretary of defense delved into the subject, using the Vietnam War as his laboratory.

4   Kim Parker, Anthony Cilluffo, and Renee Stepler, "6 Facts About the U.S. Military and Its Changing Demographics," Pew Research Center, April 13, 2017.

5   Rosen, "Military Effectiveness."

6   Rosa Brooks, *How Everything Became War and the Military Became Everything* (New York: Simon & Schuster, 2016). "Discretionary" refers to the portion of the annual budget not already committed from previous years.

7   U.S. Department of the Army, *Department of the Army Fiscal Year (FY) 2019 Budget Estimates Vol. I, Operation and Maintenance, Army: Justification Estimates, February 2018.* The Pentagon's budget for 2019 was over $700 billion; for 2020, it will exceed $750 billion.

8   Curt Mills, "US Still Paying Civil War Pension," *US News & World Report* (March 8, 2016).

9   Kristen Bialik, "The Changing Face of America's Veteran Population," *Fact Tank News,* Pew Research Center, November 10, 2017. Bialik indicates that in 2016, there were 9.8 million veterans from the Vietnam War, 7.1 million who served in the Gulf War and 1.6 million from the Korean War.

10 Philadelphia.cbslocal.com (June 14, 2019). This study is part of the Costs of War Project at Brown University's Watson Institute. See Neta Crawford, "United States Budgetary Costs of Post 9/11 Wars Through 2019," online at http://watson.brown.edu/files/Watson/imce/news/research.

11 It is worth noting that the Defense Department has climate change among the forefront of its concerns.

12 William Greider, *Secrets of the Temple: How the Federal Reserve Runs the Country* (New York: Simon & Schuster, 1987; *Who Will Tell the People: The Betrayal of American Democracy* (New York: Simon & Schuster, 1993); and *One World, Ready or Not* (New York: Simon & Schuster, 1997).

13 The Global South and the Socialist bloc never saw the U.S. policy orientation as neutral.

14 The undermining of security by these violations should be evident.

15 See some trade figures in "China's Imports from the US Plunge in Tariff War," *Boston Globe* (July 13, 2019), p. A8.

16 Richard Perez-Pena and Martina Stevis-Gridneff, "Amazon Fires Prompt Anger, Alarm in Europe," *Boston Globe* (August 24, 2019), p. A6.

17 Roberto Mangabeira Unger, "A Way to Save the Amazon," *New York Times* (August 27, 2019), p. A23. Stockholm refers to the 1972 conference on the environment held in Stockholm; the Rio Conference came twenty years later.

18 An example of the problems that arise when the United States uses the dollar as a "national currency" is when allies differ from Washington in policy toward Iran.

19 Gov. Mark Carney made that call on CNBC's business program on August 23, 2019; he was invited for that interview because he had taken this position earlier on that day at a Scottish Economics Conference at Edinburgh University. He contended that over two-thirds of world securities and over half of world trade are priced in dollars—far beyond the U.S. share of the world's economy. A "new virtual currency" could be the SDR or some other.

20 Rosa Brooks, *How Everything Became War*, pp. 14–24.

21 See "Overview" in "The Cost of War Project," p. 1, online at www.costofwar.org. See also William D. Cohan, "The Debt Crisis is Coming," *New York Times* (September 1, 2019), p. SR2. Cohan is a former investment banker.

22 See Matthew 12:25 (King James Version) for this statement from Jesus of Nazareth.

23 See some of Robert T. Curr's pioneering work in this area in "A Causal Model of Civil Strife: A Comprehensive Analysis Using New Indices," *American Political Science Review*, vol. 62 (December 1968), pp. 1104–1124. See also Robert T. Curr and Barbara Harff, *Ethnic Conflict in World Politics* (Boulder, CO: Westview Press, 1994), and Winston Langley, "What Have We Learned from the Wars of the Twentieth Century?" in Padraig O'Malley, Paul Atwood, and Patricia Patterson (eds.), *Sticks & Stones: Living with Uncertain Wars* (Amherst: University of Massachusetts Press, 2006), pp. 19–32. The reference about that to which one can aspire is linked to change because the promise of change has always been a balm for leaders and the led. When many years of promised change prove unavailing, relative deprivation increases.

24 Jacob S. Hacker, "Strong Economy, Worried Americans," *New York Times* (May 23, 2019), p. A21. See also Jeanna Smialek, "Many Adults in the US would Struggle to Find an Extra $400, Fed Study Finds," *New York Times* (May 24, 2019), p. B4.

25 Quoted in Thomas Gibbons-Neff, "Mattis Says U.S. Is Dividing into 'Hostile

Tribes' and Defends Importance of Allies," *New York Times* (August 29, 2019), p. A17. Mattis was seeing the problem primarily from a military security point of view, but he understood the socially rippling effects on the country.

26 See William Appleman Williams, *Empire as a Way of Life* (New York: Oxford University Press, 1980), p. x. Williams brought some of this data to the attention of the public in the 1980s, but new data shows even greater disparities in favor of the military in the use of national talent. For example, see Stanislava Ilic-Godfrey and William Lawhorn, "Military and Civilian Work: Comparing Personnel Shares by Occupation," *Career Outlook,* U.S. Bureau of Labor Statistics, November 2018.

27 Brooks, *How Everything Became War*, p. 19.

28 This is in contrast with a degrading, denigrated welfare system.

29 His outlook can be garnered from Milton Friedman, *Capitalism and Freedom* (Chicago: University of Chicago Press, 1962), and Milton Friedman and Rose Friedman, *Free to Choose* (New York: Harcourt, 1980).

30 Binyamin Appelbaum, *The Economists' Hour: False Prophets, Free Markets, and the Fracture of Society* (New York: Little, Brown and Company, 2019), p. 33.

31 Ibid., pp. 29–45. Here, one gets a good sense of the debate on the issue.

32 Sean McFate, "American Addiction to Mercenaries," *The Atlantic* (August 12, 2016).

33 Brooks, *How Everything Became War,* p. 13. Brooks notes that "American military personnel now operate in nearly every country on earth."

34 Among the many research institutions are the Hoover Institute at Stanford, the National Bureau of Economic Research, the American Enterprise Institute, and Brookings Institution. As for Wall Street, some of the most favored investments are in companies that supply the military.

35 See Articles 45, 46, and 47 of the UN Charter. Other, more parallel changes will have to be effected, but they are unlikely to take place at this time. If this course of action were embraced, there would be greater trust, out of which the grounds would be created for other changes.

36 "Other means" today would include the internet.

37 See Articles 41, 42, and 43 of the UN Charter.

38 This so-called Tobin tax is a modest proposed by Nobel laureate James Tobin in the 1970s. It would more than finance UN activities, especially in a world more open for trade and investments.

39 This is what Immo Stabreit called for. See the speech he delivered to the German American Business Council on September 30, 1992, while serving as Germany's ambassador to the United States. He anticipated further mutual development of Germany, the European Union, the Transatlantic area, the

North–South areas, and the environment.

40 See Article 1, Section 6, Clause 1 of the U.S. Constitution for the Speech and Debate Clause. See also Peter N. Stearns (ed.), *Peacebuilding Through Dialogue* (Fairfax, VA: George Mason University Press, 2018), as well as Daisaku Ikeda, "Mahayana Buddhism and the Twenty-first Century Civilization," a speech delivered at Harvard University on September 24, 1993.

41 Brooks, *How Everything Became War,* p. 13. One may also want to examine Paul Kennedy, *The Rise and Fall of the Great Powers* (New York: Vintage Books, 1987). Kennedy sees this type of military commitment as predictive of decline in great power status.

42 In respect to projections of interest on the debt from post-9/11 wars only, see Crawford, "United States Budgetary Costs." See also Jeff Jacoby, "Our Forgotten Mountain of Debt," *Boston Globe* (September 22, 2019), p. K6. Jacoby is a conservative who is troubled that the debt (and his figures, in some sense, underestimate things). If the public were to understand what this debt could mean for the nation's economic future, conservatives could be in some political trouble. However, this debt will be used to inveigh against "social programs."

43 This would not be the cryptocurrencies such as the Libra, which Facebook, noting the inadequacy of the dollar, would like to foist on the world.

44 When former secretary of state James Baker spoke of a U.S.-led community of democracies that would "stretch from Vancouver to Vladivostok," he was actually focusing on a liberalism that, in the post-USSR period, was not seeking democracy. Quoted in Kishore Mahbubani, *The New Asian Hemisphere* (New York: Public Affairs, 2008), p. 42.

45 Arthur Herman, *Freedom's Forge: How American Business Produced Victory in World War II* (New York: Random House, 2012), pp. 164–199.

46 This would have to be done carefully, of course. Military production will have to continue but on a different scale to ensure common military security. If successful, that security could later ensure complete disarmament.

47 The target of 2015 was two degrees Celsius, with one and a half urged for aspirational purposes. By 2018, the aspirational had become the required.

48 For an exemplary article, see Hiroko Tabuchi's "Oil Giants Defensive as Pressure Mounts," *New York Times* (September 24, 2019), p. A13.

49 Palko Karasz and Stanley Reed, "Saudi Oil Supply Is Put in Danger By Drone Strikes," *New York Times* (September 15, 2019), p. A1.

50 As quoted in Tabuchi's "Oil Giants Defensive."

51 This overall focus on the environment will likely help deal with some issues linked to the transborder movement of peoples. Fewer will flee economic distress and social displacement caused or induced by climate change.

52 See www.politico.com/story/2019/09/24/trump-speech-at-un-1507923.

53 See "Full Transcript of Greta Thunberg's Speech at the UN Climate Action Summit, September 23, 2019," *NPR News* (September 23, 2019).

54 Richard Dawkins, *The Selfish Gene* (New York: Oxford University Press, 1989). This work, often misunderstood, has been sometimes misused to justify the claim.

55 Paul Collier, *The Future of Capitalism* (New York: Harpers Collins, 2018). In particular, it could be helpful to read pp. 225–246.

56 Ibid., pp. 29-31.

57 See Shoshana Zuboff, *The Age of Surveillance Capitalism.*

58 Ibid.; see also Byron Reese, *The Fourth Age* (New York: ATRIA Books, 2018).

59 See, for example, "Exceptionalism as A Civic Religion," in Jeffrey Sachs, *A New Foreign Policy*, pp. 21–41, for the forty-one U.S. interventions in Latin America to effect regime change between 1898 and 2004; "America at War" in *Smithsonian* (Special Issue), vol. 49, no. 9 (January–February 2019), p. 29; Stephen Wertheim, "The Only Way to End 'Endless War,'" *New York Times* (September 15, 2019), p. SR7.

60 H. J. Mackinder, "The Geographical Pivot of History," *The Geographical Journal,* vol. XXIII, no. 4 (April 1904), pp. 298–321. By the 1990s, the United States had dominant influence in what is called the "Inner Marginal Crescent," composed of the Mediterranean, Turkey, Arabia, Iran, Afghanistan, Southeast Asia, Korea, and Japan. See also Nickolas J. Spykman, *American Strategy in World Politics* (New York: Harcourt, Brace and Company, 1942), and *The Geography of Peace* (New York: Harcourt, Brace and Company, 1944). Spykman has been called "the grandfather of containment."

61 The push by the United Kingdom to leave the European Union and forge closer ties with the United States (as would Israel later) will not significantly help.

62 See Rabindranath Tagore, *Rabindranath Tagore: An Anthology*, edited by Krishna Dutta and Andrew Robinson (New York: St. Martin's Press, 1997). See Tagore's letter on p. 11.

63 Joseph Conrad, *Nostromo* (New York: Penguin Classics, 2007), pp. 62–63.

64 Washington's farewell address contains a roughly similar definition of an American.

65 Norimitsu Onishi, "Man Behind Slogan Promoting White Supremacy," *New York Times* (September 21, 2019), p. A6. While white supremacy is not something advanced by a single person, Renaud Camus authored the term, capturing much that will become part of future cultural history.

66 See Michael Crowley and David E. Sanger, "Trump Celebrates Nationalism and Plays Down Crisis with Iran," *New York Times* (September 25, 2019),

p. A10. It should be noted that the mass murderer at Walmart in El Paso, Texas, wrote a manifesto that focused on replacement by Mexicans. A most compelling volume is James S. Robbins's *Erasing America: Losing Our Future by Destroying Our Past* (Washington, D.C.: Regnery Publishing, 2018).

67 See Seketu Mehta, *This Land Is Our Land: An Immigrant's Manifesto* (New York: Farrar, Straus and Giroux, 2019).

68 465 U.S. 567 (1846); 585 U.S. — 2018. In the second case, the court supposedly overruled the conclusion of the former but not the purported "plenary power" of the executive.

69 Bethany R. Berger, "'Power Over This Unfortunate Race': Race, Politics, and Indian Law in *United States v. Rogers*," *William and Mary Review,* vol. 45, no. 5 (2004), pp. 1957–2020.

70 *Korematsu v. United States* 323 U.S. 214 (1944).

71 See Maggie Blackhawk, "Where the Walls Began," *New York Times* (May 27, 2019); see also Caitlin Dickerson, "US Relocates Children from Migrant Site," *Boston Globe* (June 25, 2019), p. 1.

72 See Appelbaum, *The Economists' Hour*; Greider, *Secrets of the Temple;* John McDermott, *Economics in Real Time* (Ann Arbor: University of Michigan Press, 2004); Thomas Picketty, *Capitalism in the Twenty-First Century* (Cambridge: Harvard University Press, 2014); Thomas L. Friedman, "The Dots Show Where Trump Is Taking US," *New York Times* (June 12, 2019), p. A23. Friedman mistakenly attributes to President Trump that which is, in fact, societal—certainly that of the economic part of society.

73 Shoshana Zuboff, *The Age of Surveillance Capitalism;* Byron Reese, *The Fourth Age* (New York: ATRIA Books, 2018).

74 Reinhold Niebuhr, *The Children of Light and the Children of Darkness* (New York: Scribner's Sons, 1944), p. 9.

Index

A

A Raisin in the Sun, 80
Abrahamic tradition, 95
academy, xiii, 73, 84, 173
Adams, Brooks H., 51, 115
advertisers, 78
Aeschylus, 113, 115
Afghanistan, 12, 123
Africa, 3, 12, 38, 40–41, 48, 54, 57,
        92, 101–2, 107, 124, 163n49
African Americans, 48
African and Asian, 53
Agenda 21, *90*
Alaska, 94, 99
Albania, 36
Albert, 172
Albright, Madeleine J., 37–38, 163n49
Alcoff, Linda M., 48, 57
Algeria, 6
Alliance on Climate Change, 93
"American principles," 116
American Revolution, 18, 65–66, 78
Amazon, 40, 69, 124
Amazon forests, 124
"America First," 68, 76, 116
Amoral culture, 76
Anglo-Saxon, 6, 53, 57

Anglo-Saxon heritage or virtues, 6
Anti-Ballistic Missile Treaty (also
        called the ABM Treaty), 12, 15
Apollo Program, 131
Apple, 69, 73
arbitration, 2–3, 5
Aristotle, 77
Arizona, 21, 93
Ark, Wong Kim, 46–47, 165
Aryan, 47
arms limitation, 7
Arms race, 3, 5, 9
Asian Infrastructure Investment
        Bank, 40
Asians, 45, 55, 101
"Asphyxiating gasses," 2
Associated Press (AP), 70
Assyria, 115
Atlantic Charter, 54
Augustine, 77
Australia, 57, 99, 102

B

Bacon, Francis, 95–96
Balkans, 102
Baltic, 99, 117
"Banality of evil," 79
Bandung Conference, 53

Bangladesh, 80, 102
Bank of England, 125
Bannon, Stephen, 59
Belt and Road Initiative, 40
Berry, Thomas, 95
Biological lineage, 47, 72
"Black Tariff," 20
blacks, 57
Boer War (1899–1902), 3
Borah, William Edgar, 8
Bolshevik Revolution, 64–65
Bolsonaro, Jair, 125
Boxer Uprising (1899–1901), 3
Brand loyalty, 47, 72
Brazil, 40, 58, 89, 102, 116, 124, 131
Bretton Woods institution (also called
    Bretton Woods system), xii,
    29–30, 161n26, 161
Breyer, Stephen G., 77
British Commonwealth, 117
British Empire, 116
Brown v. Board of Education, 52
Brundtland, Gro Harlem, 88
Buddhist tradition, 96
Burden, Joanna, 45
Bush, George H. W., 14, 58
Bush, George W., 33, 38
Bush-Cheney team, 119

C

California, 21, 84, 93, 174–75
Cambridge Analytica, 111
Campbell-Bannerman, Sir Henry, 3
Canada, 5, 27, 41, 131
Cancun, 56
Cape Horne, 135
Capital in slaves, 62
Carbon emissions, 81, 109
Carbon-free sources of energy, 94
Caribbean, 6, 8, 50, 54, 57, 102
Carter, James E., 56, 76

Carter administration, xii, 31, 56, 84
Catholics, 47–48
Caucasians, 47
Celts, 48
Center for Election Systems, 73
Central America, 12, 92, 102
Central Asia, 99
Charlottesville, 59, 136
Changing Climate, xiii, 84–85
Charter on the Economic Rights and
    Duties of States, 29
charter schools, 74
Chernobyl, 12
Chile, 56
Chinese Exclusion Act, 46
Chinese markets, 2
Chlorofluorocarbons (CFCs), 84
Christian civilization, 80
Churchill, Winston, 54
Citizen, 45–47
Civil rights movement, xii, 53, 56,
    166n49
Civil War, 20, 44–45, 48, 63, 113, 123,
    139, 180
Civil Works Administration, 23
Civilian life, 127
Civilian Conservation Corps, 23
Civilization, 78, 172
Clean Air Act, 82
Clean Water Act, 82
Clinton, William J., 33, 60
Club of Rome, 82
Clybourne Park, 48
Cold War, 13, 39, 52–54, 76, 89, 91,
    99, 104, 113
Collective learning, 83, 95
Collective security, 100
Colorado, 21
Columbia, 3, 49, 74
Commander in chief, 134

Committee on Commerce, Science, and Transportation, 32
Common good, 16–17, 20, 44, 53, 68–70, 73–74, 130
common security, 112, 128
Communism, 14–15, 25, 36–37, 55, 65–66, 98
Communist Party, 11, 14, 65, 100
Comprehensive Environmental Response, Compensation, and Liability Act (CERCLA), 84–85
Compulsory arbitration, 4
conditionality, 33
Conference of Parties (CoP), 109
Confucian culture, 34
Confucian tradition, 96
Congress, iv, xiv, 3–4, 6, 9, 15, 18–20, 24, 44, 56, 64, 70, 85, 87–88, 119
Constitution, xii, 18, 44–47, 56, 62, 64, 70, 77, 104, 120–21, 128–29, 141
Consumer, 170
Consumerism, 76, 100
Consumer predictability, 71
Convention on Biological Diversity, 90, 92
Corporate culture, 68–69
corporations, 68
Cortez, Alexandria Ocasio, 97, 105
Cosmopolitanism, 113–14
Creditor nation, 8, 21, 25
CBS News, 123
Cuba, 7, 21, 36, 52, 63–65, 106, 117
Cultural ancestry, 102
Cultural message, 95
Cultural security, 120
Cyberwarriors, 125

D

Declaration of Independence, 76, 180n1
Declaration on the Environment (also known as the Rio Declaration), 90
Declaration on the Establishment of a New International Economic Order, 29
Defense Advanced Research Project Agency (DARPA), 35
Defense Department, 13, 123, 180n11
De Gaulle, Charles, 54
Democratic Party, xi, 52, 93
Demographic Challenges, 101, 106
Demographic changes, xiii, 58, 60, 80, 99, 101, 110
Denmark, 3, 106
Detention camps, 137
Dewey, George, 6
Dignity of labor, 107
Discretionary budget, 122
Discrimination, xii, 42, 53, 63, 77, 103, 125
Doctor Zhivago, 15
Doha Development Round, 35
Domestic slavery, 134
Dominican Republic, 49
Dostoevsky, Fyodor, 112
Dred Scott v. Sanford, 45
Dulles, John Foster, 66

E

Earth's ecology, 108, 110
Earth Summit. *See* United Nations Conference on the Environment and Development (UNCED, also called the Earth Summit)
Eastern Europe, 24, 26, 48, 55, 59, 65, 99–100, 104, 117, 134

East Germany, 14
East-West, 2
Economic animal, 67, 105–6, 133
Economic security, 120
Egypt, 54
Eisenhower, Dwight D., 53–54,
168n81
Emanuel African American Methodist
Episcopal Church, 59
embeddedness, 72
Emerson, Waldo R., 59
Endangered Species Act, 82
Environmental Movement, xiii, 82,
91–92, 97
Environmental Protection Agency
(EPA), 82, 85
Ethiopia, 10, 124
Europe, 1–2, 7, 19–20, 22, 24, 26–27,
41, 48, 55, 64–65, 70–71, 99–
101, 104, 124, 134
European Imperialism in Africa, 48
European Recovery Program, 26
European Union, 27, 39, 81, 101–2,
104, 109, 111, 116–17
Evil, 66, 78–79, 119, 138
Exceptional nation, 37
Expansion of whiteness, 49

F

Facebook, 40, 69, 71–72, 111, 183
"Fair Harvard," 51
Fair Housing Act, 53
Fair Labor Standard Act, 23, 50
"Fake news," 72, 119
Fallows, James, 35
False "essences," 103
Farewell Address, 18, 61–63
Fascism, 65, 102
Federal Communications Commission
(FCC), 69

Federal Emergency Relief
Administration (FERA), 23
Federal Housing Administration
(FHA), 50
Federal Reserve Bank, 18
federation of the world, 119
Fifteenth Amendment, 45
Figueres, Christiana, 92
First Amendment, 70, 77, 129, 137
Ford Motor, 131
Fordney-McCumber Tariff, 20, 22
Foreign Affairs, 57
Foreign direct investment, 100
Founding Fathers, 18, 63, 77
Fourteenth Amendment, 45–46, 58
Fourth National Climate Assessment,
94
France, 3–5, 9, 18, 31, 54, 65, 70, 99,
136
Francis, 171
Franco-Prussian War (1870), 5
Freedom from, 22, 104
Freedom to, 128
Free market, 28, 33, 66–68, 73, 101,
105, 172n60, 182
Free white persons, 47
Free world, 52, 58, 66, 136
"From savagery . . . to civilization,"
57
Fundamental fairness, 139
Fundamental rights and principles of
the Stockholm Declaration, 83

G

General Agreement on Tariff and
Trade (GATT), 25
General Assembly (also known as the
UN General Assembly), 27, 85,
89, 129, 132, 136
General Data Protection Regulation,
111

general welfare, 128
Genocide, 102
Georgia, 73, 117
Germany, 3–5, 9–10, 14, 20, 22, 31, 48, 58, 69–70, 102, 106, 116, 124, 131, 169n20
Glasnost (openness), 11
Glass-Steagall Act, 23
Global citizenship, 41, 103
Global currency, 41, 103, 124, 130–31
Globalism, 59
globalization, 56
"Global New Deal," 25
Global North, 90, 93, 101, 125, 130
Global order, 39, 118
Global South, xii, 19, 28–29, 31–32, 48, 50, 54, 56, 58, 66, 76, 82–83, 87, 90, 101
Global urbanization, 102
Global warming, 89, 94
Global Warming. See IPCC Special Report, *Global Warming*
Glorious Revolution, 78
Goddard Institute for Space Studies, 89
Gorbachev, Mikhail, xi, 11–15, 34, 36, 38, 117–19, 159n42, 163n47
Gorbachev-Reagan Initiative (also called the Reagan-Gorbachev Initiative), 11
Gore, Albert, 89
"Gratified spectatorship," 71
Great Depression, xii, 20, 22, 28, 50, 68, 105
Great nation, 24
Great Recession, 68, 105
"Great Republic," 25
Great Society, 53, 166, 167n57
Great White Fleet, 7
Greece, 25
Greek, 49

Greenhouse gas emissions, 81, 90–91
Green New Deal, 97, 105
Group of 7, 89, 173n26
Group of 77, 29, 31, 39, 53–54, 69, 83, 89, 132
Grozier, Michael, 75
Guam, 7, 21, 52, 63
Guantanamo, 76
Guatemala, 27, 53
Gulf War, 99, 128

H

Hague conferences (1899 and 1907), xi, 1, 3, 7, 10
Hannah, 172
Hansen, James, 89
Harvard University, ix, 26, 37, 59
Havas, 70
Hawaii, 7, 21, 52, 63–64, 99, 137
Helsinki Accords, 56
Hinduism, 96, 131
Hiroshima, 12
Hispanics, 49, 55, 57, 80, 101, 116
Historical revolution, 78
Historical truth, 11, 25, 28, 34, 36
Hitler, Adolf, 9, 22
Holland, 3, 18, 89
Holmes, Oliver Wendell Jr., 113–15, 119
Home Owners' Loan Corporation, 50
Host population, 102
Human dignity, 138
Human Genome Project, 70
human rights, 27, 51, 55, 75, 103–4, 110, 118, 171, 177–78
Human rights movement, xii, 111, 138
Humphrey, Hubert H., 52, 128
Hungarians, 50

I

immigrants, 57

immigration, 47, 56
"Immigration as reparation," 136
Imperialism, 7, 64. *See also* The large
    policy
"Incremental problems," 85
Independent Commission on
    International Development, 69
India, 19, 38–40, 54, 65, 93, 101, 103,
    116, 131, 135
Indonesia, 6, 53, 56
Infant industries, 20, 27
Information Age, 69
Information revolution, 110–12, 116
Insecurity, 74, 79, 122, 125, 127,
    133–34
Instruments of coercion, 98
Intellectual property, 35, 116
Intergovernmental Panel on Climate
    Change (IPCC), xiii
IPCC Special Report, *Global
    Warming*, 94
Intermediate-Range Nuclear Forces
    Treaty (1987), 15
international arbitration, 3
International Bank for Reconstruction
    and Development (IBRD), 25
International Bill of Human Rights,
    51
International Convention on
    International Trade in
    Endangered Species of Wild
    Fauna and Flora, 82
International Covenant on Civil and
    Political Rights (ICCPR), xii
International Covenant on Economic,
    Social, and Cultural Rights
    (ICESCR), xii
International Development Finance
    Corporation, 41
International Monetary Fund (IMF),
    25

Inter-Parliamentary Union, 4
Interracial marriage, 49
Iran, 27, 31, 53, 56, 101, 139
Iraq, 33, 38, 76, 117, 123, 139
Irish, 48–49
Islam, 28, 34–35, 38, 76, 95, 107, 131
Islamic culture, 34
Islamic finance, 34
Israel, 54, 116, 169n20
Italian, 47, 49
Italy, 3, 10, 64–65

J

James, William, 51
Japan, 4, 9–10, 30, 34–36, 40, 49–50,
    64–65, 76, 116, 131, 169n20
Japanese, 3–4, 6, 10, 34–35, 50, 58,
    73, 80, 102, 118, 137
Jews, 48, 59, 102, 116, 136
Johnson, Lyndon B., 27, 53
Joint chiefs of staff, 129
Joint Disarmament Committee, 129
Judaism, 95
"Judgement of nations," 121, 128

K

Kashmiri, 139
Katowice, 109
Katowice Agreement, 109
Kellogg-Briand Pact, 1928 (also called
    the Pact of Paris), xi, 158n31
Kennedy, Paul, 99
Kennedy Round of tariffs, 27
Key currency, 25, 41, 101, 124, 131
King, Steve A., 58–59
Kissinger, Henry A., 74
Kurds, 139
Kuwait, 109, 117
Kyoto Protocol, 90, 92

L

Laissez-faire capitalism (also referred to as the self-regulating market or free market), 17, 66–67
Land-grant public colleges, 21
Latin America, 38–41, 57, 99, 124
Lauer, Matt, 38, 163
leadership, 107, 112
Leadership security, 120
League of Nations, xi, 7–10, 21, 25, 65
League of Nations Covenant, 161
Less developed countries (LDCs), 27
"Less than," 102
Liberal democracy, 25, 36, 38, 66, 104–5, 131, 139
liberalism, 16
Light in August, 45
Limits to Growth (1972), 82
"Locksley Hall," 119
Lodge, Henry Cabot, 7, 50, 59
Lone superpower, 37, 116–17, 124

M

MacBride, Sean, 32
MacBride Report, 32
Madison, James, 18, 44, 67, 121
Manchuria, 9–10
Manhattan Project, 131
Manifest Destiny, 63
manufacturing, 19
"Marginal utility," 71
Markers, 102
Marshall, George C., 26
Marshall, T. H., 44, 164
Marshall Plan, xii, 26
Marx, Karl, 22
Mass consumption, 71
Mass production, 71
Mattis, James, 126, 182n25
McCain, John, 76

McKinley, William, 2, 64, 76
Medicaid, 33
Megacities, 102
Mehta, Seketu, 136
mercantilism, 16, 28, 123
Mercantilist model of development, xii, 18–19, 34–35, 40
Mercantilist period (1789–1930), 18
"Merlin and the Gleam," 114
Mexico, 21, 41, 56, 93, 99, 113, 176
Microsoft, 69, 73
Middle East (also called West Asia), 12, 28, 34, 38, 99, 102, 161n25
Militarization, 14, 100, 109
Military-industrial complex, 112, 139
Military-related technology, 134
Military security, 120, 122, 129–32
Military Staff Committee, 129
Millennium Development Goals, xiii, 93, 109, 174n38
Ministry of Industry and International Trade (MITI), 35
Minorities, 27, 50, 52–53, 55, 75, 122, 136, 139
MIT, 21
Mitchell, George, 89
Mohonk Conference, 3
Molina, Mario, 84
Molotov Plan, 26
Monroe Doctrine, 8, 76, 99
Montreal Protocol on Substances that Deplete the Ozone Layer (1985), 84, 87
Moral actors, 70
Moroccan Crises (1905 and 1906), 3
Morrill Act, 20
Morrill Tariff, 20
Multiculturalism, 102
Murphy, Edgar G., 51, 53
"Murphy's Spirit," 51, 53
Muslim, 28–29, 34, 137, 139

Mutual assured destruction (MAD), 11

N

Nagasaki, 12
Naipaul, V. S., 78
Nasser, Gamal A., 54
Nation, 61
National Academy of Sciences, xiii, 84
National community, 62, 127
National debt, 20, 39, 41, 125, 130
National Energy Policy Act (NEPA), 89
National interest, xiii, 74, 115, 125, 134
nationalism, 24, 177
National Labor Relations Act, 23
National Labor Relations Board, 23
National Recovery Administration (NRA), 23, 50
Nationals, 62
National Security Council, 13
nations, great, 18
Native Americans, 49, 75, 99, 113, 135, 137, 139
Naval College, 115
Negative freedom, 17, 22
Neo-Confucianism, 28, 38, 107
neoliberalism, 17, 28, 34–35, 137
"Neutral third party," 124
Nevada, 21, 93
New Deal, xii, 25, 28, 49–50, 53, 97, 105, 167n57, 177
New Delhi, 40
New Development Bank, 40
New International Economic Order (NIEO), 29
New Mexico, 21, 93
"New Nationalism," 24
News agencies, 70

New world information and communication order, 31
New World Order, 136
Nicholas II, 1, 4
Niebuhr, Reinhold, xiv, 74–76, 78–79, 119, 138
Nietzsche, Friedrich, 96, 98
Nixon, Richard M., 56, 58, 127
Nobel Peace Prize, 4
Non-Aligned Movement (NAM), 53
Non-carbon energy systems, 92
Nondiscrimination, xii, 52, 59
Nongovernmental organizations (NGOs), 56, 82
Nonproliferation, 9
Nonwhites, 46, 49, 53, 55, 57, 63, 116, 135
"No Plan B," 134
Nordwijk conference, 91
North Atlantic Treaty Organization (NATO), 14, 37
North Korea, 36
North-South, 2, 56, 93, 125, 129
Norway, 3, 88, 106
Nostromo, 135
Novum Organum, 95
Nuclear utilization thinker (NUT), 11

O

Obama, Barack H., 33, 74
Office of Technology Assessment, 32
Open Door Policy, 21, 99
Open markets, 17, 100
Operation Enduring Freedom, 76
Optional clause, 8
Organization for Economic Co-operation and Development (OECD), 27
Organization for European Economic Co-operation (OEEC), 26
"Orientals," 103

Our Common Future, 88, 92
Outer Space, 13, 82
Outer Space Treaty (1967), 13
ozone-depleting substances (ODS),
     87–88

P

Pact of Paris, 1928. *See* Kellogg-
     Briand Pact
Painter, Nell Irvin, 48–49
Palestinians, 139
Palladium of political safety, 63
Panama, 3, 7, 63–64, 99
Panama Canal, 3, 7, 99
"Paradise of domestic security," 75
Paris Agreement, xiii, 81, 91, 93–95,
     109
Paris Climate Agreement, 81, 92. *See
     also* Paris Agreement
"Parking charges," 88
Pasternak, Boris, 15
Pauncefort, Sir Julian, 2
Paupers, convicts, and diseased
     persons, 50
Peace congresses, 3
Peace movement, 1
Pearl Harbor, 131
People's Republic of China, 24
Perestroika (restructuring), 11
Permanent Court of Arbitration, 2, 5
Permanent Court of International
     Justice, 8
Permanent national success, 62
Personal identity data, 71
Philip, 178
Philippines, 6–7, 21, 52, 63–64
Plan B, 134, 139
plenary power, 137
Plessy, Homer, 46–47, 49, 52
Plessy v. Ferguson, 46–47, 52
Plummer, Brad, 93

Pole, 49
Political culture, xiii, 18, 69–70, 73–
     74, 126, 128
political rights, 44
Population subgroups, 101
Positive freedom, 23
Program of Action, 29
Prometheus Bound, 113, 115
Protective duties, 19
Protestants, 57
Public education, 52, 74
Public intellectuals, 73
"Public trust" theory, 130
Public Works Administration, 23
Puerto Rico, 7, 21, 52, 63, 93
Puritan ethic, 80
Puritans, 59, 73
Puritan values, xiii

R

Racial and social class security, 120
Racial atrocities, xii
Racial Formation in the United States,
     57
Radio Free Europe, 71
Read, Thomas, 7
Reagan-Gorbachev disarmament
     initiative, xi
Reciprocal Tariff Act (1934), 24
Relative deprivation, 126, 128, 133,
     135–36, 181n23
Religious institutions, 73–74
"Relocation centers," 137
Reparation, 135–36
Replacement, 25, 136–37
Reporters, 72
Reproductive vigor, 48
Republican ideal, 79
Republican Party, 4
Reserve capacity, 27
Reuters, 70

Reykjavik, xii, 12–14, 159n44
Rhode Island, 115
Ricardo, David, 22
Ridgway, Rozanne L., 14
Rio Conference (also known as the
    Rio Summit), 90–91, 125,
    181n17
Rio de Janeiro, Brazil, 89
Rio Summit. *See* United Nations
    Conference on the Environment
    and Development (UNCED,
    also called the Earth Summit)
Robinson, Marilynne, 111
Rockefeller Center, 35
Roosevelt, Franklin D. (FDR), 9, 49,
    105–7, 137
Roosevelt, Theodore, 3, 24–25, 51,
    107, 114–15, 157, 161, 166, 177,
    179
Root, Elihu, 6, 64
Rowland, Sherwood F., 84
Royal Dutch Shell, 132
Rumsfeld, Donald, 100
Rusk, Dean, 66
Russia, 1, 4–5, 14–15, 21, 31, 36–38,
    40, 64, 73, 99, 101, 109–10,
    116–17, 126, 134
Russian Federation, 15
Russian-Japanese War (also called the
    Russo-Japanese War, 1904–
    1905), 3
Russian Revolution, 49, 65, 78

S

Sakharov, Andrei, 75–76
Saudi Arabia, 34, 93, 109
Schurz, Carl, 4
Scotland, 3
Scottish Irish, 48
security, 1, 13, 23, 50, 84, 112, 120,
    125, 128–29, 132

Security Council, 13, 129, 132
Self-determination, 61–62, 64, 71,
    100, 104, 111, 138
Self-making person, 126–27
SEMATECH, 35
"Separate but equal," 52
Serwer, Andrew, 62
Sikh, 47
Silent Spring (1962), 82
Simone, 178
Singapore, 30, 35, 131
Single though differentiated, 108
"Slapping the white man down," 54
"Smart" wars, 99
Smith, 169
Smith, Adam, 17, 22, 67, 169
Smoot-Hawley Tariff, 20, 22
Social being, 67, 106
Social class, xii, 25, 36, 44, 59, 65, 97,
    125
Social Compact, 104
Social contract, 44, 62, 104–5
Social democracy, 15, 107
Social justice, 55, 62, 79
Social media, xiii, 71, 80, 104
social rights, 44
Social security, 23, 50
Social Security Act, 23
Socialist market economy, 36
"Soft power," 115
South Africa, 3, 40
South America, 101, 107
South Asia, 102
South Korea, 30, 35, 42, 116, 131,
    169n20
Southeast Asia, 101
Southern Africa, 12
"Southern strategy," 58
Sovereign equality, 52, 100
Soviet Union, 11–15, 24–26, 28, 30–
    31, 36–37, 54–56, 58, 65–66,

75–76, 82, 98, 100–101, 106, 131, 136
Space Force, 13, 99
Spain, 1, 4, 6, 63–64, 99, 113
Special drawing rights (SDR), 30
"Species identity," 103
Speech and Debate Clause, 77, 129
Stakeholders, 90, 106
"Starving the beast," 33, 39
Star Wars. *See* Strategic Defense Initiative (SDI)
Statement of Principles on Forests, 90
Stockholm Conference on the Human Environment, 82
Stockholm Declaration, 82–83, 86–87, 125
Strategic Defense Initiative (SDI), 12
Strong, Maurice, 91
"Subhuman state," 19, 75
Subsidies, 19–20, 33, 35–36, 50, 53, 56, 70, 75, 89
Suez Canal, 54
Supreme Court, 23, 45–47, 50, 113, 137
Sustainable Development Goals, 93–94, 108
Sweden, 3, 106
Syria, 92

T

Tagore, Rabindranath, 135
Taiwan, 6, 30, 35, 117, 131
tariffs, 35
Tea Party, 57, 135
Technologism, 69–70
Tennyson, Alfred, 114, 119, 128
Teutonic and Alpine, 48
Texas, 21
Thatcher, Margaret H., 31, 162n31, 162n37

The Age of Surveillance Capitalism, 110–11
"The Clash of Civilizations," 57
"The conquest of the earth," 48
The End of History and the Last Man, 36
"The Grand Inquisitor," 112
"The great replacement," 136
The Great Transformation, 105
The Hague, 1
The Iliad, 114
The "large policy," 7
The liberal model (1930–1971), 22
The Netherlands. *See* Holland
Theodore, 179
The "old order," 10
"The Oven Bird," 139
The Population Bomb (1968), 82
"The privileged princes," 107
The Wealth of Nations, 17
"The West and the Rest," 58
The will to global leadership, 116
The Will to Power, 98, 112
"Third generation" rights, 104
Third-party dispute settlement, 3
Thornton, A. P., 116
Three-Fifths Compromise, 44
Three models of political economy, 16, 24
Thunberg, Greta, 132
Topper, Klaus, 92
Trade Expansion Act (1962), 27
Trade liberalization, 100
Transborder movement of peoples, 11, 101–2
Trans-Pacific Partnership (TPP), 36, 163
Treaty Banning Nuclear Weapons Tests in the Atmosphere, in Outer Space, and Under Water

(also known as the Partial Test Ban Treaty), 82
Treaty of Versailles, 9, 49
Treaty on the Prohibition of Nuclear Weapons (2017), xii, 13
Tree of Life Synagogue, 59
Triple Entente, 5
Triplett, Irene, 123
Truman, Harry S., 27, 52
Truman Doctrine, 26
Trump, Donald J., xi, 33, 58–59, 68, 75–76, 81, 92, 119, 124, 132, 135–37, 141, 162n29n29
Trump administration, 13, 15, 31, 39, 41, 58, 99, 141, 163n45
Trump v. Hawaii, 137
Turkey, 25, 131
Tuskegee University, 21
TV giants, 69
Two inheritances, 134

U

Ummah, 28–29, 34, 107
UN Secretary General, 88
Union of Concerned Scientists, 93
Union of South American Nations, 39
United Kingdom, xiii, 2–7, 18, 20–22, 31–32, 48, 52, 54, 57, 70, 78, 82, 99, 116–17, 134–35
United Nations (UN), xii–xiii, 25, 29, 81–82
United Nations Charter (also known as the UN Charter), 25, 27, 50, 52, 86, 120–21, 128–29
United Nations Climate Summit (2019), 132
United Nations Conference on the Environment and Development (UNCED, also called the Earth Summit), xiii, 89–90
United Nations Conference on Trade and Development (UNCTAD), 29
United Nations Disarmament Commission, 129
United Nations Educational, Scientific, and Cultural Organization (UNESCO), 25
United Nations Environment Program (UNEP), 82
United Nations Framework Convention on Climate Change (UNFCCC), 81, 89–90
United Nations General Assembly (also called the General Assembly), 27, 85, 89, 129, 132, 136
United Nations Millenium Development Goals, xiii, 93–94, 108–9, 174
United States, ix, xi–4, 6–22, 24, 26–60, 62–67, 69–71, 73–82, 84, 87–89, 91–95, 98–104, 115–25, 130–32, 134–39
United States-Mexico-Canada Agreement (USMCA), 41
United States v. Bhagat Singh Thind, 47
United States v. Wong Kim Ark, 46
universal civilization, 78
Universal Declaration of Human Rights, 27, 51, 55, 75, 103–4, 110, 118
Universal Peace Congress, 3
University of California (Irvine), 84
Unspeakable fear, 114
Uruguay Round of Tariffs (1986–1984), 35
U.S. propaganda, 65
U.S. Senate, 89
Utah, 21

V

"Vancouver to Vladivostok," 134, 183n44
Venezuela, 106
veterans benefits, 123
Vienna Convention for the Protection of the Ozone Layer (1985), 84, 87
Vietnam, 27, 30, 36, 52–53, 56, 65, 75, 123, 127, 131, 180
Vietnam War, 30, 52, 56, 75, 127
Voice of America, 71
Volunteer army, 127

W

"War on terrorism," 76
War Production Board (WPB), 131
Warsaw Pact, 14, 37
Watanuke, Joji, 75
Webster, Daniel, 20
welfare, 128
"Welfare queens," 53
West, 2, 6, 11, 16, 24, 28, 31–32, 36–37, 58, 61, 63, 66, 94, 103, 161
Western civilization, 58, 103
Western dominance, 58
Western Europe, 15, 26–27, 36, 48, 55, 70, 94, 99–100
whiteness, 47–48, 57
whites, 57
Will to power, xiii, 96, 98, 100, 112, 117
Wilson, Woodrow, 21, 49, 64

Wilson's Fourteen Points, 21, 161
Wolff, 70
World Bank (also known as the International Bank for Reconstruction and Development or IBRD), 25–27, 29, 40, 54, 161
World Charter for Nature, 84–85, 88–90, 95
World Commission on Environment and Development (WCED), 84
World Conferences on Women, 69
"World control," 8
World Health Organization (WHO), 25
World Trade Organization (WTO), 35
World War I, xii, 5, 7–8, 22, 48–49, 64–65, 70
World War II, ix, xii, 7, 10–11, 24–25, 50–51, 53–54, 59, 64–65, 70–71, 76, 99–100, 103, 131, 137–38
Worth, Timothy, 89
Wyoming, 21

Y

Yeltsin, Boris, 15, 36

Z

Zaire, 27, 53
Zeus, 113
Zuboff, Shoshana, 110, 133